CAMBRIDGE GREEK AND LATIN CLASSICS

PLATO
SYMPOSIUM

EDITED BY

SIR KENNETH DOVER

Formerly President of Corpus Christi College, Oxford

CAMBRIDGE UNIVERSITY PRESS
Cambridge, New York, Melbourne, Madrid, Cape Town, Singapore, São Paulo,
Delhi, Dubai, Tokyo

Cambridge University Press
The Edinburgh Building, Cambridge CB2 8RU, UK

Published in the United States of America by Cambridge University Press, New York

www.cambridge.org
Information on this title: www.cambridge.org/9780521295239

First published 1980
Eighteenth printing 2009

Printed in the United Kingdom at the University Press, Cambridge

Library of Congress Cataloguing in Publication data
Plato.
Symposium.
(Cambridge Greek and Latin classics)
Bibliography: p. 13
Includes indexes.
I. Love. II. Socrates.
I. Dover, Kenneth James. II. Title.
B385.A5D68 1979 184 78-67301

ISBN 978-0-521-20081-3 hardback
ISBN 978-0-521-29523-9 paperback

CONTENTS

PREFACE

The main purpose of this edition and commentary is to enable the learner to read and enjoy Plato's *Symposium* in Greek, to understand its arguments and to appreciate its artistry. The secondary purpose is to improve the learner's knowledge of Greek in order that he may find it easier to read other texts. In an edition which is meant to be brief and relatively inexpensive, these two purposes compete for space, and the need to increase the reader's speed by telling him the meanings of words rather than making him seek them all in the lexicon is also a claim on space.

My information about the text of the *Symposium* is derived from the text and apparatus criticus of Burnet's Oxford Classical Text and of Robin's Budé edition, supplemented by some further data helpfully communicated to me by Dr W. S. McD. Nicoll. I have not collated any Plato manuscripts myself, but I have exercised my own judgement throughout in editing the text on the evidence available to me. Textual problems are not discussed in the commentary, nor are variants and emendations recorded in the apparatus, except where they are important. Users of this or any edition are warned that the textual variants presented by citations from Plato in later literature are not yet as fully investigated as is desirable.

The *Symposium*, like most of what Plato wrote, is about how life should be lived; not just the life of an ancient Athenian, but your life and mine. Since he is a highly original thinker and a writer of remarkable imagination, skill, dramatic power and sensitivity in the use of language, what he says is worth reading, and the minimum requirement of any commentary on any work of his is that it should ask in respect of each passage: what does he mean? why does he say it? does it follow? and is it true? His distinctive values, attitudes, assumptions, cravings and passions are not mine, and for that reason I do not find his philosophical arguments even marginally persuasive. Much that is written about him is marked, in my view, by an uncritical enthusiasm for the abstract and immutable, as if such an enthusiasm always and necessarily afforded better access to the truth about man, nature and divinity than is afforded by a love of the particular, material and perishable. One consequence of this is that Plato is sometimes welcomed as an ally by people who would not like what they found if they attended less selectively and more precisely to what he actually says. Another consequence is that the Platonic Socrates is taken, in all seriousness, as if he were a man with a genuinely open and enquiring mind, and the quality of other Greek intellectuals, some of whom are best known to us through Plato's portrayal of them, is underrated. The working hypothesis adopted in my commentary and introduction is that Plato writes not as a scholar or scientist but from first to last as an advocate, an heir to the tradition of didactic poetry, a nursling of Attic drama and a product, no less than the politicians and litigants whom he criticised so articulately, of a culture which admired the art of the persuader.

Oxford, April 1978   K.J.D.

PREFACE TO 1982 REPRINT

Reviewers and other friends have persuaded me that some of my statements look intemperate, and I should clarify these statements. In the first line of this page, emphasise 'distinctive'; many of the values and attitudes which Plato shares with most people are mine too. In the last sentence of the Preface 'from first to last as an advocate' does not mean that Plato discarded reason in favour of advocacy when reasoning seemed to him cogent in itself. On p. 6, line 20, emphasise 'dictated'; many people's 'reasoned reflection on experience' leads them away from the Theory of Ideas. On p. 8, line 13, emphasise 'assumptions'.

                                                             K.J.D.

ABBREVIATIONS AND REFERENCES

ANCIENT AUTHORS AND WORKS

Aesch. = Aeschylus

Ar. = Aristophanes; *Ach.* = *Acharnians*

Arist. = Aristotle

Dem. = Demosthenes

Eur. = Euripides

Hdt. = Herodotus

Hes. = Hesiod; *Theog.* = *Theogony*; *WD* = *Works and Days*

Hipp. = Hippocrates

Hom. = Homer; *Il.* = *Iliad*; *Od.* = *Odyssey*

Lys. = Lysias

Pl. = Plato; *Ap.* = *Apology*; *Chrm.* = *Charmides*; *Euthd.* = *Euthydemus*; *Grg.* = *Gorgias*; *Phd.* = *Phaedo*; *Phdr.* = *Phaedrus*; *Phlb.* = *Philebus*; *Prt.* = *Protagoras*; *Rep.* = *Republic*; *Smp.* = *Symposium*; *Tht.* = *Theaetetus*

Soph. = Sophocles

Thuc. = Thucydides

Xen. = Xenophon; *Anab.* = *Anabasis*; *Hell.* = *Hellenica*; *Mem.* = *Memorabilia*; *Smp.* = *Symposium*

MODERN WORKS

DK = (ed.) Diels, H., revised by Kranz, W., *Die Fragmente der Vorsokratiker*, sixth edition (Berlin 1951)

GH = Dover, K. J., *Greek homosexuality* (London 1978)

GP = Denniston, J. D., *Greek particles*, second edition (Oxford 1954)

GPM = Dover, K. J., *Greek popular morality in the time of Plato and Aristotle* (Oxford 1974)

HGP = Guthrie, W. K. C., *A history of Greek philosophy* (Cambridge 1967–)

KR = Kirk, G. S., and Raven, J. E., *The Presocratic philosophers* (Cambridge 1957)

LSJ = Liddell, H. G., and Scott, R., *Greek–English Lexicon*, revised by Sir Henry Stuart Jones and R. McKenzie, with Supplement (Oxford 1968)

MT = Goodwin, W. W., *Syntax of the moods and tenses of the Greek verb*, revised edition (London 1910).

Collections of fragments

Fragments of Aeschylus, Euripides, Sophocles and minor tragic poets are cited from Nauck, *Tragicorum Graecorum fragmenta*; of Alcaeus and Sappho, from Lobel and Page, *Poetarum Lesbiorum fragmenta*; of Alcman, from Page, *Poetae lyrici Graeci*; of Archilochus, Solon and Theognis, from West, *Iambi et elegi Graeci*; of Aristophanes, Alexis, Antiphanes, Eupolis, Pherecrates and Plato Comicus, from Kock's *Comicorum Atticorum fragmenta* and Demiańczuk's *Supplementum comicum*; of Critias, Democritus, Empedocles, Gorgias, Heraclitus, Parmenides and Prodicus, from DK and (where applicable) from KR also; of Hesiod, from Merkelbach and West, *Fragmenta Hesiodea*; and of Ion of Chios and Philochorus, from Jacoby, *Die Fragmente der griechischen Historiker*.

INTRODUCTION

1 EROS

Plato's *Symposium* depicts a gathering of guests in the house of the tragic poet Agathon. After dinner they decide that instead of hard drinking and singing they will take it in turns to make a speech in praise of ἔρως. This word, which can denote any very strong desire (e.g. for victory) and is used also by Homer (in the form ἔρος) to denote appetite for food and drink, usually means 'love' in the sense which that word bears in our expressions 'be in love (with...)' (ἐρᾶν, epic and poetic ἔρασθαι) and 'fall in love (with...)' (ἐρασθῆναι): that is, intense desire for a particular individual as a sexual partner. The word is not used, except rhetorically or humorously, of the relations between parents and children, brothers and sisters, masters and servants or rulers and subjects.

Like rivers, mountains, abstractions (e.g. justice, piety) and forces (e.g. shame, terror) which are felt by the individual as acting upon him from outside, eros was constantly spoken of as a deity and was so portrayed in the visual arts. Since Greek script did not distinguish between capital and small letters, only the context can show whether a writer who uses the word 'eros' is saying something about a youthful winged deity or about an aspect of human feeling and behaviour. In translating, we must keep 'he' and 'it' both at our disposal and use whichever is appropriate to any given context. It would be mistaken to say that the deity Eros is 'only' the symbol of a natural force, since his characteristics (especially as described by Agathon in 195c6–196b3, in accordance with representation in the visual arts) are characteristics of the outward form of objects of eros, or of temperaments susceptible to eros, but not of the natural force itself.

'Love' in general is φιλία in Greek (verb φιλεῖν); it can denote non-belligerency between nations, the affection we may feel for a colleague and the great love which we commonly feel for a parent, child, close friend or (combined with sexual desire) for a spouse or lover. 'Do you love me?' is φιλεῖς ἐμέ; whether in a sexual (e.g. Xen.

Smp. 9.6) or familial (e.g. Ar. *Clouds* 82) context.[1] Sexual intercourse was regarded as the province of the goddess Aphrodite and was called τὰ ἀφροδίσια (verb ἀφροδισιάζειν); sexual desire was most commonly denoted by words for desire in general, ἐπιθυμία and ἐπιθυμεῖν. Since it is common to desire relief of sexual tension without caring much about the identity of one's partner, while sexual intercourse may in turn generate a great love for a particular partner, Greek literature does not draw a consistent and precise distinction between the role of Aphrodite and the role of Eros (cf. 180c3f. n.).

The Greeks generally agreed, however, in treating the difference between eros and ordinary sexual desire as quantitative (Prodicus (B7) defined eros as 'desire doubled', adding that 'eros doubled' is 'madness') and in treating both as essentially a response to the stimulus afforded by the sight of a person who is καλός. This word, when applied to a person, means 'beautiful', 'pretty', 'handsome', 'attractive', and its antonym is αἰσχρός 'ugly'. The words are also applied to objects, sights and sounds and whatever can be heard about and thought about, such as an institution, an achievement or failure, or a virtuous or vicious action; καλός expresses a favourable reaction ('admirable', 'creditable', 'honourable') and αἰσχρός an unfavourable reaction ('disgraceful', 'repulsive', 'contemptible').[2]

Four speakers in *Smp.*, including Socrates, treat eros as a response to what is καλός. Aristophanes (as we shall see) holds a different view, and Eryximachus comprehends under eros all forms and degrees of harmonious relationship. Socrates, as might be expected (see §3 below), regards the eros excited by beautiful persons as simply the first step towards satisfaction of the soul's desire for transcendent beauty.

---

[1] There are several other words for love. In Christian Greek ἀγάπη and ἀγαπᾶν are favoured, but it should be noted that in classical Greek these words can denote love of which a sexual relationship is an ingredient (on an early Attic red-figure vase a woman lolling 'topless' on a bed and drinking wine is named Ἀγάπη).

[2] In later Greek καλός replaced ἀγαθός and χρηστός as the most general word for 'good'. The process began early with the synonymy of the adverbs καλῶς and εὖ: *GPM* 69–73.

2 HOMOSEXUALITY

In *Smp.* we hear a great deal more of homosexual than of heterosexual eros; and this is not an eccentricity of Plato's, but consonant
with the behaviour of his time and place. It is clear from Greek
literature, art and myth that at least by the early sixth century B.C.
the Greeks had come to think it natural[1] that a good-looking boy or
youth should excite in an older male the same desire for genital
contact and orgasm as is excited by a pretty girl. They did not
consider homosexual relations incompatible with concurrent heterosexual relations or with marriage; some men were no doubt predominantly homosexual, but the sustained relationship between
Pausanias and Agathon which we encounter in *Smp.* (177d, 193bc) is
something unusual.

The language of sex in serious Greek literature (as distinct from
comedy and some minor genres) is always circumspect, and the
reader should not be misled by the recurrent terms ὑπουργεῖν 'render
a service', and χαρίζεσθαι 'grant a favour'. The ultimate 'service' or
'favour' desired by the older male is bodily contact leading to
orgasm, though no doubt a smile or a friendly word would be treasured
by the besotted lover as an interim favour. It is clear that a homosexual lover was thought capable of all the obsessive longing, despair,
self-abasement and devoted self-sacrifice which our most romantic
literature associates with heterosexual love.[2]

Wherever and whenever the homosexual ethos of the Greek world
originated (cf. 182b1 n.), the simple answer to the question, 'Why
were the Athenians of Plato's time so fond of homosexual relations?'
is 'Because their fathers and grandfathers were'. The structure of
Athenian society, and in particular the segregation of the sexes,
reinforced and maintained this ethos. At least in families which owned
enough slaves to exempt their womenfolk from running errands and
working out-of-doors, it was difficult and dangerous for an Athenian
youth to have a love-affair with the daughter of a neighbour of
citizen status. It was easy for him, if he had some pocket-money, to
pay for the use of the body of a woman of foreign or servile status; with
more money, he could make a more permanent arrangement; but
only by courting and seducing a younger male of freeborn status could

[1] *GH* 60–8.   [2] *GH* 50–2, 123f.

he achieve the satisfaction of being accepted for his own sake (and of being admired and envied by his fellows for his 'conquest') without incurring the risks attendant on adultery.[1]

The Greeks did not think of a homosexual love-affair as involving mutual desire on the part of two males of the same age-group. The more mature male, motivated by eros, 'pursues', and the younger, if he 'yields', is motivated by affection, gratitude and admiration. The older male is the ἐραστής ('lover'), the younger is his ἐρώμενος (passive participle of ἐρᾶν) or his παιδικά (a neuter plural, 'things to do with boys', designating a person).[2] Society sympathised with the persistent ἐραστής and encouraged him, but did not tolerate forwardness or deliberate seductiveness on the part of the ἐρώμενος; we may compare heterosexual societies in which women are expected to say 'no' but men are expected to go on trying to make them say 'yes'.[3]

Plato's Socrates enters urbanely into the conventions of Athenian homosexuality.[4] For example, in *Chrm.* 155c he professes to have been thrown into a confused and excited state by a glimpse inside Charmides' cloak, just as if he were speaking of glimpsing a girl's breasts; in *Lysis* 206a he advises Hippothales, who is madly in love with Lysis, that the more one praises a good-looking boy, the more conceited he becomes and 'the harder he is to get' (δυσαλωτότερος); and in *Smp.* 177d6–e3 he welcomes Phaedrus' proposal of speeches in praise of Eros with enthusiasm, saying, 'I don't claim to understand anything but τὰ ἐρωτικά!' What *he* means by τὰ ἐρωτικά, we learn by the time we have finished reading *Smp.*, and not least from Alcibiades' story of his own vain attempt to seduce Socrates. The description of Aristodemus as an ἐραστής of Socrates (173b3) is half a joke,[5] half an acknowledgement that the Socratics used the language of eros more freely, and with less specialised connotations, than most people.

Any relationship between an older and a younger male in a Greek community had an educational dimension which was necessarily lacking in a relationship between a man and a woman, since the younger, destined to become an adult male, could take the older as a model to be imitated, and this stimulated the older to become, and

[1] *GH* 149–51, *GPM* 209–16.   [2] *GH* 16f.
[3] *GH* 81–109.   [4] *GH* 153–7.
[5] Cf. *Prt.* 317c, where Socrates speaks of himself and Hippocrates as ἐρασταί (i.e. 'fans') of Protagoras.

remain, worth imitating. That is why the homosexual response of a man to the visual stimulus afforded by a handsome boy or youth seemed to Plato a good foundation upon which first a teacher–pupil relationship, and then a cooperative intellectual enterprise, could be built. He also considered that our response to visual beauty (*Phdr.* 250d) is the clearest glimpse of eternity that our senses afford us (modern metaphysicians are apt to think first of a Beethoven symphony, though some prefer a Highland sunrise); and there can be little doubt that homosexual response was the most powerful emotional experience known to most of the people for whom he was writing. Whether he himself was a stranger to heterosexual response cannot be decided on existing evidence. Equally, we do not know whether Socrates experienced homosexual temptation as strongly as others did, or less; Aristoxenus in the late fourth century reported (fr. 54a) a tradition (which Platonists have been inclined to treat contemptuously) that Socrates' heterosexual appetite was abnormally strong.

3 PHILOSOPHY

Plato was born in 428/7 and was therefore 28 when Socrates was executed. He has nowhere given us a comprehensive statement of his philosophy as it was at any one period of his life, declaring its axioms, explaining its methods systematically and offering proof of its conclusions. In each work he explores a problem or group of problems without indicating, any further than is necessary for the purpose of that work, its relation to other problems. If we knew the exact date of every one of his works, it would be easier to plot the course of his intellectual development and fill in the gaps. As it is, we know only the relative order of some works, and our ordering of the rest depends on reconciliation of observable changes in style with acceptable hypotheses about the development of his thought. Hence it is possible to ask, e.g., 'When he wrote *Smp.*, did Plato believe in the immortality of the soul?', and different scholars have given different answers to that question.

The philosophical portions[1] of *Smp.* can be followed by any reader

---

[1] What precedes Socrates' interrogation of Agathon (with the doubtful exception of Eryximachus' speech) and what follows the arrival of Alcibiades are not philosophical, though Plato no doubt wishes us to draw

who attends carefully to what is said, even if he has no previous acquaintance with Platonic or any other philosophy. He may, however, be surprised to find so much unjustified and implausible assertion and so little rigorous argument. He will be less surprised if he is aware of Plato's fundamental assumptions.

In life we encounter many things, people and events. Each of these 'particulars' is limited in time and space: it comes into being, it exists here or there, it changes, it ceases to be. Since we do not encounter anything which is wholly unlike everything else, we can form and use 'universal' concepts, generalising, exemplifying, defining, deducing and predicting. In the light of experience, and in accordance with our needs in trying to understand and affect our environment, we correct our generalisations, modify our definitions, replace our axioms. To many people this situation is wholly acceptable. Others, of whom Plato was one, believe that there is something more, something which 'really exists', unchanging, independent of our indefinitely adjustable generalisations and pragmatic definitions. Whether this belief happens to be right, happens to be wrong, or is insufficiently meaningful to be called either, it is at any rate not dictated by reasoned reflection on experience; it is engendered by a kind of craving, which may itself be an operation of divine grace, a psychopathological symptom, the product of an intellectual failure to disentangle words from things, or an element of good or bad luck in the temperament which heredity and experience combine to produce in the individual. Whatever it is, Plato yielded to it, but not to it alone; a second craving made him a philosopher (rather than the kind of visionary who claims portentously to understand the 'meaning of life'), for he believed that the human soul is able to attain firm and certain knowledge of real unchanging entities (εἴδη, ἰδέαι 'ideas' or 'forms') by systematic and communicable reasoning. This knowledge is ἐπιστήμη; propositions founded upon experience, and therefore ultimately on sensory perception, are δόξαι 'opinions'. The eye can perceive an object of the kind we call 'beautiful', but the idea of beauty – 'Beauty', 'the beautiful' (τὸ καλόν), 'the beautiful (by) itself' (αὐτὸ τὸ καλόν) – is perceived only by 'the eye of the soul' (cf. 211e–212a). Plato freely uses generalisations based

from both those portions some inferences which are relevant to his philosophical argument.

upon sensory experience (e.g. 207ab) in corroboration or refutation of hypotheses about the ideas, and *how* particulars, perceptible by our senses and having dimensions in time and space, reflect or 'participate in' the ideas is never explained; indeed, in *Phd.* 100d Plato makes his ignorance of the mechanism explicit. Equally, when the poets treated, e.g., Justice or Modesty as personal deities, or when a worshipper sacrificed at an altar dedicated to Good Order, the relationship between the goddess and the attributes or actions after which she was named was not subjected to intellectual scrutiny; and Plato's 'ideas' are, historically speaking, the progeny of the personified abstractions who thronged the suburbs of Olympus.

Plato's third and most distinctive craving is revealed in a passage of *Phd.* (97b–99b) where he portrays Socrates as dissatisfied with Anaxagoras' explanation of the working of the physical universe because Anaxagoras failed to show why it is *best* that things should work as they do – in other words, because Anaxagoras seemed to him to deal with causation and explanation at a trivial mechanistic level and not to answer the questions which really matter. Plato did not make the thoughtless error of assuming that what is infinite and eternal must for that sole reason be better (or worse) than what is finite and transient. He chose, rather, to believe, or welcomed his own compulsion to believe, that Good is at the very heart of the universe, the ultimate explanation of its structure and of the functioning of all that is in it, including the interrelation of the ideas. In *Rep.* 508d the idea of good (ἡ τοῦ ἀγαθοῦ ἰδέα) is the 'cause (αἰτία) of knowledge (ἐπιστήμη) and truth', and in 509b the relation of what is known (τὰ γιγνωσκόμενα) to the good is compared to the relation of what is seen (τὰ ὁρώμενα) to the sun which not only makes what is seen visible but also brings it to life and growth.

This belief explains why Plato so readily equates knowledge and virtue, between which our everyday experience leads us to draw a considerable distinction. There is nothing man can do about reality (that is, in Plato's terms, the ideas) except understand it rationally; but man's response to good, determined by the very nature of good (cf. 204d–206a), is desire and love. Hence (Plato thinks) desire and reason continuously reinforce each other, and if the good is the ultimate explanation of everything, desire and reason actually converge upon it and will fuse at the point where 'vision' of the good is attained.

But why does anyone embark on the road whose ultimate destination is the fusion of reason and desire in knowledge of the good? In *Smp.* Plato offers an account of an operative force, an ingredient in the structure of the universe, which propels us on that road. That force is eros. The manifestations to which we give the name of eros in ordinary life are in some cases first steps on the right road, in other cases errors or perversions, just as in any other thoughts, desires or actions we can be on the right lines or badly astray. To the extent to which we share Plato's assumptions, his account will seem attractive to us. If we do not share his assumptions, we may not find any part of his account even momentarily plausible. Do not expect him to 'prove' that his account is true; he made no serious attempt, at least in his extant works, to convert his assumptions into logically demonstrable propositions. Had he succeeded in doing so, more of his pupils and successors would have been Platonists. Perhaps their familiarity with the artfulness employed by forensic speakers in seeking to implant assumptions and attitudes in the minds of a jury put them on their guard when Plato employed the same artfulness (e.g. 210b, 205a (p. 145)) in the service of metaphysics.

4 HISTORICAL BASIS

Smp. begins with a short scene in dramatic form. Apollodorus has met Glaucon and some other friends, and they have asked him to tell them the story of Agathon's party. He agrees to tell it as he himself heard it from Aristodemus, who had actually been at the party. The story begins at 174a3 ἔφη γάρ οἱ Σωκράτη ἐντυχεῖν 'Aristodemus said that Socrates met him', and right to the end the narrative framework is expressed as reported speech, while the actual words uttered by the characters in the story are mostly given in direct speech; see 174a n. for more details. We are reminded at fairly frequent intervals (e.g. 177e8–178a5) that Apollodorus is speaking not as an eye-witness but as a reporter of what he had heard from Aristodemus.

Plato uses a similar technique in *Parmenides*, where Cephalus tells how his half-brother Antiphon told the story told to him by Pythodorus about Socrates' meeting with Parmenides and Zeno (*Phd.* is a little different, in that Phaedo, who tells Echecrates the story of Socrates' death, had himself been present on that occasion). Plato's reasons for adopting this technique in a minority of his works are not known; in some others, Socrates himself is the narrator, and the majority are cast in purely dramatic form throughout. Conceivably Plato wished to give authority to his portrayal of Socrates by implicitly inviting us to check it against an independent tradition. On the other hand, he may have intended an oblique suggestion that his portrayal should be judged – like myths or moralising anecdotes – more on its intrinsic merits and the lessons to be learned from it than on its truth to fact. Although Apollodorus says (173b4–6) that he checked 'some things' in Aristodemus' account with Socrates himself, he reminds us (172e3–6) that he has kept company with Socrates for only three years, whereas it is 'many years' since Agathon left Athens, and (178a1–3) that there are gaps both in his own memory and in Aristodemus'.

It would be wrong to imagine that a man like Plato, who pursues with intellectual acuity and with every evidence of passionate concern the philosophical study of virtue and justice, necessarily observes the standards of veracity which we demand of a historian or scientist. If he is accustomed, as a metaphysician, to using words like 'reality' and 'existence' in senses which sometimes approximate to the opposite of the senses which those words bear in ordinary discourse, we may find that his notions of truth also are idiosyncratic. We cannot take it as certain that the personages of *Smp.* were ever all present at the same party in Agathon's house or anywhere else. To acknowledge this is not to assert that they cannot have been present. The occasion of the party is Agathon's first victory as a tragic poet (173a5–6). Agathon won this victory at the Lenaea early in 416,[1] and we have no grounds (of the kind which gives trouble in the 'dramatic dating' of some other Platonic works) for saying that any of the identifiable personages of the story were dead or abroad at that time. Aristophanes, as author of *Clouds*, may possibly have been so hostile to Socrates that even the most self-confident of hosts would have thought twice about inviting them to the same party; but it would be going far beyond the evidence to say that Agathon did not invite them.

---

[1] The date is given us by Athenaeus 217b, and comes ultimately from the Athenian official record of the festivals. Thus at the party Socrates is in his early fifties. Alcibiades is in his thirties; his appointment as one of the generals of the Sicilian Expedition lies over a year ahead (a persistent

Socrates in *Smp.* claims to have learned about the nature of eros from a Mantinean woman named Diotima, and he reports what she said to him. She described, he says (210a1–212a8), a systematic rational progress from admiration of particular beautiful persons and things, which are perceived by the senses, to the spiritual contemplation and understanding of that universal beauty (τὸ καλόν) which is independent, unchanging and eternal, a universal in which all perishable beautiful particulars somehow share (211b2–5). The language used of τὸ καλόν by Diotima is the language used of it also in *Phd.* 100b–d and *Rep.* 474d–479e. Now, Aristotle (*Metaphysics* 987b1–10, 1078b17–1079a4, 1086a35–b5) states that Socrates interested himself in the definition of virtues but did not separate (χωρίζειν) universals from particulars; this separation, he says, was made by Plato, who postulated ἰδέαι in which particulars 'participate'. Unless Aristotle's sources of information on Socrates were very much less numerous and varied than one would naturally suppose, his statement implies that Socrates did not talk about beauty in the terms in which Plato's Socrates talks about it. *A fortiori*, Diotima (if there ever was such a person) did not instruct Socrates in those terms.

5   DATE OF COMPOSITION

Two passages (182b6f. and 193a2f.) make historical allusions which suit Plato's own time but not the time at which Agathon was writing tragedies. The former speaks of 'many parts of Ionia and elsewhere' as being 'under the barbarians', and the latter refers to the 'splitting up' of the Arcadians by Sparta. The King's Peace of 387/6 recognised the Persians' claim to 'the cities in Asia'; and in 385 the Spartans broke up the Arcadian city of Mantinea into four separate settlements. Another consideration is that in 178e–179b3 Phaedrus speaks of an army composed of ἐρασταί and their παιδικά in extravagant and entirely hypothetical terms; but there are reasons for thinking that the 'sacred band' of Thebes, composed in just such a way, was formed in or very soon after 378. A dating of *Smp.* to the period 384–379 is consistent with its style and its philosophical content.[1]

arithmetical error in modern discussions of *Smp.* has obscured that interval).

[1] I have argued this in more detail in *Phronesis* 10 (1965) 1–20; for a different interpretation see H. B. Mattingly, *ibid.* 3 (1958) 31ff.

6 SYMPOSIA

A Greek at a party lay on a bed, turning the upper half of his body to the left, propping himself by his left elbow on cushions, and taking food and drink with his right hand from a table on the left of the bed. At Agathon's party (as we see often in vase-paintings) each bed is wide enough for two (175c6–8), who must therefore lie obliquely, one further down the bed than the other, so that each can get at his own food-table (it appears from 213a7–b7 that Agathon's bed could accommodate three). Lying on one elbow seems uncomfortable for eating and inconvenient for conversation, but it was advantageous at the kind of party which included sexual intercourse with hired women and ended with collapse into drunken sleep. At Agathon's party Phaedrus lies 'first' (177d4) and Agathon 'last' (175c7) until the arrival of Socrates, who then becomes the last. The guests are required to deliver their speeches ἐπὶ δεξιά 'from left to right' (177d3), beginning with Phaedrus and ending with Socrates. Eryximachus, whose turn is meant to follow Aristophanes', lies 'on the bed below (κάτω) Aristophanes' (185d1). Evidently the beds are disposed in a circle or rectangle, and ἐπὶ δεξιά probably denotes an anti-clockwise sequence from the door, each speaker being followed by the person whom he could more easily touch with his right hand than with his left.

Xen. *Anab.* 6.1.30 makes a passing reference to the election of a συμποσίαρχος at a symposium, and the implication of Alexis fr. 21 is that the man elected could prescribe endless toasts. Agathon and his guests do not elect anyone, but Eryximachus takes the lead in proposing how they should conduct themselves (176b5–177e6; cf. p. 85) and thereafter (189a7–c1; cf. 193d6–194a4) is inclined to behave as if he were in charge; he even manages to reassert his authority (214a6–e3) after the drunken Alcibiades has cried (213e9f.) 'I elect ἄρχοντα τῆς πόσεως – myself!'

7 ENCOMIA

The speech which each guest delivers is described indifferently as ἔπαινος 'praise' (e.g. 177d2) or an 'encomium' (e.g. 177b1) of eros. The word ἐγκώμιον seems originally to have denoted a song of welcome and felicitation addressed, e.g., to an athletic victor by a festive crowd (κῶμος), but by the early fourth century it was applied also to speeches composed in praise of any kind of person or thing. Later in the century the author of the *Rhetorica ad Alexandrum* (35) formulated rules for the genre. The speaker, he says, should praise (i) those blessings with which the subject is endowed ἔξω τῆς ἀρετῆς 'independently of (*sc.* his own) good quality', namely, his good family background, strength, beauty and wealth;[1] (ii) his ἀρετή, divided into σοφία ('skill', 'accomplishments'), δικαιοσύνη ('honesty', 'uprightness'), ἀνδρεία ('courage') and ἐπιτηδεύματα ἔνδοξα ('pursuits and activities which enhance his reputation'); (iii) his forebears; (iv) his achievements, including what he has caused to happen through the agency of others. Rhetorical rules of this kind were founded on existing practice, and an instructive example is Xenophon's *Agesilaus*, which he calls (1.1, 11.1) ἔπαινος. He begins with the king's εὐγένεια 'birth into a good family' (1.2), proceeds to narrate his notable ἔργα (ὅσα... διεπράξατο, 1.6), and goes on to τὴν ἐν τῇ ψυχῇ ἀρετήν (3.1), dealing in turn with his piety (3.2), honesty (4.1), self-control (5.1; the term σωφροσύνη is used in 5.7), courage (6.1), skill (6.4) and other specific virtues and graces (7.1). The 'cardinal virtues' (not always exactly the same ones, nor in the same order)[2] are of primary importance in encomia, and we shall encounter them in the speeches delivered by Phaedrus and Agathon. Piety towards the gods will be missing, since Eros is himself a god.

8 TEXTUAL TRANSMISSION

Substantial portions of the second half of *Smp.* are preserved in a papyrus of the second century A.D. (*Oxyrhynchus Papyri* 843). The complete work exists in nearly forty medieval manuscripts, of which the oldest is the Clarkianus (in the Bodleian Library at Oxford), written in A.D. 895. There are few marginal scholia in the manuscripts. Many authors of late antiquity quote from Plato, and occasionally in a form which makes better sense than the direct textual tradition.

In the present edition variant readings and conjectures are given in

[1] The Greeks tended to regard wealth as a matter of luck rather than as the reward of intelligent industry: *GPM* 110, 172-5.
[2] *GPM* 66f.

the apparatus criticus only where it seems to me that there is real doubt about what Plato wrote and that it really matters. The following sigla are used:

a The only reading found in the papyrus text.

a One of two or more readings found in the papyrus text.

m The only reading found in those medieval manuscripts which have so far been collated.

m One of two or more readings found in those manuscripts.

c The only reading found in ancient quotations of the passage in question, so far as editors have reported the quotations.

c One of two or more readings found in ancient quotations.

z Conjectural emendation proposed at any time from the Renaissance to the present day.

[a] From 201a to 214a and from 217b to the end this siglum means that the papyrus text is not legible. Up to 200e and from 214b to 217a we have no papyrus text, and no inference must be drawn there from absence of mention of **a**.

9 BIBLIOGRAPHY

The only edition of *Smp.* with a commentary in English is that of R. G. Bury (second edition, Cambridge 1932). Robin's edition includes a French translation, an extensive introduction and some footnotes (sixth edition, Paris 1958).

The translation by Walter Hamilton (Harmondsworth 1951) is more perceptive and felicitous than those of Benjamin Jowett (in vol. i of Jowett's Plato translation, revised by D. J. Allan and H. E. Dale, Oxford 1953) and W. R. M. Lamb (in vol. v of the Loeb Plato, London 1925); it is also closer to the Greek than that of Michael Joyce, included in (ed.) John Warrington, *Plato: the Symposium and other dialogues* (London 1964).

For a concise and lucid exposition of the issues raised in the study of the *Symposium* see *HGP* iv 365–96, where there is also a good bibliography of books and articles published before the middle of 1973. F. M. Cornford, *The unwritten philosophy and other essays* (Cambridge 1950) 68–80 says much of importance in a dozen pages. Those readers of the *Symposium*, however, whose time for supplementary reading is very limited should give precedence to Plato's *Phaedrus*.

The following should be added to the bibliography given in *HGP*: H. Buchner, *Eros und Sein: Erörterungen zu Platons Symposion* (Bonn 1965); K. J. Dover, 'Eros and Nomos (Plato, *Symposium* 182a–185c)', *Bulletin of the Institute of Classical Studies* 11 (1964) 31–42; B. Ehlers, *Eine vorplatonische Deutung des sokratischen Eros: der Dialog* Aspasia *des Sokratikers Aischines* (Munich 1966); E. Hoffmann, *Über Platons Symposion* (Heidelberg 1947). J. C. B. Gosling, *Plato* (London 1973) is more recent than *HGP* iv; chapters 2–4, 8 and 15 are particularly relevant. L. Brandwood, *Word index to Plato* (Leeds 1976) has given the study of Plato a new dimension; E. des Places, *Lexique de la langue philosophique et religieuse de Platon* (Paris 1964) provides more detailed information about selected words.

Note: in references to works of Plato (e.g. '172a1', '*Phd.* 117d') the first number and the letter represent the page and section of Stephanus' sixteenth-century edition, universally adopted as a system of reference. The line-number will be given only in references to *Smp.*

THE SYMPOSIUM

ΣΥΜΠΟΣΙΟΝ

ΑΠΟΛΛΟΔΩΡΟΣ   ΕΤΑΙΡΟΣ

ΑΠ. δοκῶ μοι περὶ ὧν πυνθάνεσθε οὐκ ἀμελέτητος
εἶναι. καὶ γὰρ ἐτύγχανον πρώην εἰς ἄστυ οἴκοθεν ἀνιὼν Φαλη-
ρόθεν· τῶν οὖν γνωρίμων τις ὄπισθεν κατιδών με πόρρωθεν
ἐκάλεσε, καὶ παίζων ἅμα τῇ κλήσει, 'ὦ Φαληρεύς,' ἔφη,
'οὗτος Ἀπολλόδωρος, οὐ περιμενεῖς;' κἀγὼ ἐπιστὰς περι- 5
έμεινα. καὶ ὅς, ''Ἀπολλόδωρε,' ἔφη, 'καὶ μὴν καὶ ἔναγχός
σε ἐζήτουν, βουλόμενος διαπυθέσθαι τὴν Ἀγάθωνος συνουσίαν
καὶ Σωκράτους καὶ Ἀλκιβιάδου καὶ τῶν ἄλλων τῶν τότε ἐν b
τῷ συνδείπνῳ παραγενομένων, περὶ τῶν ἐρωτικῶν λόγων
τίνες ἦσαν· ἄλλος γάρ τις μοι διηγεῖτο ἀκηκοὼς Φοίνικος
τοῦ Φιλίππου, ἔφη δὲ καὶ σὲ εἰδέναι. ἀλλὰ γὰρ οὐδὲν εἶχε
σαφὲς λέγειν. σὺ οὖν μοι διήγησαι· δικαιότατος γὰρ εἶ 5
τοὺς τοῦ ἑταίρου λόγους ἀπαγγέλλειν. πρότερον δέ μοι,'
ἦ δ' ὅς, 'εἰπέ, σὺ αὐτὸς παρεγένου τῇ συνουσίᾳ ταύτῃ ἢ οὔ;'
κἀγὼ εἶπον ὅτι 'παντάπασιν ἔοικέ σοι οὐδὲν διηγεῖσθαι
σαφὲς ὁ διηγούμενος, εἰ νεωστὶ ἡγῇ τὴν συνουσίαν γεγονέναι c
ταύτην ἣν ἐρωτᾷς, ὥστε καὶ ἐμὲ παραγενέσθαι.' 'ἐγώ γε
δή,' ἔφη. 'πόθεν,' ἦν δ' ἐγώ, 'ὦ Γλαύκων; οὐκ οἶσθ' ὅτι
πολλῶν ἐτῶν Ἀγάθων ἐνθάδε οὐκ ἐπιδεδήμηκεν, ἀφ' οὗ δ'
ἐγὼ Σωκράτει συνδιατρίβω καὶ ἐπιμελὲς πεποίημαι ἑκάστης 5
ἡμέρας εἰδέναι ὅτι ἂν λέγῃ ἢ πράττῃ, οὐδέπω τρία ἔτη ἐστίν;
πρὸ τοῦ δὲ περιτρέχων ὅπη τύχοιμι καὶ οἰόμενός τι ποιεῖν 173
ἀθλιώτερος ἢ ὁτουοῦν, οὐχ ἧττον ἢ σὺ νυνί, οἰόμενος δεῖν
πάντα μᾶλλον πράττειν ἢ φιλοσοφεῖν.' καὶ ὅς, 'μὴ
σκῶπτ',' ἔφη, 'ἀλλ' εἰπέ μοι πότε ἐγένετο ἡ συνουσία
αὕτη.' κἀγὼ εἶπον ὅτι 'παίδων ὄντων ἡμῶν ἔτι, ὅτε τῇ πρώτῃ 5
τραγῳδίᾳ ἐνίκησεν Ἀγάθων, τῇ ὑστεραίᾳ ἢ ᾗ τὰ ἐπινίκια
ἔθυεν αὐτός τε καὶ οἱ χορευταί.' 'πάνυ,' ἔφη, 'ἄρα πάλαι,

a 5 -μένεις vel -μενεις m   b 2 συνδειπνεῖν m   c 2 γε δή] γάρ c
173 a 6 ἢ ᾗ] ἡ (sic) m

ὡς ἔοικεν. ἀλλὰ τίς σοι διηγεῖτο; ἢ αὐτὸς Σωκράτης;'
b 'οὐ μὰ τὸν Δία,' ἦν δ' ἐγώ, 'ἀλλ' ὅσπερ Φοίνικι. 'Αριστό-
δημος ἦν τις, Κυδαθηναιεύς, σμικρός, ἀνυπόδητος ἀεί· παρ-
εγεγόνει δ' ἐν τῇ συνουσίᾳ, Σωκράτους ἐραστὴς ὢν ἐν τοῖς
μάλιστα τῶν τότε, ὡς ἐμοὶ δοκεῖ. οὐ μέντοι ἀλλὰ καὶ
5 Σωκράτη γε ἔνια ἤδη ἀνηρόμην ὧν ἐκείνου ἤκουσα, καί μοι
ὡμολόγει καθάπερ ἐκεῖνος διηγεῖτο.' 'τί οὖν,' ἔφη, 'οὐ
διηγήσω μοι; πάντως δὲ ἡ ὁδὸς ἡ εἰς ἄστυ ἐπιτηδεία
πορευομένοις καὶ λέγειν καὶ ἀκούειν.'
οὕτω δὴ ἰόντες ἅμα τοὺς λόγους περὶ αὐτῶν ἐποιούμεθα.
c ὥστε, ὅπερ ἀρχόμενος εἶπον, οὐκ ἀμελετήτως ἔχω. εἰ οὖν
δεῖ καὶ ὑμῖν διηγήσασθαι, ταῦτα χρὴ ποιεῖν. καὶ γὰρ ἔγωγε
καὶ ἄλλως, ὅταν μέν τινας περὶ φιλοσοφίας λόγους ἢ αὐτὸς
ποιῶμαι ἢ ἄλλων ἀκούω, χωρὶς τοῦ οἴεσθαι ὠφελεῖσθαι
5 ὑπερφυῶς ὡς χαίρω· ὅταν δὲ ἄλλους τινάς, ἄλλως τε καὶ
τοὺς ὑμετέρους τοὺς τῶν πλουσίων καὶ χρηματιστικῶν, αὐτός
τε ἄχθομαι ὑμᾶς τε τοὺς ἑταίρους ἐλεῶ, ὅτι οἴεσθέ τι ποιεῖν
d οὐδὲν ποιοῦντες. καὶ ἴσως αὖ ὑμεῖς ἐμὲ ἡγεῖσθε κακοδαίμονα
εἶναι, καὶ οἴομαι ὑμᾶς ἀληθῆ οἴεσθαι· ἐγὼ μέντοι ὑμᾶς οὐκ
οἴομαι ἀλλ' εὖ οἶδα.
ΕΤ. ἀεὶ ὅμοιος εἶ, ὦ 'Απολλόδωρε· ἀεὶ γὰρ σαυτόν
5 τε κακηγορεῖς καὶ τοὺς ἄλλους, καὶ δοκεῖς μοι ἀτεχνῶς
πάντας ἀθλίους ἡγεῖσθαι πλὴν Σωκράτους, ἀπὸ σαυτοῦ
ἀρξάμενος. καὶ ὁπόθεν ποτὲ ταύτην τὴν ἐπωνυμίαν ἔλαβες,
τὸ μαλακὸς καλεῖσθαι, οὐκ οἶδα ἔγωγε· ἐν μὲν γὰρ τοῖς
λόγοις ἀεὶ τοιοῦτος εἶ· σαυτῷ τε καὶ τοῖς ἄλλοις ἀγριαίνεις
10 πλὴν Σωκράτους.
e ΑΠ. ὦ φίλτατε, καὶ δῆλόν γε δὴ ὅτι οὕτω δια-
νοούμενος καὶ περὶ ἐμαυτοῦ καὶ περὶ ὑμῶν μαίνομαι καὶ
παραπαίω.
ΕΤ. οὐκ ἄξιον περὶ τούτων, 'Απολλόδωρε, νῦν ἐρίζειν·
5 ἀλλ' ὅπερ ἐδεόμεθά σου, μὴ ἄλλως ποιήσῃς, ἀλλὰ διήγησαι
τίνες ἦσαν οἱ λόγοι.
ΑΠ. ἦσαν τοίνυν ἐκεῖνοι τοιοίδε τινές — μᾶλλον δ'

d 8 μανικὸς m

ἐξ ἀρχῆς ὑμῖν, ὡς ἐκεῖνος διηγεῖτο, καὶ ἐγὼ πειράσομαι 174
διηγήσασθαι.

ἔφη γὰρ οἱ Σωκράτη ἐντυχεῖν λελουμένον τε καὶ τὰς
βλαύτας ὑποδεδεμένον, ἃ ἐκεῖνος ὀλιγάκις ἐποίει· καὶ ἐρέσθαι
αὐτὸν ὅποι ἴοι οὕτω καλὸς γεγενημένος.   5
καὶ τὸν εἰπεῖν ὅτι 'ἐπὶ δεῖπνον εἰς 'Αγάθωνος. χθὲς γὰρ
αὐτὸν διέφυγον τοῖς ἐπινικίοις, φοβηθεὶς τὸν ὄχλον· ὡμολόγησα δ' εἰς τήμερον παρέσεσθαι. ταῦτα δὴ ἐκαλλωπισάμην, ἵνα καλὸς παρὰ καλὸν ἴω. ἀλλὰ σύ,' ἦ δ' ὅς, 'πῶς
ἔχεις πρὸς τὸ ἐθέλειν ἂν ἰέναι ἄκλητος ἐπὶ δεῖπνον;'   b
κἀγώ, ἔφη, εἶπον ὅτι 'οὕτως ὅπως ἂν σὺ κελεύῃς.'
'ἕπου τοίνυν,' ἔφη, 'ἵνα καὶ τὴν παροιμίαν διαφθείρωμεν
μεταβαλόντες, ὡς ἄρα καὶ ἀγαθῶν ἐπὶ δαῖτας ἴασιν
αὐτόματοι ἀγαθοί. Ὅμηρος μὲν γὰρ κινδυνεύει οὐ μόνον   5
διαφθεῖραι ἀλλὰ καὶ ὑβρίσαι εἰς ταύτην τὴν παροιμίαν·
ποιήσας γὰρ τὸν 'Αγαμέμνονα διαφερόντως ἀγαθὸν ἄνδρα
τὰ πολεμικά, τὸν δὲ Μενέλεων μαλθακὸν αἰχμητήν,   c
θυσίαν ποιουμένου καὶ ἑστιῶντος τοῦ 'Αγαμέμνονος ἄκλητον
ἐποίησεν ἐλθόντα τὸν Μενέλεων ἐπὶ τὴν θοίνην, χείρω ὄντα
ἐπὶ τὴν τοῦ ἀμείνονος.'
ταῦτ' ἀκούσας εἰπεῖν ἔφη 'ἴσως μέντοι κινδυνεύσω καὶ   5
ἐγὼ οὐχ ὡς σὺ λέγεις, ὦ Σώκρατες, ἀλλὰ καθ' Ὅμηρον
φαῦλος ὢν ἐπὶ σοφοῦ ἀνδρὸς ἰέναι θοίνην ἄκλητος. ὅρα οὖν
ἄγων με τί ἀπολογήσῃ, ὡς ἐγὼ μὲν οὐχ ὁμολογήσω ἄκλητος
ἥκειν, ἀλλ' ὑπὸ σοῦ κεκλημένος.'   d
'σύν τε δύ',' ἔφη, 'ἐρχομένω πρὸ ὁδοῦ βουλευσόμεθα
ὅτι ἐροῦμεν. ἀλλ' ἴωμεν.'
τοιαῦτ' ἄττα σφᾶς ἔφη διαλεχθέντας ἰέναι. τὸν οὖν
Σωκράτη ἑαυτῷ πως προσέχοντα τὸν νοῦν κατὰ τὴν ὁδὸν   5
πορεύεσθαι ὑπολειπόμενον, καὶ περιμένοντος οὗ κελεύειν
προιέναι εἰς τὸ πρόσθεν. ἐπειδὴ δὲ γενέσθαι ἐπὶ τῇ οἰκίᾳ
τῇ 'Αγάθωνος, ἀνεῳγμένην καταλαμβάνειν τὴν θύραν, καί τι   e
ἔφη αὐτόθι γελοῖον παθεῖν. οἱ μὲν γὰρ εὐθὺς παῖδά τινα

b 1 ἂν ἰέναι z: ἀνιέναι m   b 4 'Αγάθων' z   c 7 ὅρα z:
ἄρα vel ἆρα m   d 2 πρὸ ὁ τοῦ z cl. Hom. Il. 10.224

τῶν ἔνδοθεν ἀπαντήσαντα ἄγειν οὗ κατέκειντο οἱ ἄλλοι, καὶ
καταλαμβάνειν ἤδη μέλλοντας δειπνεῖν· εὐθὺς δ' οὖν ὡς
5 ἰδεῖν τὸν Ἀγάθωνα, 'ὦ,' φάναι, "Ἀριστόδημε, εἰς καλὸν ἥκεις
ὅπως συνδειπνήσῃς· εἰ δ' ἄλλου τινὸς ἕνεκα ἦλθες, εἰς αὖθις
ἀναβαλοῦ, ὡς καὶ χθὲς ζητῶν σε ἵνα καλέσαιμι οὐχ οἷός τ'
ἦ ἰδεῖν. ἀλλὰ Σωκράτη ἡμῖν πῶς οὐκ ἄγεις;'

καὶ ἐγώ, ἔφη, μεταστρεφόμενος οὐδαμοῦ ὁρῶ Σωκράτη
10 ἑπόμενον· εἶπον οὖν ὅτι καὶ αὐτὸς μετὰ Σωκράτους ἥκοιμι,
κληθεὶς ὑπ' ἐκείνου δεῦρ' ἐπὶ δεῖπνον.

'καλῶς γ',' ἔφη, 'ποιῶν σύ· ἀλλὰ ποῦ ἐστιν οὗτος;'
175 'ὄπισθεν ἐμοῦ ἄρτι εἰσῄει· ἀλλὰ θαυμάζω καὶ αὐτὸς ποῦ
ἂν εἴη.'

'οὐ σκέψῃ,' ἔφη, 'παῖ,' φάναι τὸν Ἀγάθωνα, 'καὶ εἰσάξεις
Σωκράτη; σὺ δ',' ἦ δ' ὅς, "Ἀριστόδημε, παρ' Ἐρυξίμαχον
5 κατακλίνου.'

καὶ ἓ μὲν ἔφη ἀπονίζειν τὸν παῖδα ἵνα κατακέοιτο· ἄλλον
δέ τινα τῶν παίδων ἥκειν ἀγγέλλοντα ὅτι 'Σωκράτης οὗτος
ἀναχωρήσας ἐν τῷ τῶν γειτόνων προθύρῳ ἕστηκεν, κἀμοῦ
καλοῦντος οὐκ ἐθέλει εἰσιέναι.'

10 'ἄτοπόν γ',' ἔφη, 'λέγεις· οὔκουν καλεῖς αὐτὸν καὶ μὴ
ἀφήσεις;'

b καὶ ὃς ἔφη εἰπεῖν 'μηδαμῶς, ἀλλ' ἐᾶτε αὐτόν. ἔθος γάρ
τι τοῦτ' ἔχει· ἐνίοτε ἀποστὰς ὅποι ἂν τύχῃ ἕστηκεν. ἥξει
δ' αὐτίκα, ὡς ἐγὼ οἶμαι. μὴ οὖν κινεῖτε, ἀλλ' ἐᾶτε.'

'ἀλλ' οὕτω χρὴ ποιεῖν, εἰ σοὶ δοκεῖ,' ἔφη φάναι τὸν
5 Ἀγάθωνα. 'ἀλλ' ἡμᾶς, ὦ παῖδες, τοὺς ἄλλους ἑστιᾶτε.
πάντως παρατίθετε ὅτι ἂν βούλησθε, ἐπειδάν τις ὑμῖν μὴ
ἐφεστήκῃ, ὃ ἐγὼ οὐδεπώποτε ἐποίησα· νῦν οὖν, νομίζοντες
καὶ ἐμὲ ὑφ' ὑμῶν κεκλῆσθαι ἐπὶ δεῖπνον καὶ τούσδε τοὺς
c ἄλλους, θεραπεύετε, ἵν' ὑμᾶς ἐπαινῶμεν.'

μετὰ ταῦτα ἔφη σφᾶς μὲν δειπνεῖν, τὸν δὲ Σωκράτη
οὐκ εἰσιέναι. τὸν οὖν Ἀγάθωνα πολλάκις κελεύειν μετα-
πέμψασθαι τὸν Σωκράτη, ἓ δὲ οὐκ ἐᾶν. ἥκειν οὖν αὐτὸν οὐ
5 πολὺν χρόνον ὡς εἰώθει διατρίψαντα, ἀλλὰ μάλιστα σφᾶς

e 3 τῶν c: om. m

μεσοῦν δειπνοῦντας. τὸν οὖν Ἀγάθωνα (τυγχάνειν γὰρ
ἔσχατον κατακείμενον μόνον) 'δεῦρ',' ἔφη φάναι, 'Σώκρατες,
παρ' ἐμὲ κατάκεισο, ἵνα καὶ τοῦ σοφοῦ ἁπτόμενός σου
ἀπολαύσω ὅ σοι προσέστη ἐν τοῖς προθύροις. δῆλον γὰρ d
ὅτι ηὗρες αὐτὸ καὶ ἔχεις· οὐ γὰρ ἂν προαπέστης.'
καὶ τὸν Σωκράτη καθίζεσθαι καὶ εἰπεῖν ὅτι 'εὖ ἂν ἔχοι,'
φάναι, 'ὦ Ἀγάθων, εἰ τοιοῦτον εἴη ἡ σοφία ὥστ' ἐκ τοῦ πληρε-
στέρου εἰς τὸ κενώτερον ῥεῖν ἡμῶν, ἐὰν ἁπτώμεθα ἀλλήλων, 5
ὥσπερ τὸ ἐν ταῖς κύλιξιν ὕδωρ τὸ διὰ τοῦ ἐρίου ῥέον ἐκ τῆς
πληρεστέρας εἰς τὴν κενωτέραν. εἰ γὰρ οὕτως ἔχει καὶ ἡ
σοφία, πολλοῦ τιμῶμαι τὴν παρὰ σοὶ κατάκλισιν· οἶμαι γάρ e
με παρὰ σοῦ πολλῆς καὶ καλῆς σοφίας πληρωθήσεσθαι. ἡ μὲν
γὰρ ἐμὴ φαύλη τις ἂν εἴη, ἢ καὶ ἀμφισβητήσιμος ὥσπερ ὄναρ
οὖσα, ἡ δὲ σὴ λαμπρά τε καὶ πολλὴν ἐπίδοσιν ἔχουσα, ἥ γε
παρὰ σοῦ νέου ὄντος οὕτω σφόδρα ἐξέλαμψεν καὶ ἐκφανὴς 5
ἐγένετο πρώην ἐν μάρτυσι τῶν Ἑλλήνων πλέον ἢ τρισ-
μυρίοις.'
'ὑβριστὴς εἶ,' ἔφη, 'ὦ Σώκρατες,' ὁ Ἀγάθων. 'καὶ ταῦτα
μὲν καὶ ὀλίγον ὕστερον διαδικασόμεθα ἐγώ τε καὶ σὺ περὶ
τῆς σοφίας, δικαστῇ χρώμενοι τῷ Διονύσῳ· νῦν δὲ πρὸς τὸ
δεῖπνον πρῶτα τρέπου.' 10
μετὰ ταῦτα, ἔφη, κατακλινέντος τοῦ Σωκράτους καὶ 176
δειπνήσαντος καὶ τῶν ἄλλων, σπονδάς τε σφᾶς ποιήσασθαι
καὶ ᾄσαντας τὸν θεὸν καὶ τἆλλα τὰ νομιζόμενα τρέπεσθαι
πρὸς τὸν πότον· τὸν οὖν Παυσανίαν ἔφη λόγου τοιούτου
τινὸς κατάρχειν. 'εἶεν, ἄνδρες,' φάναι, 'τίνα τρόπον ῥᾷστα 5
πιόμεθα; ἐγὼ μὲν οὖν λέγω ὑμῖν ὅτι τῷ ὄντι πάνυ χαλεπῶς
ἔχω ὑπὸ τοῦ χθὲς πότου καὶ δέομαι ἀναψυχῆς τινος, οἶμαι
δὲ καὶ ὑμῶν τοὺς πολλούς· παρῆστε γὰρ χθές. σκοπεῖσθε
οὖν τίνι τρόπῳ ἂν ὡς ῥᾷστα πίνοιμεν.' b
τὸν οὖν Ἀριστοφάνη εἰπεῖν, 'τοῦτο μέντοι εὖ λέγεις, ὦ
Παυσανία, τὸ παντὶ τρόπῳ παρασκευάσασθαι ῥᾳστώνην τινὰ
τῆς πόσεως· καὶ γὰρ αὐτός εἰμι τῶν χθὲς βεβαπτισμένων.'
ἀκούσαντα οὖν αὐτῶν ἔφη Ἐρυξίμαχον τὸν Ἀκουμενοῦ 5
'ἦ καλῶς,' φάναι, 'λέγετε. καὶ ἔτι ἑνὸς δέομαι ὑμῶν ἀκοῦσαι

πῶς ἔχει πρὸς τὸ ἐρρῶσθαι πίνειν 'Αγάθων.'

'οὐδαμῶς,' φάναι, 'οὐδ' αὐτὸς ἔρρωμαι.'

c   'ἕρμαιον ἂν εἴη ἡμῖν,' ἦ δ' ὅς, 'ὡς ἔοικεν, ἐμοί τε καὶ
'Αριστοδήμῳ καὶ Φαίδρῳ καὶ τοῖσδε, εἰ ὑμεῖς οἱ δυνατώτατοι
πίνειν νῦν ἀπειρήκατε· ἡμεῖς μὲν γὰρ ἀεὶ ἀδύνατοι. Σωκράτη δ' ἐξαιρῶ λόγου· ἱκανὸς γὰρ κατ' ἀμφότερα, ὥστ'
5 ἐξαρκέσει αὐτῷ ὁπότερ' ἂν ποιῶμεν. ἐπειδὴ οὖν μοι δοκεῖ
οὐδεὶς τῶν παρόντων προθύμως ἔχειν πρὸς τὸ πολὺν πίνειν
οἶνον, ἴσως ἂν ἐγὼ περὶ τοῦ μεθύσκεσθαι οἷόν ἐστι τἀληθῆ
λέγων ἧττον ἂν εἴην ἀηδής. ἐμοὶ γὰρ δὴ τοῦτό γε οἶμαι
d κατάδηλον γεγονέναι ἐκ τῆς ἰατρικῆς ὅτι χαλεπὸν τοῖς
ἀνθρώποις ἡ μέθη ἐστίν· καὶ οὔτε αὐτὸς ἑκὼν εἶναι πόρρω
ἐθελήσαιμι ἂν πιεῖν οὔτε ἄλλῳ συμβουλεύσαιμι, ἄλλως τε
καὶ κραιπαλῶντα ἔτι ἐκ τῆς προτεραίας.'

5   'ἀλλὰ μήν,' ἔφη φάναι ὑπολαβόντα Φαῖδρον τὸν Μυρρινούσιον, 'ἔγωγέ σοι εἴωθα πείθεσθαι ἄλλως τε καὶ ἅττ' ἂν περὶ
ἰατρικῆς λέγῃς· νῦν δ', ἂν εὖ βουλεύωνται, καὶ οἱ λοιποί.'
e ταῦτα δὴ ἀκούσαντας συγχωρεῖν πάντας μὴ διὰ μέθης
ποιήσασθαι τὴν ἐν τῷ παρόντι συνουσίαν, ἀλλ' οὕτω πίνοντας
πρὸς ἡδονήν.

'ἐπειδὴ τοίνυν,' φάναι τὸν 'Ερυξίμαχον, 'τοῦτο μὲν δέ-
5 δοκται, πίνειν ὅσον ἂν ἕκαστος βούληται, ἐπάναγκες δὲ μηδὲν
εἶναι, τὸ μετὰ τοῦτο εἰσηγοῦμαι τὴν μὲν ἄρτι εἰσελθοῦσαν
αὐλητρίδα χαίρειν ἐᾶν, αὐλοῦσαν ἑαυτῇ ἤ, ἂν βούληται, ταῖς
γυναιξὶ ταῖς ἔνδον, ἡμᾶς δὲ διὰ λόγων ἀλλήλοις συνεῖναι
τὸ τήμερον· καὶ δι' οἵων λόγων, εἰ βούλεσθε, ἐθέλω ὑμῖν
10 εἰσηγήσασθαι.'

177 φάναι δὴ πάντας καὶ βούλεσθαι καὶ κελεύειν αὐτὸν
εἰσηγεῖσθαι. εἰπεῖν οὖν τὸν 'Ερυξίμαχον ὅτι 'ἡ μέν μοι
ἀρχὴ τοῦ λόγου ἐστὶ κατὰ τὴν Εὐριπίδου Μελανίππην· οὐ
γὰρ ἐμὸς ὁ μῦθος, ἀλλὰ Φαίδρου τοῦδε, ὃν μέλλω λέγειν.
5 Φαῖδρος γὰρ ἑκάστοτε πρός με ἀγανακτῶν λέγει "οὐ δεινόν,"
φησίν, "ὦ 'Ερυξίμαχε, ἄλλοις μέν τισι θεῶν ὕμνους καὶ
παιῶνας εἶναι ὑπὸ τῶν ποιητῶν πεποιημένους, τῷ δὲ "Ερωτι,

b 7 πίνειν, 'Αγάθωνος z   d 7 βουλεύωνται z: βούλωνται m

τηλικούτῳ ὄντι καὶ τοσούτῳ θεῷ, μηδὲ ἕνα πώποτε τοσούτων
γεγονότων ποιητῶν πεποιηκέναι μηδὲν ἐγκώμιον; εἰ δὲ βούλει b
αὖ σκέψασθαι τοὺς χρηστοὺς σοφιστάς, Ἡρακλέους μὲν καὶ
ἄλλων ἐπαίνους καταλογάδην συγγράφειν, ὥσπερ ὁ βέλτιστος
Πρόδικος· καὶ τοῦτο μὲν ἧττον καὶ θαυμαστόν, ἀλλ' ἔγωγε
ἤδη τινὶ ἐνέτυχον βιβλίῳ ἀνδρὸς σοφοῦ, ἐν ᾧ ἐνῆσαν ἅλες 5
ἔπαινον θαυμάσιον ἔχοντες πρὸς ὠφελίαν, καὶ ἄλλα τοιαῦτα
συχνὰ ἴδοις ἂν ἐγκεκωμιασμένα. / τὸ οὖν τοιούτων μὲν πέρι c
πολλὴν σπουδὴν ποιήσασθαι, Ἔρωτα δὲ μηδένα πω ἀνθρώπων
τετολμηκέναι εἰς ταυτηνὶ τὴν ἡμέραν ἀξίως ὑμνῆσαι, ἀλλ'
οὕτως ἠμέληται τοσοῦτος θεός." ταῦτα δή μοι δοκεῖ εὖ
λέγειν Φαῖδρος. ἐγὼ οὖν ἐπιθυμῶ ἅμα μὲν τούτῳ ἔρανον 5
εἰσενεγκεῖν καὶ χαρίσασθαι, ἅμα δ' ἐν τῷ παρόντι πρέπον
μοι δοκεῖ εἶναι ἡμῖν τοῖς παροῦσι κοσμῆσαι τὸν θεόν. εἰ οὖν
συνδοκεῖ καὶ ὑμῖν, γένοιτ' ἂν ἡμῖν ἐν λόγοις ἱκανὴ διατριβή· d
δοκεῖ γάρ μοι χρῆναι ἕκαστον ἡμῶν λόγον εἰπεῖν ἔπαινον
Ἔρωτος ἐπὶ δεξιὰ ὡς ἂν δύνηται κάλλιστον, ἄρχειν δὲ
Φαῖδρον πρῶτον, ἐπειδὴ καὶ πρῶτος κατάκειται καί ἐστιν
ἅμα πατὴρ τοῦ λόγου.' 5

'οὐδείς σοι, ὦ Ἐρυξίμαχε,' φάναι τὸν Σωκράτη, 'ἐναντία
ψηφιεῖται. οὔτε γὰρ ἄν που ἐγὼ ἀποφήσαιμι, ὃς οὐδέν
φημι ἄλλο ἐπίστασθαι ἢ τὰ ἐρωτικά, οὔτε που Ἀγάθων καὶ
Παυσανίας, οὐδὲ μὴν Ἀριστοφάνης, ᾧ περὶ Διόνυσον καὶ e
Ἀφροδίτην πᾶσα ἡ διατριβή, οὐδὲ ἄλλος οὐδεὶς τουτωνὶ ὧν
ἐγὼ ὁρῶ. καίτοι οὐκ ἐξ ἴσου γίγνεται ἡμῖν τοῖς ὑστάτοις
κατακειμένοις· ἀλλ' ἐὰν οἱ πρόσθεν ἱκανῶς καὶ καλῶς
εἴπωσιν, ἐξαρκέσει ἡμῖν. ἀλλὰ τύχῃ ἀγαθῇ καταρχέτω 5
Φαῖδρος καὶ ἐγκωμιαζέτω τὸν Ἔρωτα.'

ταῦτα δὴ καὶ οἱ ἄλλοι πάντες ἄρα συνέφασάν τε καὶ
ἐκέλευον ἅπερ ὁ Σωκράτης. πάντων μὲν οὖν ἃ ἕκαστος 178
εἶπεν οὔτε πάνυ ὁ Ἀριστόδημος ἐμέμνητο οὔτ' αὖ ἐγὼ
ἃ ἐκεῖνος ἔλεγε πάντα· ἃ δὲ μάλιστα καὶ ὧν ἔδοξέ
μοι ἀξιομνημόνευτον, τούτων ὑμῖν ἐρῶ ἑκάστου τὸν
λόγον. 5

a 4 ἀξιομνημόνευτον εἶναι, τούτων m

πρῶτον μὲν γάρ, ὥσπερ λέγω, ἔφη Φαῖδρον ἀρξάμενον
ἐνθένδε ποθὲν λέγειν, ὅτι μέγας θεὸς εἴη ὁ Ἔρως καὶ
θαυμαστὸς ἐν ἀνθρώποις τε καὶ θεοῖς, πολλαχῇ μὲν καὶ ἄλλῃ,
οὐχ ἥκιστα δὲ κατὰ τὴν γένεσιν. 'τὸ γὰρ ἐν τοῖς πρεσβύ-
b τατον εἶναι τὸν θεὸν τίμιον,' ἦ δ' ὅς, 'τεκμήριον δὲ τούτου·
γονῆς γὰρ Ἔρωτος οὔτ' εἰσὶν οὔτε λέγονται ὑπ' οὐδενὸς οὔτε
ἰδιώτου οὔτε ποιητοῦ, ἀλλ' Ἡσίοδος πρῶτον μὲν Χάος φησὶ
γενέσθαι,
5   αὐτὰρ ἔπειτα
          Γαῖ' εὐρύστερνος, πάντων ἕδος ἀσφαλὲς αἰεί,
          ἠδ' Ἔρος.

Ἡσιόδῳ δὲ καὶ Ἀκουσίλεως σύμφησιν μετὰ τὸ Χάος δύο
τούτω γενέσθαι, Γῆν τε καὶ Ἔρωτα. Παρμενίδης δὲ τὴν
10 γένεσιν λέγει·
          πρώτιστον μὲν Ἔρωτα θεῶν μητίσατο πάντων.

c οὕτω πολλαχόθεν ὁμολογεῖται ὁ Ἔρως ἐν τοῖς πρεσβύτατος εἶναι. πρεσβύτατος δὲ ὢν μεγίστων ἀγαθῶν ἡμῖν
αἴτιός ἐστιν. οὐ γὰρ ἔγωγ' ἔχω εἰπεῖν ὅτι μεῖζόν ἐστιν
ἀγαθὸν εὐθὺς νέῳ ὄντι ἢ ἐραστὴς χρηστὸς καὶ ἐραστῇ
5 παιδικά. ὃ γὰρ χρὴ ἀνθρώποις ἡγεῖσθαι παντὸς τοῦ βίου
τοῖς μέλλουσι καλῶς βιώσεσθαι, τοῦτο οὔτε συγγένεια οἷα
τε ἐμποιεῖν οὕτω καλῶς οὔτε τιμαὶ οὔτε πλοῦτος οὔτ' ἄλλο
d οὐδὲν ὡς ἔρως. λέγω δὲ δὴ τί τοῦτο; τὴν ἐπὶ μὲν τοῖς
αἰσχροῖς αἰσχύνην, ἐπὶ δὲ τοῖς καλοῖς φιλοτιμίαν· οὐ γάρ
ἐστιν ἄνευ τούτων οὔτε πόλιν οὔτε ἰδιώτην μεγάλα καὶ
καλὰ ἔργα ἐξεργάζεσθαι. φημὶ τοίνυν ἐγὼ ἄνδρα ὅστις
5 ἐρᾷ, εἴ τι αἰσχρὸν ποιῶν κατάδηλος γίγνοιτο ἢ πάσχων
ὑπό του δι' ἀνανδρίαν μὴ ἀμυνόμενος, οὔτ' ἂν ὑπὸ πατρὸς
ὀφθέντα οὕτως ἀλγῆσαι οὔτε ὑπὸ ἑταίρων οὔτε ὑπ' ἄλλου
e οὐδενὸς ὡς ὑπὸ παιδικῶν. ταὐτὸν δὲ τοῦτο καὶ τὸν ἐρώμενον ὁρῶμεν, ὅτι διαφερόντως τοὺς ἐραστὰς αἰσχύνεται,
ὅταν ὀφθῇ ἐν αἰσχρῷ τινι ὤν. εἰ οὖν μηχανή τις γένοιτο
ὥστε πόλιν γενέσθαι ἢ στρατόπεδον ἐραστῶν τε καὶ παι-

δικῶν, οὐκ ἔστιν ὅπως ἂν ἄμεινον οἰκήσειαν τὴν ἑαυτῶν ἢ 5
ἀπεχόμενοι πάντων τῶν αἰσχρῶν καὶ φιλοτιμούμενοι πρὸς
ἀλλήλους, καὶ μαχόμενοί γ' ἂν μετ' ἀλλήλων οἱ τοιοῦτοι 179
νικῷεν ἂν ὀλίγοι ὄντες ὡς ἔπος εἰπεῖν πάντας ἀνθρώπους.
ἐρῶν γὰρ ἀνὴρ ὑπὸ παιδικῶν ὀφθῆναι ἢ λιπὼν τάξιν ἢ
ὅπλα ἀποβαλὼν ἧττον ἂν δήπου δέξαιτο ἢ ὑπὸ πάντων τῶν
ἄλλων, καὶ πρὸ τούτου τεθνάναι ἂν πολλάκις ἕλοιτο. καὶ 5
μὴν ἐγκαταλιπεῖν γε τὰ παιδικὰ ἢ μὴ βοηθῆσαι κινδυνεύοντι —
οὐδεὶς οὕτω κακὸς ὅντινα οὐκ ἂν αὐτὸς ὁ Ἔρως ἔνθεον
ποιήσειε πρὸς ἀρετήν, ὥστε ὅμοιον εἶναι τῷ ἀρίστῳ φύσει·
καὶ ἀτεχνῶς, ὃ ἔφη Ὅμηρος, μένος ἐμπνεῦσαι ἐνίοις b
τῶν ἡρώων τὸν θεόν, τοῦτο ὁ Ἔρως τοῖς ἐρῶσι παρέχει
γιγνόμενον παρ' αὐτοῦ.
   καὶ μὴν ὑπεραποθνήσκειν γε μόνοι ἐθέλουσιν οἱ ἐρῶντες,
οὐ μόνον ὅτι ἄνδρες, ἀλλὰ καὶ αἱ γυναῖκες.   τούτου δὲ καὶ 5
ἡ Πελίου θυγάτηρ Ἄλκηστις ἱκανὴν μαρτυρίαν παρέχεται
ὑπὲρ τοῦδε τοῦ λόγου εἰς τοὺς Ἕλληνας, ἐθελήσασα μόνη
ὑπὲρ τοῦ αὑτῆς ἀνδρὸς ἀποθανεῖν, ὄντων αὐτῷ πατρός τε
καὶ μητρός, οὓς ἐκείνη τοσοῦτον ὑπερεβάλετο τῇ φιλίᾳ διὰ c
τὸν ἔρωτα, ὥστε ἀποδεῖξαι αὐτοὺς ἀλλοτρίους ὄντας τῷ υἱεῖ
καὶ ὀνόματι μόνον προσήκοντας· καὶ τοῦτ' ἐργασαμένη τὸ
ἔργον οὕτω καλὸν ἔδοξεν ἐργάσασθαι οὐ μόνον ἀνθρώποις
ἀλλὰ καὶ θεοῖς, ὥστε πολλῶν πολλὰ καὶ καλὰ ἐργασαμένων 5
εὐαριθμήτοις δή τισιν ἔδοσαν τοῦτο γέρας οἱ θεοί, ἐξ Ἅιδου
ἀνεῖναι πάλιν τὴν ψυχήν, ἀλλὰ τὴν ἐκείνης ἀνεῖσαν ἀγα-
σθέντες τῷ ἔργῳ. οὕτω καὶ θεοὶ τὴν περὶ τὸν ἔρωτα σπουδήν d
τε καὶ ἀρετὴν μάλιστα τιμῶσιν.   Ὀρφέα δὲ τὸν Οἰάγρου
ἀτελῆ ἀπέπεμψαν ἐξ Ἅιδου, φάσμα δείξαντες τῆς γυναικὸς
ἐφ' ἣν ἧκεν, αὐτὴν δὲ οὐ δόντες, ὅτι μαλθακίζεσθαι ἐδόκει, ἅτε ὢν κιθαρῳδός, καὶ οὐ τολμᾶν ἕνεκα τοῦ ἔρωτος 5
ἀποθνήσκειν ὥσπερ Ἄλκηστις, ἀλλὰ διαμηχανᾶσθαι ζῶν
εἰσιέναι εἰς Ἅιδου. τοιγάρτοι διὰ ταῦτα δίκην αὐτῷ ἐπέ-
θεσαν, καὶ ἐποίησαν τὸν θάνατον αὐτοῦ ὑπὸ γυναικῶν
γενέσθαι, οὐχ ὥσπερ Ἀχιλλέα τὸν τῆς Θέτιδος υἱὸν ἐτίμη- e

178 e 5 ἢ del. z   b 5 ὅτι] om. m: οἱ c   c 7 ἀνιέναι z

σαν καὶ εἰς μακάρων νήσους ἀπέπεμψαν, ὅτι πεπυσμένος
παρὰ τῆς μητρὸς ὡς ἀποθανοῖτο ἀποκτείνας "Εκτορα, μὴ
ποιήσας δὲ τοῦτο οἴκαδε ἐλθὼν γηραιὸς τελευτήσοι,
5 ἐτόλμησεν ἑλέσθαι βοηθήσας τῷ ἐραστῇ Πατρόκλῳ καὶ
180 τιμωρήσας οὐ μόνον ὑπεραποθανεῖν ἀλλὰ καὶ ἐπαποθανεῖν
τετελευτηκότι· ὅθεν δὴ καὶ ὑπεραγασθέντες οἱ θεοὶ διαφερόντως αὐτὸν ἐτίμησαν, ὅτι τὸν ἐραστὴν οὕτω περὶ πολλοῦ
ἐποιεῖτο. Αἰσχύλος δὲ φλυαρεῖ φάσκων Ἀχιλλέα Πα-
5 τρόκλου ἐρᾶν, ὃς ἦν καλλίων οὐ μόνον Πατρόκλου ἀλλ᾽
ἄρα καὶ τῶν ἡρώων ἁπάντων, καὶ ἔτι ἀγένειος, ἔπειτα
νεώτερος πολύ, ὥς φησιν Ὅμηρος. ἀλλὰ γὰρ τῷ ὄντι
μάλιστα μὲν ταύτην τὴν ἀρετὴν οἱ θεοὶ τιμῶσιν τὴν περὶ
b τὸν ἔρωτα, μᾶλλον μέντοι θαυμάζουσιν καὶ ἄγανται καὶ
εὖ ποιοῦσιν ὅταν ὁ ἐρώμενος τὸν ἐραστὴν ἀγαπᾷ ἢ ὅταν
ὁ ἐραστὴς τὰ παιδικά. θειότερον γὰρ ἐραστὴς παιδικῶν·
ἔνθεος γάρ ἐστι. διὰ ταῦτα καὶ τὸν Ἀχιλλέα τῆς Ἀλκήσ-
5 τιδος μᾶλλον ἐτίμησαν, εἰς μακάρων νήσους ἀποπέμψαντες.
    οὕτω δὴ ἔγωγέ φημι Ἔρωτα θεῶν καὶ πρεσβύτατον καὶ
τιμιώτατον καὶ κυριώτατον εἶναι εἰς ἀρετῆς καὶ εὐδαιμονίας
κτῆσιν ἀνθρώποις καὶ ζῶσι καὶ τελευτήσασιν.᾽
c   Φαῖδρον μὲν τοιοῦτόν τινα λόγον ἔφη εἰπεῖν, μετὰ δὲ
Φαῖδρον ἄλλους τινὰς εἶναι ὧν οὐ πάνυ διεμνημόνευε· οὓς
παρεὶς τὸν Παυσανίου λόγον διηγεῖτο. εἰπεῖν δ᾽ αὐτὸν
ὅτι ‘οὐ καλῶς μοι δοκεῖ, ὦ Φαῖδρε, προβεβλῆσθαι ἡμῖν
5 ὁ λόγος, τὸ ἁπλῶς οὕτως παρηγγέλθαι ἐγκωμιάζειν Ἔρωτα.
εἰ μὲν γὰρ εἷς ἦν ὁ Ἔρως, καλῶς ἂν εἶχε, νῦν δὲ οὐ γάρ
ἐστιν εἷς· μὴ ὄντος δὲ ἑνὸς ὀρθότερόν ἐστι πρότερον προρ-
d ρηθῆναι ὁποῖον δεῖ ἐπαινεῖν. ἐγὼ οὖν πειράσομαι τοῦτο
ἐπανορθώσασθαι, πρῶτον μὲν Ἔρωτα φράσαι ὃν δεῖ ἐπαινεῖν, ἔπειτα ἐπαινέσαι ἀξίως τοῦ θεοῦ. πάντες γὰρ ἴσμεν
ὅτι οὐκ ἔστιν ἄνευ Ἔρωτος Ἀφροδίτη. μιᾶς μὲν οὖν
5 οὔσης εἷς ἂν ἦν Ἔρως· ἐπεὶ δὲ δὴ δύο ἐστόν, δύο ἀνάγκη
καὶ Ἔρωτε εἶναι. πῶς δ᾽ οὐ δύο τὼ θεά; ἡ μέν γε που
πρεσβυτέρα καὶ ἀμήτωρ Οὐρανοῦ θυγάτηρ, ἣν δὴ καὶ

a 6 ἄρα om. m: ἅμα z

Οὐρανίαν ἐπονομάζομεν· ἡ δὲ νεωτέρα Διὸς καὶ Διώνης,
ἣν δὴ Πάνδημον καλοῦμεν. ἀναγκαῖον δὴ καὶ Ἔρωτα τὸν e
μὲν τῇ ἑτέρᾳ συνεργὸν Πάνδημον ὀρθῶς καλεῖσθαι, τὸν δὲ
Οὐράνιον. ἐπαινεῖν μὲν οὖν δεῖ πάντας θεούς, ἃ δ᾽ οὖν
ἑκάτερος εἴληχε πειρατέον εἰπεῖν. πᾶσα γὰρ πρᾶξις ὧδ᾽
ἔχει· αὐτὴ ἐφ᾽ ἑαυτῆς πραττομένη οὔτε καλὴ οὔτε αἰσχρά. 5
οἷον ὃ νῦν ἡμεῖς ποιοῦμεν, ἢ πίνειν ἢ ᾄδειν ἢ διαλέγεσθαι, 181
οὐκ ἔστι τούτων αὐτὸ καλὸν οὐδέν, ἀλλ᾽ ἐν τῇ πράξει, ὡς
ἂν πραχθῇ, τοιοῦτον ἀπέβη· καλῶς μὲν γὰρ πραττόμενον
καὶ ὀρθῶς καλὸν γίγνεται, μὴ ὀρθῶς δὲ αἰσχρόν. οὕτω δὴ
καὶ τὸ ἐρᾶν καὶ ὁ Ἔρως οὐ πᾶς ἐστι καλὸς οὐδὲ ἄξιος 5
ἐγκωμιάζεσθαι, ἀλλὰ ὁ καλῶς προτρέπων ἐρᾶν.

ὁ μὲν οὖν τῆς Πανδήμου Ἀφροδίτης ὡς ἀληθῶς πάν-
δημός ἐστι καὶ ἐξεργάζεται ὅτι ἂν τύχῃ· καὶ οὗτός ἐστιν b
ὃν οἱ φαῦλοι τῶν ἀνθρώπων ἐρῶσιν. ἐρῶσι δὲ οἱ τοιοῦτοι
πρῶτον μὲν οὐχ ἧττον γυναικῶν ἢ παίδων, ἔπειτα ὧν καὶ
ἐρῶσι τῶν σωμάτων μᾶλλον ἢ τῶν ψυχῶν, ἔπειτα ὡς ἂν
δύνωνται ἀνοητοτάτων, πρὸς τὸ διαπράξασθαι μόνον βλέ- 5
ποντες, ἀμελοῦντες δὲ τοῦ καλῶς ἢ μή· ὅθεν δὴ συμβαίνει
αὐτοῖς, ὅτι ἂν τύχωσι, τοῦτο πράττειν, ὁμοίως μὲν ἀγαθόν,
ὁμοίως δὲ τοὐναντίον. ἔστι γὰρ καὶ ἀπὸ τῆς θεοῦ νεωτέρας
τε οὔσης πολὺ ἢ τῆς ἑτέρας, καὶ μετεχούσης ἐν τῇ γενέσει c
καὶ θήλεος καὶ ἄρρενος. ὁ δὲ τῆς Οὐρανίας πρῶτον μὲν οὐ
μετεχούσης θήλεος ἀλλ᾽ ἄρρενος μόνον (καί ἐστιν οὗτος ὁ
τῶν παίδων ἔρως), ἔπειτα πρεσβυτέρας, ὕβρεως ἀμοίρου· ὅθεν
δὴ ἐπὶ τὸ ἄρρεν τρέπονται οἱ ἐκ τούτου τοῦ ἔρωτος ἔπιπνοι, 5
τὸ φύσει ἐρρωμενέστερον καὶ νοῦν μᾶλλον ἔχον ἀγαπῶντες.
καί τις ἂν γνοίη καὶ ἐν αὐτῇ τῇ παιδεραστίᾳ τοὺς εἰλικρινῶς
ὑπὸ τούτου τοῦ ἔρωτος ὡρμημένους· οὐ γὰρ ἐρῶσι παίδων, d
ἀλλ᾽ ἐπειδὰν ἤδη ἄρχωνται νοῦν ἴσχειν, τοῦτο δὲ πλησιάζει
τῷ γενειάσκειν. παρεσκευασμένοι γὰρ οἶμαί εἰσιν οἱ ἐντεῦθεν ἀρχόμενοι ἐρᾶν ὡς τὸν βίον ἅπαντα συνεσόμενοι
καὶ κοινῇ συμβιωσόμενοι, ἀλλ᾽ οὐκ ἐξαπατήσαντες, ἐν 5
ἀφροσύνῃ λαβόντες ὡς νέον, καταγελάσαντες οἰχήσεσθαι
ἐπ᾽ ἄλλον ἀποτρέχοντες. χρῆν δὲ καὶ νόμον εἶναι μὴ ἐρᾶν

e παίδων, ἵνα μὴ εἰς ἄδηλον πολλὴ σπουδὴ ἀνηλίσκετο· τὸ
γὰρ τῶν παίδων τέλος ἄδηλον οἷ τελευτᾷ κακίας καὶ ἀρετῆς
ψυχῆς τε πέρι καὶ σώματος. ⌐οἱ μὲν οὖν ἀγαθοὶ τὸν νόμον
τοῦτον αὐτοὶ αὐτοῖς ἑκόντες τίθενται, χρῆν δὲ καὶ τούτους
5 τοὺς πανδήμους ἐραστὰς προσαναγκάζειν τὸ τοιοῦτον, ὥσπερ
καὶ τῶν ἐλευθέρων γυναικῶν προσαναγκάζομεν αὐτοὺς καθ'
182 ὅσον δυνάμεθα μὴ ἐρᾶν. οὗτοι γάρ εἰσιν οἱ καὶ τὸ ὄνειδος
πεποιηκότες, ὥστε τινὰς τολμᾶν λέγειν ὡς αἰσχρὸν χαρίζεσθαι ἐρασταῖς· λέγουσι δὲ εἰς τούτους ἀποβλέποντες,
ὁρῶντες αὐτῶν τὴν ἀκαιρίαν καὶ ἀδικίαν, ἐπεὶ οὐ δήπου
5 κοσμίως γε καὶ νομίμως ὁτιοῦν πρᾶγμα πραττόμενον ψόγον
ἂν δικαίως φέροι.

καὶ δὴ καὶ ὁ περὶ τὸν ἔρωτα νόμος ἐν μὲν ταῖς ἄλλαις
πόλεσι νοῆσαι ῥάδιος, ἁπλῶς γὰρ ὥρισται· ὁ δ' ἐνθάδε
b καὶ ἐν Λακεδαίμονι ποικίλος. ἐν Ἤλιδι μὲν γὰρ καὶ ἐν
Βοιωτοῖς, καὶ οὗ μὴ σοφοὶ λέγειν, ἁπλῶς νενομοθέτηται
καλὸν τὸ χαρίζεσθαι ἐρασταῖς, καὶ οὐκ ἄν τις εἴποι οὔτε
νέος οὔτε παλαιὸς ὡς αἰσχρόν, ἵνα οἶμαι μὴ πράγματ'
5 ἔχωσιν λόγῳ πειρώμενοι πείθειν τοὺς νέους, ἅτε ἀδύνατοι λέγειν· τῆς δὲ Ἰωνίας καὶ ἄλλοθι πολλαχοῦ αἰσχρὸν
νενόμισται, ὅσοι ὑπὸ βαρβάροις οἰκοῦσιν. τοῖς γὰρ βαρβάροις διὰ τὰς τυραννίδας αἰσχρὸν τοῦτό γε, καὶ ἥ γε
c φιλοσοφία καὶ ἡ φιλογυμναστία. οὐ γὰρ οἶμαι συμφέρει
τοῖς ἄρχουσι φρονήματα μεγάλα ἐγγίγνεσθαι τῶν ἀρχομένων, οὐδὲ φιλίας ἰσχυρὰς καὶ κοινωνίας· ὃ δὴ μάλιστα
φιλεῖ τά τε ἄλλα πάντα καὶ ὁ ἔρως ἐμποιεῖν. ἔργῳ δὲ
5 τοῦτο ἔμαθον καὶ οἱ ἐνθάδε τύραννοι· ὁ γὰρ Ἀριστογεί-
τονος ἔρως καὶ ἡ Ἁρμοδίου φιλία βέβαιος γενομένη κατ-
έλυσεν αὐτῶν τὴν ἀρχήν. οὕτως οὗ μὲν αἰσχρὸν ἐτέθη
d χαρίζεσθαι ἐρασταῖς, κακίᾳ τῶν θεμένων κεῖται, τῶν μὲν
ἀρχόντων πλεονεξίᾳ, τῶν δὲ ἀρχομένων ἀνανδρίᾳ· οὗ δὲ
καλὸν ἁπλῶς ἐνομίσθη, διὰ τὴν τῶν θεμένων τῆς ψυχῆς
ἀργίαν. ἐνθάδε δὲ πολὺ τούτων κάλλιον νενομοθέτηται, καὶ

a 5 πρᾶγμα om. m   b 1 καὶ ἐν Λακεδαίμονι del. vel post γὰρ
transp. z

ὅπερ εἶπον, οὐ ῥᾴδιον κατανοῆσαι. ἐνθυμηθέντι γὰρ ὅτι 5
λέγεται κάλλιον τὸ φανερῶς ἐρᾶν τοῦ λάθρᾳ, καὶ μάλιστα
τῶν γενναιοτάτων καὶ ἀρίστων, κἂν αἰσχίους ἄλλων ὦσι, καὶ
ὅτι αὖ ἡ παρακέλευσις τῷ ἐρῶντι παρὰ πάντων θαυμαστή,
οὐχ ὡς τι αἰσχρὸν ποιοῦντι, καὶ ἑλόντι τε καλὸν δοκεῖ εἶναι
καὶ μὴ ἑλόντι αἰσχρόν, καὶ πρὸς τὸ ἐπιχειρεῖν ἑλεῖν ἐξου- e
σίαν ὁ νόμος δέδωκε τῷ ἐραστῇ θαυμαστὰ ἔργα ἐργαζομένῳ
ἐπαινεῖσθαι, ἃ εἴ τις τολμῴη ποιεῖν ἄλλ' ὁτιοῦν διώκων καὶ
βουλόμενος διαπράξασθαι πλὴν τοῦτο, [φιλοσοφίας] τὰ μέ- 183
γιστα καρποῖτ' ἂν ὀνείδη — εἰ γὰρ ἢ χρήματα βουλόμενος
παρά του λαβεῖν ἢ ἀρχὴν ἄρξαι ἤ τινα ἄλλην δύναμιν
ἐθέλοι ποιεῖν οἷάπερ οἱ ἐρασταὶ πρὸς τὰ παιδικά, ἱκετείας
τε καὶ ἀντιβολήσεις ἐν ταῖς δεήσεσιν ποιούμενοι, καὶ ὅρκους 5
ὀμνύντες, καὶ κοιμήσεις ἐπὶ θύραις, καὶ ἐθέλοντες δουλείας
δουλεύειν οἵας οὐδ' ἂν δοῦλος οὐδείς, ἐμποδίζοιτο ἂν μὴ
πράττειν οὕτω τὴν πρᾶξιν καὶ ὑπὸ φίλων καὶ ὑπὸ ἐχθρῶν,
τῶν μὲν ὀνειδιζόντων κολακείας καὶ ἀνελευθερίας, τῶν δὲ b
νουθετούντων καὶ αἰσχυνομένων ὑπὲρ αὐτῶν. τῷ δ' ἐρῶντι
πάντα ταῦτα ποιοῦντι χάρις ἔπεστι, καὶ δέδοται ὑπὸ τοῦ
νόμου ἄνευ ὀνείδους πράττειν, ὡς πάγκαλόν τι πρᾶγμα
διαπραττομένου. ὁ δὲ δεινότατον, ὡς γε λέγουσιν οἱ πολ- 5
λοί, ὅτι καὶ ὀμνύντι μόνῳ συγγνώμη παρὰ θεῶν ἐκβάντι
τῶν ὅρκων· ἀφροδίσιον γὰρ ὅρκον οὔ φασιν εἶναι· οὕτω
καὶ οἱ θεοὶ καὶ οἱ ἄνθρωποι πᾶσαν ἐξουσίαν πεποιήκασι τῷ c
ἐρῶντι, ὡς ὁ νόμος φησὶν ὁ ἐνθάδε. ταύτῃ μὲν οὖν οἰηθείη
ἄν τις πάγκαλον νομίζεσθαι ἐν τῇδε τῇ πόλει καὶ τὸ ἐρᾶν
καὶ τὸ φίλους γίγνεσθαι τοῖς ἐρασταῖς. ἐπειδὰν δὲ παι-
δαγωγοὺς ἐπιστήσαντες οἱ πατέρες τοῖς ἐρωμένοις μὴ ἐῶσι 5
διαλέγεσθαι τοῖς ἐρασταῖς, καὶ τῷ παιδαγωγῷ ταῦτα προστεταγμένα ᾖ, ἡλικιῶται δὲ καὶ ἑταῖροι ὀνειδίζωσιν ἐάν τι
ὁρῶσιν τοιοῦτον γιγνόμενον, καὶ τοὺς ὀνειδίζοντας αὖ οἱ
πρεσβύτεροι μὴ διακωλύωσι μηδὲ λοιδορῶσιν ὡς οὐκ ὀρθῶς d
λέγοντας, εἰς δὲ ταῦτά τις αὖ βλέψας ἡγήσαιτ' ἂν πάλιν
αἴσχιστον τὸ τοιοῦτον ἐνθάδε νομίζεσθαι. τὸ δὲ οἶμαι ὧδ'

a 1 φιλοσοφίας del. z   c 7 ἑταῖροι z: ἕτεροι m

ἔχει· οὐχ ἁπλοῦν ἐστιν, ὅπερ ἐξ ἀρχῆς ἐλέχθη οὔτε καλὸν
5 εἶναι αὐτὸ καθ' αὑτὸ οὔτε αἰσχρόν, ἀλλὰ καλῶς μὲν πραττόμενον καλόν, αἰσχρῶς δὲ αἰσχρόν. αἰσχρῶς μὲν οὖν
ἐστι πονηρῷ τε καὶ πονηρῶς χαρίζεσθαι, καλῶς δὲ χρηστῷ
τε καὶ καλῶς. πονηρὸς δ' ἐστὶν ἐκεῖνος ὁ ἐραστὴς ὁ πάν-
e δημος, ὁ τοῦ σώματος μᾶλλον ἢ τῆς ψυχῆς ἐρῶν· καὶ γὰρ
οὐδὲ μόνιμός ἐστιν, ἅτε οὐδὲ μονίμου ἐρῶν πράγματος·
ἅμα γὰρ τῷ τοῦ σώματος ἄνθει λήγοντι, οὗπερ ἤρα, οἴχεται ἀποπτάμενος, πολλοὺς λόγους καὶ ὑποσχέσεις καται-
5 σχύνας· ὁ δὲ τοῦ ἤθους χρηστοῦ ὄντος ἐραστὴς διὰ βίου
μένει, ἅτε μονίμῳ συντακείς. τούτους δὴ βούλεται ὁ
184 ἡμέτερος νόμος εὖ καὶ καλῶς βασανίζειν, καὶ τοῖς μὲν
χαρίσασθαι, τοὺς δὲ διαφεύγειν. διὰ ταῦτα οὖν τοῖς μὲν
διώκειν παρακελεύεται, τοῖς δὲ φεύγειν, ἀγωνοθετῶν καὶ
βασανίζων ποτέρων ποτέ ἐστιν ὁ ἐρῶν καὶ ποτέρων ὁ
5 ἐρώμενος. οὕτω δὴ ὑπὸ ταύτης τῆς αἰτίας πρῶτον μὲν τὸ
ἁλίσκεσθαι ταχὺ αἰσχρὸν νενόμισται, ἵνα χρόνος ἐγγένηται,
ὃς δὴ δοκεῖ τὰ πολλὰ καλῶς βασανίζειν, ἔπειτα τὸ ὑπὸ
χρημάτων καὶ ὑπὸ πολιτικῶν δυνάμεων ἁλῶναι αἰσχρόν,
b ἐάν τε κακῶς πάσχων πτήξῃ καὶ μὴ καρτερήσῃ, ἄν τ'
εὐεργετούμενος εἰς χρήματα ἢ εἰς διαπράξεις πολιτικὰς μὴ
καταφρονήσῃ· οὐδὲν γὰρ δοκεῖ τούτων οὔτε βέβαιον οὔτε
μόνιμον εἶναι, χωρὶς τοῦ μηδὲ πεφυκέναι ἀπ' αὐτῶν γεν-
5 ναίαν φιλίαν. μία δὴ λείπεται τῷ ἡμετέρῳ νόμῳ ὁδός, εἰ
μέλλει καλῶς χαριεῖσθαι ἐραστῇ παιδικά. ἔστι γὰρ ἡμῖν
νόμος, ὥσπερ ἐπὶ τοῖς ἐρασταῖς ἦν δουλεύειν ἐθέλοντα
c ἡντινοῦν δουλείαν παιδικοῖς μὴ κολακείαν εἶναι μηδὲ ἐπο-
νείδιστον, οὕτω δὴ καὶ ἄλλη μία μόνη δουλεία ἑκούσιος
λείπεται οὐκ ἐπονείδιστος· αὕτη δ' ἐστὶν ἡ περὶ τὴν ἀρετήν.
νενόμισται γὰρ δὴ ἡμῖν, ἐάν τις ἐθέλῃ τινὰ θεραπεύειν
5 ἡγούμενος δι' ἐκεῖνον ἀμείνων ἔσεσθαι ἢ κατὰ σοφίαν τινὰ
ἢ κατὰ ἄλλο ὁτιοῦν μέρος ἀρετῆς, αὕτη αὖ ἡ ἐθελοδουλεία
οὐκ αἰσχρὰ εἶναι οὐδὲ κολακεία. δεῖ δὴ τὼ νόμω τούτω
συμβαλεῖν εἰς ταὐτόν, τόν τε περὶ τὴν παιδεραστίαν καὶ

d 7 καλὸν m   b 7 ὅσπερ c m: ὥσπερ ⟨γὰρ⟩ z

τὸν περὶ τὴν φιλοσοφίαν τε καὶ τὴν ἄλλην ἀρετήν, εἰ d
μέλλει συμβῆναι καλὸν γενέσθαι τὸ ἐραστῇ παιδικὰ χαρίσασθαι.   ὅταν γὰρ εἰς τὸ αὐτὸ ἔλθωσιν ἐραστής τε καὶ
παιδικά, νόμον ἔχων ἑκάτερος, ὁ μὲν χαρισαμένοις παιδικοῖς
ὑπηρετῶν ὁτιοῦν δικαίως ἂν ὑπηρετεῖν, ὁ δὲ τῷ ποιοῦντι 5
αὐτὸν σοφόν τε καὶ ἀγαθὸν δικαίως αὖ ὁτιοῦν ἂν ὑπουργῶν, καὶ ὁ μὲν δυνάμενος εἰς φρόνησιν καὶ τὴν
ἄλλην ἀρετὴν συμβάλλεσθαι, ὁ δὲ δεόμενος εἰς παίδευσιν e
καὶ τὴν ἄλλην σοφίαν κτᾶσθαι, τότε δή, τούτων συνιόντων
εἰς ταὐτὸν τῶν νόμων, μοναχοῦ ἐνταῦθα συμπίπτει τὸ καλὸν
εἶναι παιδικὰ ἐραστῇ χαρίσασθαι, ἄλλοθι δὲ οὐδαμοῦ. ἐπὶ
τούτῳ καὶ ἐξαπατηθῆναι οὐδὲν αἰσχρόν, ἐπὶ δὲ τοῖς ἄλλοις 5
πᾶσι καὶ ἐξαπατωμένῳ αἰσχύνην φέρει καὶ μή. εἰ γάρ τις
ἐραστῇ ὡς πλουσίῳ πλούτου ἕνεκα χαρισάμενος ἐξαπατηθείη 185
καὶ μὴ λάβοι χρήματα, ἀναφανέντος τοῦ ἐραστοῦ πένητος,
οὐδὲν ἧττον αἰσχρόν· δοκεῖ γὰρ ὁ τοιοῦτος τό γε αὑτοῦ
ἐπιδεῖξαι, ὅτι ἕνεκα χρημάτων ὁτιοῦν ἂν ὁτῳοῦν ὑπηρετοῖ,
τοῦτο δὲ οὐ καλόν. κατὰ τὸν αὐτὸν δὴ λόγον κἂν εἴ τις 5
ὡς ἀγαθῷ χαρισάμενος καὶ αὐτὸς ὡς ἀμείνων ἐσόμενος διὰ
τὴν φιλίαν ἐραστοῦ ἐξαπατηθείη, ἀναφανέντος ἐκείνου κακοῦ
καὶ οὐ κεκτημένου ἀρετήν, ὅμως καλὴ ἡ ἀπάτη· δοκεῖ γὰρ b
αὖ καὶ οὗτος τὸ καθ' αὑτὸν δεδηλωκέναι, ὅτι ἀρετῆς γ'
ἕνεκα καὶ τοῦ βελτίων γενέσθαι πᾶν ἂν παντὶ προθυμηθείη,
τοῦτο δὲ αὖ πάντων κάλλιστον· οὕτω πᾶν πάντως γε καλὸν
ἀρετῆς γ' ἕνεκα χαρίζεσθαι. οὗτός ἐστιν ὁ τῆς οὐρανίας θεοῦ 5
ἔρως καὶ οὐράνιος καὶ πολλοῦ ἄξιος καὶ πόλει καὶ ἰδιώταις,
πολλὴν ἐπιμέλειαν ἀναγκάζων ποιεῖσθαι πρὸς ἀρετὴν τόν
τε ἐρῶντα αὐτὸν αὑτοῦ καὶ τὸν ἐρώμενον· οἱ δ' ἕτεροι c
πάντες τῆς ἑτέρας, τῆς πανδήμου. ταῦτά σοι,' ἔφη, 'ὡς ἐκ
τοῦ παραχρῆμα, ὦ Φαῖδρε, περὶ Ἔρωτος συμβάλλομαι.'
   Παυσανίου δὲ παυσαμένου (διδάσκουσι γάρ με ἴσα λέγειν
οὑτωσὶ οἱ σοφοί) ἔφη ὁ Ἀριστόδημος δεῖν μὲν Ἀριστοφάνη 5
λέγειν, τυχεῖν δὲ αὐτῷ τινα ἢ ὑπὸ πλησμονῆς ἢ ὑπό τινος

ἄλλου λύγγα ἐπιπεπτωκυῖαν καὶ οὐχ οἷόν τε εἶναι λέγειν

d ἀλλ' εἰπεῖν αὐτόν (ἐν τῇ κάτω γὰρ αὐτοῦ τὸν ἰατρὸν Ἐρυξίμαχον κατακεῖσθαι) 'ὦ Ἐρυξίμαχε, δίκαιος εἶ ἢ παῦσαί
με τῆς λυγγὸς ἢ λέγειν ὑπὲρ ἐμοῦ, ἕως ἂν ἐγὼ παύσωμαι.'
καὶ τὸν Ἐρυξίμαχον εἰπεῖν 'ἀλλὰ ποιήσω ἀμφότερα ταῦτα·

5 ἐγὼ μὲν γὰρ ἐρῶ ἐν τῷ σῷ μέρει, σὺ δ' ἐπειδὰν παύσῃ, ἐν
τῷ ἐμῷ. ἐν ᾧ δ' ἂν ἐγὼ λέγω, ἐὰν μέν σοι ἐθέλῃ ἀπνευστὶ
ἔχοντι πολὺν χρόνον παύεσθαι ἡ λύγξ· εἰ δὲ μή, ὕδατι

e ἀνακογχυλίασον. εἰ δ' ἄρα πάνυ ἰσχυρά ἐστιν, ἀναλαβών
τι τοιοῦτον οἵῳ κινήσαις ἂν τὴν ῥῖνα, πτάρε· καὶ ἐὰν τοῦτο
ποιήσῃς ἅπαξ ἢ δίς, καὶ εἰ πάνυ ἰσχυρά ἐστι, παύσεται.'
'οὐκ ἂν φθάνοις λέγων,' φάναι τὸν Ἀριστοφάνη· 'ἐγὼ

5 δὲ ταῦτα ποιήσω.'

εἰπεῖν δὴ τὸν Ἐρυξίμαχον, 'δοκεῖ τοίνυν μοι ἀναγκαῖον
εἶναι, ἐπειδὴ Παυσανίας ὁρμήσας ἐπὶ τὸν λόγον καλῶς οὐχ

186 ἱκανῶς ἀπετέλεσε, δεῖν ἐμὲ πειρᾶσθαι τέλος ἐπιθεῖναι τῷ
λόγῳ. τὸ μὲν γὰρ διπλοῦν εἶναι τὸν Ἔρωτα δοκεῖ μοι
καλῶς διελέσθαι· ὅτι δὲ οὐ μόνον ἐστὶν ἐπὶ ταῖς ψυχαῖς
τῶν ἀνθρώπων πρὸς τοὺς καλοὺς ἀλλὰ καὶ πρὸς ἄλλα πολλὰ

5 καὶ ἐν τοῖς ἄλλοις, τοῖς τε σώμασι τῶν πάντων ζῴων καὶ
τοῖς ἐν τῇ γῇ φυομένοις καὶ ὡς ἔπος εἰπεῖν ἐν πᾶσι τοῖς
οὖσι, καθεωρακέναι μοι δοκῶ ἐκ τῆς ἰατρικῆς, τῆς ἡμετέρας

b τέχνης, ὡς μέγας καὶ θαυμαστὸς καὶ ἐπὶ πᾶν ὁ θεὸς τείνει
καὶ κατ' ἀνθρώπινα καὶ κατὰ θεῖα πράγματα. ἄρξομαι δὲ
ἀπὸ τῆς ἰατρικῆς λέγων, ἵνα καὶ πρεσβεύωμεν τὴν τέχνην.
ἡ γὰρ φύσις τῶν σωμάτων τὸν διπλοῦν Ἔρωτα τοῦτον ἔχει·

5 τὸ γὰρ ὑγιὲς τοῦ σώματος καὶ τὸ νοσοῦν ὁμολογουμένως
ἕτερόν τε καὶ ἀνόμοιόν ἐστι, τὸ δὲ ἀνόμοιον ἀνομοίων ἐπιθυμεῖ καὶ ἐρᾷ. ἄλλος μὲν οὖν ὁ ἐπὶ τῷ ὑγιεινῷ ἔρως, ἄλλος
δὲ ὁ ἐπὶ τῷ νοσώδει. ἔστιν δή, ὥσπερ ἄρτι Παυσανίας
ἔλεγεν τοῖς μὲν ἀγαθοῖς καλὸν χαρίζεσθαι τῶν ἀνθρώπων,

c τοῖς δ' ἀκολάστοις αἰσχρόν, οὕτω καὶ ἐν αὐτοῖς τοῖς σώμασιν
τοῖς μὲν ἀγαθοῖς ἑκάστου τοῦ σώματος καὶ ὑγιεινοῖς καλὸν
χαρίζεσθαι καὶ δεῖ, καὶ τοῦτό ἐστιν ᾧ ὄνομα τὸ ἰατρικόν,

b 5 ὁμολογοῦμεν ὡς c m

τοῖς δὲ κακοῖς καὶ νοσώδεσιν αἰσχρόν τε καὶ δεῖ ἀχαριστεῖν,
εἰ μέλλει τις τεχνικὸς εἶναι. ἔστι γὰρ ἰατρική, ὡς ἐν 5
κεφαλαίῳ εἰπεῖν, ἐπιστήμη τῶν τοῦ σώματος ἐρωτικῶν πρὸς
πλησμονὴν καὶ κένωσιν, καὶ ὁ διαγιγνώσκων ἐν τούτοις τὸν
καλόν τε καὶ αἰσχρὸν ἔρωτα, οὗτός ἐστιν ὁ ἰατρικώτατος· d
καὶ ὁ μεταβάλλειν ποιῶν, ὥστε ἀντὶ τοῦ ἑτέρου ἔρωτος τὸν
ἕτερον κτᾶσθαι, καὶ οἷς μὴ ἔνεστιν ἔρως, (δεῖ δ᾽ ἐγγενέσθαι,)
ἐπιστάμενος ἐμποιῆσαι καὶ ἐνόντα ἐξελεῖν ἀγαθὸς ἂν εἴη
δημιουργός. δεῖ γὰρ δὴ τὰ ἔχθιστα ὄντα ἐν τῷ σώματι 5
φίλα οἷόν τ᾽ εἶναι ποιεῖν καὶ ἐρᾶν ἀλλήλων. ἔστι δὲ ἔχθιστα
τὰ ἐναντιώτατα, ψυχρὸν θερμῷ, πικρὸν γλυκεῖ, ξηρὸν ὑγρῷ,
πάντα τὰ τοιαῦτα· τούτοις ἐπιστηθεὶς ἔρωτα ἐμποιῆσαι καὶ e
ὁμόνοιαν ὁ ἡμέτερος πρόγονος Ἀσκληπιός, ὡς φασιν οἵδε οἱ
ποιηταὶ καὶ ἐγὼ πείθομαι, συνέστησεν τὴν ἡμετέραν τέχνην.
ἥ τε οὖν ἰατρική, ὥσπερ λέγω, πᾶσα διὰ τοῦ θεοῦ τούτου
κυβερνᾶται, ὡσαύτως δὲ καὶ γυμναστικὴ καὶ γεωργία· μουσικὴ 187
δὲ καὶ παντὶ κατάδηλος τῷ καὶ σμικρὸν προσέχοντι τὸν νοῦν
ὅτι κατὰ ταὐτὰ ἔχει τούτοις, ὥσπερ ἴσως καὶ Ἡράκλειτος
βούλεται λέγειν, ἐπεὶ τοῖς γε ῥήμασιν οὐ καλῶς λέγει. τὸ
ἓν γάρ φησι διαφερόμενον αὐτὸ αὑτῷ συμφέρεσθαι 5
ὥσπερ ἁρμονίαν τόξου τε καὶ λύρας. ἔστι δὲ πολλὴ
ἀλογία ἁρμονίαν φάναι διαφέρεσθαι ἢ ἐκ διαφερομένων ἔτι
εἶναι. ἀλλὰ ἴσως τόδε ἐβούλετο λέγειν, ὅτι ἐκ διαφερομένων
πρότερον τοῦ ὀξέος καὶ βαρέος, ἔπειτα ὕστερον ὁμολογη- b
σάντων γέγονεν ὑπὸ τῆς μουσικῆς τέχνης. οὐ γὰρ δήπου
ἐκ διαφερομένων γε ἔτι τοῦ ὀξέος καὶ βαρέος ἁρμονία ἂν
εἴη. ἡ γὰρ ἁρμονία συμφωνία ἐστίν, συμφωνία δὲ ὁμολογία
τις, ὁμολογίαν δὲ ἐκ διαφερομένων, ἕως ἂν διαφέρωνται, 5
ἀδύνατον εἶναι, διαφερόμενον δὲ αὖ καὶ μὴ ὁμολογοῦν ἀδύνατον ἁρμόσαι, ὥσπερ γε καὶ ὁ ῥυθμὸς ἐκ τοῦ ταχέος καὶ
βραδέος, ἐκ διενηνεγμένων πρότερον, ὕστερον δὲ ὁμολογη- c
σάντων γέγονε. τὴν δὲ ὁμολογίαν πᾶσι τούτοις, ὥσπερ
ἐκεῖ ἡ ἰατρική, ἐνταῦθα ἡ μουσικὴ ἐντίθησιν, ἔρωτα καὶ
ὁμόνοιαν ἀλλήλων ἐμποιήσασα· καί ἐστιν αὖ μουσικὴ περὶ
187 c 4 ἀλλήλοις m

5 ἁρμονίαν καὶ ῥυθμὸν ἐρωτικῶν ἐπιστήμη. καὶ ἐν μέν γε
αὐτῇ τῇ συστάσει ἁρμονίας τε καὶ ῥυθμοῦ οὐδὲν χαλεπὸν τὰ
ἐρωτικὰ διαγιγνώσκειν, οὐδὲ ὁ διπλοῦς ἔρως ἐνταῦθά πω
ἐστίν· ἀλλ᾽ ἐπειδὰν δέῃ πρὸς τοὺς ἀνθρώπους καταχρῆσθαι
d ῥυθμῷ τε καὶ ἁρμονίᾳ ἢ ποιοῦντα, ὃ δὴ μελοποιίαν καλοῦσιν,
ἢ χρώμενον ὀρθῶς τοῖς πεποιημένοις μέλεσί τε καὶ μέτροις,
ὃ δὴ παιδεία ἐκλήθη, ἐνταῦθα δὴ καὶ χαλεπὸν καὶ ἀγαθοῦ
δημιουργοῦ δεῖ. πάλιν γὰρ ἥκει ὁ αὐτὸς λόγος, ὅτι τοῖς μὲν
5 κοσμίοις τῶν ἀνθρώπων, καὶ ὡς ἂν κοσμιώτεροι γίγνοιντο
οἱ μήπω ὄντες, δεῖ χαρίζεσθαι καὶ φυλάττειν τὸν τούτων
ἔρωτα, καὶ οὗτός ἐστιν ὁ καλός, ὁ οὐράνιος, ὁ τῆς Οὐρανίας
e μούσης Ἔρως· ὁ δὲ Πολυμνίας, ὁ πάνδημος, ὃν δεῖ εὐλαβούμενον προσφέρειν οἷς ἂν προσφέρῃ, ὅπως ἂν τὴν μὲν ἡδονὴν
αὐτοῦ καρπώσηται, ἀκολασίαν δὲ μηδεμίαν ἐμποιήσῃ, ὥσπερ
ἐν τῇ ἡμετέρᾳ τέχνῃ μέγα ἔργον ταῖς περὶ τὴν ὀψοποιικὴν
5 τέχνην ἐπιθυμίαις καλῶς χρῆσθαι, ὥστ᾽ ἄνευ νόσου τὴν
ἡδονὴν καρπώσασθαι. καὶ ἐν μουσικῇ δὴ καὶ ἐν ἰατρικῇ
καὶ ἐν τοῖς ἄλλοις πᾶσι καὶ τοῖς ἀνθρωπείοις καὶ τοῖς θείοις,
καθ᾽ ὅσον παρείκει, φυλακτέον ἑκάτερον τὸν Ἔρωτα· ἔνεστον
188 γάρ. ἐπεὶ καὶ ἡ τῶν ὡρῶν τοῦ ἐνιαυτοῦ σύστασις μεστή
ἐστιν ἀμφοτέρων τούτων, καὶ ἐπειδὰν μὲν πρὸς ἄλληλα τοῦ
κοσμίου τύχῃ ἔρωτος ἃ νυνδὴ ἐγὼ ἔλεγον, τά τε θερμὰ καὶ
τὰ ψυχρὰ καὶ ξηρὰ καὶ ὑγρά, καὶ ἁρμονίαν καὶ κρᾶσιν λάβῃ
5 σώφρονα, ἥκει φέροντα εὐετηρίαν τε καὶ ὑγίειαν ἀνθρώποις
καὶ τοῖς ἄλλοις ζῴοις τε καὶ φυτοῖς, καὶ οὐδὲν ἠδίκησεν·
ὅταν δὲ ὁ μετὰ τῆς ὕβρεως Ἔρως ἐγκρατέστερος περὶ τὰς
τοῦ ἐνιαυτοῦ ὥρας γένηται, διέφθειρέν τε πολλὰ καὶ ἠδίκησεν.
b οἵ τε γὰρ λοιμοὶ φιλοῦσι γίγνεσθαι ἐκ τῶν τοιούτων καὶ
ἄλλα ἀνόμοια πολλὰ νοσήματα καὶ τοῖς θηρίοις καὶ τοῖς
φυτοῖς· καὶ γὰρ πάχναι καὶ χάλαζαι καὶ ἐρυσῖβαι ἐκ
πλεονεξίας καὶ ἀκοσμίας περὶ ἄλληλα τῶν τοιούτων γίγνεται
5 ἐρωτικῶν, ὧν ἐπιστήμη περὶ ἄστρων τε φορὰς καὶ ἐνιαυτῶν
ὥρας ἀστρονομία καλεῖται. ἔτι τοίνυν καὶ αἱ θυσίαι πᾶσαι
καὶ οἷς μαντικὴ ἐπιστατεῖ — ταῦτα δ᾽ ἐστὶν ἡ περὶ θεούς τε

καὶ ἀνθρώπους πρὸς ἀλλήλους κοινωνία — οὐ περὶ ἄλλο τί c
ἐστιν ἢ περὶ Ἔρωτος φυλακήν τε καὶ ἴασιν. πᾶσα γὰρ
ἀσέβεια φιλεῖ γίγνεσθαι ἐὰν μή τις τῷ κοσμίῳ Ἔρωτι
χαρίζηται μηδὲ τιμᾷ τε αὐτὸν καὶ πρεσβεύῃ ἐν παντὶ ἔργῳ,
ἀλλὰ τὸν ἕτερον, καὶ περὶ γονέας καὶ ζῶντας καὶ τετελευ- 5
τηκότας καὶ περὶ θεούς· ἃ δὴ προστέτακται τῇ μαντικῇ
ἐπισκοπεῖν τοὺς ἐρῶντας καὶ ἰατρεύειν, καί ἐστιν αὖ ἡ
μαντικὴ φιλίας θεῶν καὶ ἀνθρώπων δημιουργὸς τῷ ἐπί- d
στασθαι τὰ κατὰ ἀνθρώπους ἐρωτικά, ὅσα τείνει πρὸς θέμιν
καὶ εὐσέβειαν.

οὕτω πολλὴν καὶ μεγάλην, μᾶλλον δὲ πᾶσαν δύναμιν ἔχει
συλλήβδην μὲν ὁ πᾶς Ἔρως, ὁ δὲ περὶ τἀγαθὰ μετὰ σωφρο- 5
σύνης καὶ δικαιοσύνης ἀποτελούμενος καὶ παρ' ἡμῖν καὶ
παρὰ θεοῖς, οὗτος τὴν μεγίστην δύναμιν ἔχει καὶ πᾶσαν ἡμῖν
εὐδαιμονίαν παρασκευάζει καὶ ἀλλήλοις δυναμένους ὁμιλεῖν
καὶ φίλους εἶναι καὶ τοῖς κρείττοσιν ἡμῶν θεοῖς. ἴσως μὲν
οὖν καὶ ἐγὼ τὸν Ἔρωτα ἐπαινῶν πολλὰ παραλείπω, οὐ μέντοι e
ἑκών γε. ἀλλ' εἴ τι ἐξέλιπον, σὸν ἔργον, ὦ 'Αριστόφανες,
ἀναπληρῶσαι· ἢ εἴ πως ἄλλως ἐν νῷ ἔχεις ἐγκωμιάζειν τὸν
θεόν, ἐγκωμίαζε, ἐπειδὴ καὶ τῆς λυγγὸς πέπαυσαι.'

ἐκδεξάμενον οὖν ἔφη εἰπεῖν τὸν 'Αριστοφάνη ὅτι 'καὶ 189
μάλ' ἐπαύσατο, οὐ μέντοι πρίν γε τὸν πταρμὸν προσενεχθῆναι
αὐτῇ, ὥστε με θαυμάζειν εἰ τὸ κόσμιον τοῦ σώματος ἐπιθυμεῖ τοιούτων ψόφων καὶ γαργαλισμῶν, οἷον καὶ ὁ πταρμός
ἐστιν· πάνυ γὰρ εὐθὺς ἐπαύσατο, ἐπειδὴ αὐτῷ τὸν πταρμὸν 5
προσήνεγκα.'

καὶ τὸν 'Ερυξίμαχον, 'ὦγαθέ,' φάναι, ''Αριστόφανες, ὅρα
τί ποιεῖς. γελωτοποιεῖς μέλλων λέγειν, καὶ φύλακά με τοῦ
λόγου ἀναγκάζεις γίγνεσθαι τοῦ σεαυτοῦ, ἐάν τι γελοῖον b
εἴπῃς, ἐξόν σοι ἐν εἰρήνῃ λέγειν.'

καὶ τὸν 'Αριστοφάνη γελάσαντα εἰπεῖν 'εὖ λέγεις, ὦ
'Ερυξίμαχε, καί μοι ἔστω ἄρρητα τὰ εἰρημένα. ἀλλὰ μή με
φύλαττε, ὡς ἐγὼ φοβοῦμαι περὶ τῶν μελλόντων ῥηθήσεσθαι, 5

οὔ τι μὴ γελοῖα εἴπω — τοῦτο μὲν γὰρ ἂν κέρδος εἴη καὶ τῆς
ἡμετέρας μούσης ἐπιχώριον — ἀλλὰ μὴ καταγέλαστα.'
    'βαλών γε,' φάναι, 'ὦ Ἀριστόφανες, οἴει ἐκφεύξεσθαι·
ἀλλὰ πρόσεχε τὸν νοῦν καὶ οὕτως λέγε ὡς δώσων λόγον.
c ἴσως μέντοι, ἂν δόξῃ μοι, ἀφήσω σε.'
    'καὶ μήν, ὦ Ἐρυξίμαχε,' εἰπεῖν τὸν Ἀριστοφάνη, 'ἄλλῃ
γέ πῃ ἐν νῷ ἔχω λέγειν ἢ ᾗ σύ τε καὶ Παυσανίας εἰπέτην.
ἐμοὶ γὰρ δοκοῦσιν ἄνθρωποι παντάπασι τὴν τοῦ ἔρωτος
5 δύναμιν οὐκ ᾐσθῆσθαι, ἐπεὶ αἰσθανόμενοί γε μέγιστ' ἂν
αὐτοῦ ἱερὰ κατασκευάσαι καὶ βωμούς, καὶ θυσίας ἂν ποιεῖν
μεγίστας, οὐχ ὥσπερ νῦν τούτων οὐδὲν γίγνεται περὶ αὐτόν,
δέον πάντων μάλιστα γίγνεσθαι. ἔστι γὰρ θεῶν φιλαν-
d θρωπότατος, ἐπίκουρός τε ὢν τῶν ἀνθρώπων καὶ ἰατρὸς
τούτων ὧν ἰαθέντων μεγίστη εὐδαιμονία ἂν τῷ ἀνθρωπείῳ
γένει εἴη. ἐγὼ οὖν πειράσομαι ὑμῖν εἰσηγήσασθαι τὴν
δύναμιν αὐτοῦ, ὑμεῖς δὲ τῶν ἄλλων διδάσκαλοι ἔσεσθε.
5 δεῖ δὲ πρῶτον ὑμᾶς μαθεῖν τὴν ἀνθρωπίνην φύσιν καὶ τὰ
παθήματα αὐτῆς. ἡ γὰρ πάλαι ἡμῶν φύσις οὐχ αὕτη ἦν
ἥπερ νῦν, ἀλλ' ἀλλοία. πρῶτον μὲν γὰρ τρία ἦν τὰ γένη
τὰ τῶν ἀνθρώπων, οὐχ ὥσπερ νῦν δύο, ἄρρεν καὶ θῆλυ,
e ἀλλὰ καὶ τρίτον προσῆν κοινὸν ὂν ἀμφοτέρων τούτων, οὗ
νῦν ὄνομα λοιπόν, αὐτὸ δὲ ἠφάνισται· ἀνδρόγυνον γὰρ ἓν
τότε μὲν ἦν καὶ εἶδος καὶ ὄνομα ἐξ ἀμφοτέρων κοινὸν τοῦ
τε ἄρρενος καὶ θήλεος, νῦν δὲ οὐκ ἔστιν ἀλλ' ἢ ἐν ὀνείδει
5 ὄνομα κείμενον. ἔπειτα ὅλον ἦν ἑκάστου τοῦ ἀνθρώπου τὸ
εἶδος στρογγύλον, νῶτον καὶ πλευρὰς κύκλῳ ἔχον, χεῖρας
δὲ τέτταρας εἶχε, καὶ σκέλη τὰ ἴσα ταῖς χερσίν, καὶ πρόσωπα
190 δύ' ἐπ' αὐχένι κυκλοτερεῖ, ὅμοια πάντῃ, κεφαλὴν δ' ἐπ'
ἀμφοτέροις τοῖς προσώποις ἐναντίοις κειμένοις μίαν, καὶ
ὦτα τέτταρα, καὶ αἰδοῖα δύο, καὶ τἆλλα πάντα ὡς ἀπὸ
τούτων ἄν τις εἰκάσειεν. ἐπορεύετο δὲ καὶ ὀρθὸν ὥσπερ
5 νῦν, ὁποτέρωσε βουληθείη· καὶ ὁπότε ταχὺ ὁρμήσειεν θεῖν,
ὥσπερ οἱ κυβιστῶντες καὶ εἰς ὀρθὸν τὰ σκέλη περιφερό-
μενοι κυβιστῶσι κύκλῳ, ὀκτὼ τότε οὖσι τοῖς μέλεσιν

        d 6 αὕτη m   e 2 ἓν om. c m

ἀπερειδόμενοι ταχὺ ἐφέροντο κύκλῳ. ἦν δὲ διὰ ταῦτα τρία
τὰ γένη καὶ τοιαῦτα, ὅτι τὸ μὲν ἄρρεν ἦν τοῦ ἡλίου τὴν b
ἀρχὴν ἔκγονον, τὸ δὲ θῆλυ τῆς γῆς, τὸ δὲ ἀμφοτέρων μετέχον
τῆς σελήνης, ὅτι καὶ ἡ σελήνη ἀμφοτέρων μετέχει· περιφερῆ
δὲ δὴ ἦν καὶ αὐτὰ καὶ ἡ πορεία αὐτῶν διὰ τὸ τοῖς γονεῦσιν
ὅμοια εἶναι. ἦν οὖν τὴν ἰσχὺν δεινὰ καὶ τὴν ῥώμην, καὶ 5
τὰ φρονήματα μεγάλα εἶχον, ἐπεχείρησαν δὲ τοῖς θεοῖς,
καὶ ὃ λέγει Ὅμηρος περὶ Ἐφιάλτου τε καὶ Ὤτου, περὶ
ἐκείνων λέγεται, τὸ εἰς τὸν οὐρανὸν ἀνάβασιν ἐπιχειρεῖν
ποιεῖν, ὡς ἐπιθησομένων τοῖς θεοῖς. ὁ οὖν Ζεὺς καὶ οἱ c
ἄλλοι θεοὶ ἐβουλεύοντο ὅτι χρὴ αὐτοὺς ποιῆσαι, καὶ ἠπό-
ρουν· οὔτε γὰρ ὅπως ἀποκτείναιεν εἶχον καὶ ὥσπερ τοὺς
γίγαντας κεραυνώσαντες τὸ γένος ἀφανίσαιεν (αἱ τιμαὶ
γὰρ αὐτοῖς καὶ ἱερὰ τὰ παρὰ τῶν ἀνθρώπων ἠφανίζετο) 5
οὔτε ὅπως ἐῷεν ἀσελγαίνειν. μόγις δὴ ὁ Ζεὺς ἐννοήσας
λέγει ὅτι "δοκῶ μοι," ἔφη, "ἔχειν μηχανήν, ὡς ἂν εἶέν
τε ἄνθρωποι καὶ παύσαιντο τῆς ἀκολασίας ἀσθενέστεροι
γενόμενοι. νῦν μὲν γὰρ αὐτούς," ἔφη, "διατεμῶ δίχα ἕκαστον, d
καὶ ἅμα μὲν ἀσθενέστεροι ἔσονται, ἅμα δὲ χρησιμώτεροι
ἡμῖν διὰ τὸ πλείους τὸν ἀριθμὸν γεγονέναι· καὶ βαδιοῦνται
ὀρθοὶ ἐπὶ δυοῖν σκελοῖν. ἐὰν δ' ἔτι δοκῶσιν ἀσελγαίνειν
καὶ μὴ 'θέλωσιν ἡσυχίαν ἄγειν, πάλιν αὖ," ἔφη, "τεμῶ δίχα, 5
ὥστ' ἐφ' ἑνὸς πορεύσονται σκέλους ἀσκωλιάζοντες." ταῦτα
εἰπὼν ἔτεμνε τοὺς ἀνθρώπους δίχα, ὥσπερ οἱ τὰ ὀὰ τέμ-
νοντες καὶ μέλλοντες ταριχεύειν, ἢ ὥσπερ οἱ τὰ ᾠὰ ταῖς e
θριξίν· ὅντινα δὲ τέμοι, τὸν Ἀπόλλω ἐκέλευεν τό τε
πρόσωπον μεταστρέφειν καὶ τὸ τοῦ αὐχένος ἥμισυ πρὸς
τὴν τομήν, ἵνα θεώμενος τὴν αὐτοῦ τμῆσιν κοσμιώτερος
εἴη ὁ ἄνθρωπος, καὶ τἆλλα ἰᾶσθαι ἐκέλευεν. ὁ δὲ τό τε 5
πρόσωπον μετέστρεφε, καὶ συνέλκων πανταχόθεν τὸ δέρμα
ἐπὶ τὴν γαστέρα νῦν καλουμένην, ὥσπερ τὰ σύσπαστα
βαλλάντια, ἓν στόμα ποιῶν ἀπέδει κατὰ μέσην τὴν γαστέρα,
ὃ δὴ τὸν ὀμφαλὸν καλοῦσι. καὶ τὰς μὲν ἄλλας ῥυτίδας
τὰς πολλὰς ἐξελέαινε καὶ τὰ στήθη διήρθρου, ἔχων τι 191

d 7 ὀὰ z cl. c: ᾠὰ vel ᾠὰ c m

τοιοῦτον ὄργανον οἷον οἱ σκυτοτόμοι περὶ τὸν καλάποδα
λεαίνοντες τὰς τῶν σκυτῶν ῥυτίδας· ὀλίγας δὲ κατέλιπε,
τὰς περὶ αὐτὴν τὴν γαστέρα καὶ τὸν ὀμφαλόν, μνημεῖον
5 εἶναι τοῦ παλαιοῦ πάθους. ἐπειδὴ οὖν ἡ φύσις δίχα
ἐτμήθη, ποθοῦν ἕκαστον τὸ ἥμισυ τὸ αὑτοῦ συνῄει, καὶ
περιβάλλοντες τὰς χεῖρας καὶ συμπλεκόμενοι ἀλλήλοις,
ἐπιθυμοῦντες συμφῦναι, ἀπέθνησκον ὑπὸ λιμοῦ καὶ τῆς
b ἄλλης ἀργίας διὰ τὸ μηδὲν ἐθέλειν χωρὶς ἀλλήλων ποιεῖν.
καὶ ὁπότε τι ἀποθάνοι τῶν ἡμίσεων, τὸ δὲ λειφθείη, τὸ
λειφθὲν ἄλλο ἐζήτει καὶ συνεπλέκετο, εἴτε γυναικὸς τῆς
ὅλης ἐντύχοι ἡμίσει, ὃ δὴ νῦν γυναῖκα καλοῦμεν, εἴτε
5 ἀνδρός· καὶ οὕτως ἀπώλλυντο. ἐλεήσας δὲ ὁ Ζεὺς ἄλλην
μηχανὴν πορίζεται, καὶ μετατίθησιν αὐτῶν τὰ αἰδοῖα εἰς
τὸ πρόσθεν. τέως γὰρ καὶ ταῦτα ἐκτὸς εἶχον, καὶ ἐγέννων
c καὶ ἔτικτον οὐκ εἰς ἀλλήλους ἀλλ’ εἰς γῆν, ὥσπερ οἱ τέττιγες. μετέθηκέ τε οὖν οὕτω αὐτῶν εἰς τὸ πρόσθεν καὶ
διὰ τούτων τὴν γένεσιν ἐν ἀλλήλοις ἐποίησεν, διὰ τοῦ
ἄρρενος ἐν τῷ θήλει, τῶνδε ἕνεκα, ἵνα ἐν τῇ συμπλοκῇ
5 ἅμα μὲν εἰ ἀνὴρ γυναικὶ ἐντύχοι, γεννῷεν καὶ γίγνοιτο τὸ
γένος, ἅμα δ’ εἰ καὶ ἄρρην ἄρρενι, πλησμονὴ γοῦν γίγνοιτο
τῆς συνουσίας καὶ διαπαύοιντο καὶ ἐπὶ τὰ ἔργα τρέποιντο
καὶ τοῦ ἄλλου βίου ἐπιμελοῖντο. ἔστι δὴ οὖν ἐκ τόσου
d ὁ ἔρως ἔμφυτος ἀλλήλων τοῖς ἀνθρώποις καὶ τῆς ἀρχαίας
φύσεως συναγωγεὺς καὶ ἐπιχειρῶν ποιῆσαι ἓν ἐκ δυοῖν καὶ
ἰάσασθαι τὴν φύσιν τὴν ἀνθρωπίνην. ἕκαστος οὖν ἡμῶν
ἐστιν ἀνθρώπου σύμβολον, ἅτε τετμημένος ὥσπερ αἱ ψῆτται,
5 ἐξ ἑνὸς δύο· ζητεῖ δὴ ἀεὶ τὸ αὑτοῦ ἕκαστος σύμβολον.
ὅσοι μὲν οὖν τῶν ἀνδρῶν τοῦ κοινοῦ τμῆμά εἰσιν, ὃ δὴ
τότε ἀνδρόγυνον ἐκαλεῖτο, φιλογύναικές τε εἰσὶ καὶ οἱ
πολλοὶ τῶν μοιχῶν ἐκ τούτου τοῦ γένους γεγόνασιν, καὶ
e ὅσαι αὖ γυναῖκες φίλανδροί τε καὶ μοιχεύτριαι ἐκ τούτου
τοῦ γένους γίγνονται. ὅσαι δὲ τῶν γυναικῶν γυναικὸς
τμῆμά εἰσιν, οὐ πάνυ αὗται τοῖς ἀνδράσι τὸν νοῦν προσ-
έχουσιν, ἀλλὰ μᾶλλον πρὸς τὰς γυναῖκας τετραμμέναι

e 1 ἐκ τούτου...2 γίγνονται del. z

εἰσί, καὶ αἱ ἑταιρίστριαι ἐκ τούτου τοῦ γένους γίγνονται. 5
ὅσοι δὲ ἄρρενος τμῆμά εἰσι, τὰ ἄρρενα διώκουσι, καὶ τέως
μὲν ἂν παῖδες ὦσιν, ἅτε τεμάχια ὄντα τοῦ ἄρρενος, φιλοῦσι
τοὺς ἄνδρας καὶ χαίρουσι συγκατακείμενοι καὶ συμπεπλε-
γμένοι τοῖς ἀνδράσι, καί εἰσιν οὗτοι βέλτιστοι τῶν παίδων 192
καὶ μειρακίων, ἅτε ἀνδρειότατοι ὄντες φύσει. φασὶ δὲ δή
τινες αὐτοὺς ἀναισχύντους εἶναι, ψευδόμενοι· οὐ γὰρ ὑπ'
ἀναισχυντίας τοῦτο δρῶσιν ἀλλ' ὑπὸ θάρρους καὶ ἀνδρείας
καὶ ἀρρενωπίας, τὸ ὅμοιον αὐτοῖς ἀσπαζόμενοι. μέγα δὲ 5
τεκμήριον· καὶ γὰρ τελεωθέντες μόνοι ἀποβαίνουσιν εἰς
τὰ πολιτικὰ ἄνδρες οἱ τοιοῦτοι. ἐπειδὰν δὲ ἀνδρωθῶσι,
παιδεραστοῦσι καὶ πρὸς γάμους καὶ παιδοποιίας οὐ προσ- b
έχουσι τὸν νοῦν φύσει, ἀλλ' ὑπὸ τοῦ νόμου ἀναγκάζονται·
ἀλλ' ἐξαρκεῖ αὐτοῖς μετ' ἀλλήλων καταζῆν ἀγάμοις. πάντως
μὲν οὖν ὁ τοιοῦτος παιδεραστής τε καὶ φιλεραστὴς γίγνεται,
ἀεὶ τὸ συγγενὲς ἀσπαζόμενος. ὅταν μὲν οὖν καὶ αὐτῷ 5
ἐκείνῳ ἐντύχῃ τῷ αὑτοῦ ἡμίσει καὶ ὁ παιδεραστὴς καὶ
ἄλλος πᾶς, τότε καὶ θαυμαστὰ ἐκπλήττονται φιλίᾳ τε καὶ
οἰκειότητι καὶ ἔρωτι, οὐκ ἐθέλοντες ὡς ἔπος εἰπεῖν χωρί- c
ζεσθαι ἀλλήλων οὐδὲ σμικρὸν χρόνον. καὶ οἱ διατελοῦντες
μετ' ἀλλήλων διὰ βίου οὗτοί εἰσιν, οἳ οὐδ' ἂν ἔχοιεν εἰπεῖν
ὅτι βούλονται σφίσι παρ' ἀλλήλων γίγνεσθαι. οὐδενὶ
γὰρ ἂν δόξειεν τοῦτ' εἶναι ἡ τῶν ἀφροδισίων συνουσία, ὡς 5
ἄρα τούτου ἕνεκα ἕτερος ἑτέρῳ χαίρει συνὼν οὕτως ἐπὶ
μεγάλης σπουδῆς· ἀλλ' ἄλλο τι βουλομένη ἑκατέρου ἡ ψυχὴ
δήλη ἐστίν, ὃ οὐ δύναται εἰπεῖν, ἀλλὰ μαντεύεται ὃ βού- d
λεται, καὶ αἰνίττεται. καὶ εἰ αὐτοῖς ἐν τῷ αὐτῷ κατακει-
μένοις ἐπιστὰς ὁ Ἥφαιστος, ἔχων τὰ ὄργανα, ἔροιτο· "τί
ἐσθ' ὃ βούλεσθε, ὦ ἄνθρωποι, ὑμῖν παρ' ἀλλήλων γενέσθαι;" καὶ εἰ ἀποροῦντας αὐτοὺς πάλιν ἔροιτο· "ἆρά γε 5
τοῦδε ἐπιθυμεῖτε, ἐν τῷ αὐτῷ γενέσθαι ὅτι μάλιστα ἀλλήλοις, ὥστε καὶ νύκτα καὶ ἡμέραν μὴ ἀπολείπεσθαι ἀλλήλων; εἰ γὰρ τούτου ἐπιθυμεῖτε, θέλω ὑμᾶς συντῆξαι καὶ
συμφυσῆσαι εἰς τὸ αὐτό, ὥστε δύ' ὄντας ἕνα γεγονέναι e

c 4 οὐδενὶ c: οὐδὲν m   d 8 ἐντῆξαι m   e 1 συμφῦσαι m

καὶ ἕως τ᾽ ἂν ζῆτε, ὡς ἕνα ὄντα, κοινῇ ἀμφοτέρους ζῆν,
καὶ ἐπειδὰν ἀποθάνητε, ἐκεῖ αὖ ἐν ᾍδου ἀντὶ δυοῖν ἕνα
εἶναι κοινῇ τεθνεῶτε· ἀλλ᾽ ὁρᾶτε εἰ τούτου ἐρᾶτε καὶ
5 ἐξαρκεῖ ὑμῖν ἂν τούτου τύχητε," ταῦτ᾽ ἀκούσας ἴσμεν ὅτι
οὐδ᾽ ἂν εἷς ἐξαρνηθείη οὐδ᾽ ἄλλο τι ἂν φανείη βουλόμενος,
ἀλλ᾽ ἀτεχνῶς οἴοιτ᾽ ἂν ἀκηκοέναι τοῦτο ὃ πάλαι ἄρα ἐπε-
θύμει, συνελθὼν καὶ συντακεὶς τῷ ἐρωμένῳ ἐκ δυοῖν εἷς
γενέσθαι. τοῦτο γάρ ἐστι τὸ αἴτιον, ὅτι ἡ ἀρχαία φύσις
10 ἡμῶν ἦν αὕτη καὶ ἦμεν ὅλοι· τοῦ ὅλου οὖν τῇ ἐπιθυμίᾳ
193 καὶ διώξει ἔρως ὄνομα. καὶ πρὸ τοῦ, ὥσπερ λέγω, ἓν
ἦμεν, νυνὶ δὲ διὰ τὴν ἀδικίαν διῳκίσθημεν ὑπὸ τοῦ θεοῦ,
καθάπερ Ἀρκάδες ὑπὸ Λακεδαιμονίων· φόβος οὖν ἐστιν,
ἐὰν μὴ κόσμιοι ὦμεν πρὸς τοὺς θεούς, ὅπως μὴ καὶ αὖθις
5 διασχισθησόμεθα, καὶ περίιμεν ἔχοντες ὥσπερ οἱ ἐν ταῖς
στήλαις καταγραφὴν ἐκτετυπωμένοι, διαπεπρισμένοι κατὰ
τὰς ῥῖνας, γεγονότες ὥσπερ λίσπαι. ἀλλὰ τούτων ἕνεκα
πάντ᾽ ἄνδρα χρὴ ἅπαντα παρακελεύεσθαι εὐσεβεῖν περὶ
b θεούς, ἵνα τὰ μὲν ἐκφύγωμεν, τῶν δὲ τύχωμεν, ὡς ὁ Ἔρως
ἡμῖν ἡγεμὼν καὶ στρατηγός. ᾧ μηδεὶς ἐναντία πραττέτω
(πράττει δ᾽ ἐναντία ὅστις θεοῖς ἀπεχθάνεται)· φίλοι γὰρ
γενόμενοι καὶ διαλλαγέντες τῷ θεῷ ἐξευρήσομέν τε καὶ
5 ἐντευξόμεθα τοῖς παιδικοῖς τοῖς ἡμετέροις αὐτῶν, ὃ τῶν νῦν
ὀλίγοι ποιοῦσι. καὶ μή μοι ὑπολάβῃ Ἐρυξίμαχος, κωμῳδῶν
τὸν λόγον, ὡς Παυσανίαν καὶ Ἀγάθωνα λέγω· ἴσως μὲν
c γὰρ καὶ οὗτοι τούτων τυγχάνουσιν ὄντες καί εἰσιν ἀμφότεροι
τὴν φύσιν ἄρρενες, λέγω δὲ οὖν ἔγωγε καθ᾽ ἁπάντων καὶ
ἀνδρῶν καὶ γυναικῶν, ὅτι οὕτως ἂν ἡμῶν τὸ γένος εὔδαιμον
γένοιτο, εἰ ἐκτελέσαιμεν τὸν ἔρωτα καὶ τῶν παιδικῶν τῶν
5 αὐτοῦ ἕκαστος τύχοι εἰς τὴν ἀρχαίαν ἀπελθὼν φύσιν. εἰ
δὲ τοῦτο ἄριστον, ἀναγκαῖον καὶ τῶν νῦν παρόντων τὸ
τούτου ἐγγυτάτω ἄριστον εἶναι· τοῦτο δ᾽ ἐστὶ παιδικῶν τυχεῖν
κατὰ νοῦν αὐτῷ πεφυκότων· οὗ δὴ τὸν αἴτιον θεὸν ὑμνοῦντες
d δικαίως ἂν ὑμνοῖμεν Ἔρωτα, ὃς ἔν τε τῷ παρόντι ἡμᾶς
πλεῖστα ὀνίνησιν εἰς τὸ οἰκεῖον ἄγων, καὶ εἰς τὸ ἔπειτα
ἐλπίδας μεγίστας παρέχεται, ἡμῶν παρεχομένων πρὸς θεοὺς

εὐσέβειαν, καταστήσας ἡμᾶς εἰς τὴν ἀρχαίαν φύσιν καὶ
ἰασάμενος μακαρίους καὶ εὐδαίμονας ποιῆσαι.   5
οὗτος,' ἔφη, 'ὦ 'Ερυξίμαχε, ὁ ἐμὸς λόγος ἐστὶ περὶ
"Ερωτος, ἀλλοῖος ἢ ὁ σός. ὥσπερ οὖν ἐδεήθην σου, μὴ
κωμῳδήσῃς αὐτόν, ἵνα καὶ τῶν λοιπῶν ἀκούσωμεν τί ἕκαστος
ἐρεῖ, μᾶλλον δὲ τί ἑκάτερος· 'Αγάθων γὰρ καὶ Σωκράτης e
λοιποί.'
'ἀλλὰ πείσομαί σοι,' ἔφη φάναι τὸν 'Ερυξίμαχον· 'καὶ
γάρ μοι ὁ λόγος ἡδέως ἐρρήθη. καὶ εἰ μὴ συνήδη Σωκράτει τε καὶ 'Αγάθωνι δεινοῖς οὖσι περὶ τὰ ἐρωτικά, πάνυ 5
ἂν ἐφοβούμην μὴ ἀπορήσωσι λόγων διὰ τὸ πολλὰ καὶ
παντοδαπὰ εἰρῆσθαι· νῦν δὲ ὅμως θαρρῶ.'
τὸν οὖν Σωκράτη εἰπεῖν 'καλῶς γὰρ αὐτὸς ἠγώνισαι, 194
ὦ 'Ερυξίμαχε· εἰ δὲ γένοιο οὗ νῦν ἐγώ εἰμι, μᾶλλον δὲ
ἴσως οὗ ἔσομαι ἐπειδὰν καὶ 'Αγάθων εἴπῃ εὖ, καὶ μάλ' ἂν
φοβοῖο καὶ ἐν παντὶ εἴης ὥσπερ ἐγὼ νῦν.'
'φαρμάττειν βούλει με, ὦ Σώκρατες,' εἰπεῖν τὸν 'Αγάθωνα, 5
'ἵνα θορυβηθῶ διὰ τὸ οἴεσθαι τὸ θέατρον προσδοκίαν μεγάλην
ἔχειν ὡς εὖ ἐροῦντος ἐμοῦ.'
'ἐπιλήσμων μεντἂν εἴην, ὦ 'Αγάθων,' εἰπεῖν τὸν Σωκράτη, 'εἰ ἰδὼν τὴν σὴν ἀνδρείαν καὶ μεγαλοφροσύνην b
ἀναβαίνοντος ἐπὶ τὸν ὀκρίβαντα μετὰ τῶν ὑποκριτῶν, καὶ
βλέψαντος ἐναντία τοσούτῳ θεάτρῳ, μέλλοντος ἐπιδείξεσθαι
σαυτοῦ λόγους, καὶ οὐδ' ὁπωστιοῦν ἐκπλαγέντος, νῦν
οἰηθείην σε θορυβήσεσθαι ἕνεκα ἡμῶν ὀλίγων ἀνθρώπων.' 5
'τί δέ, ὦ Σώκρατες;' τὸν 'Αγάθωνα φάναι, 'οὐ δήπου με
οὕτω θεάτρου μεστὸν ἡγῇ ὥστε καὶ ἀγνοεῖν ὅτι νοῦν ἔχοντι
ὀλίγοι ἔμφρονες πολλῶν ἀφρόνων φοβερώτεροι.'
'οὐ μεντἂν καλῶς ποιοίην,' φάναι, 'ὦ 'Αγάθων, περὶ σοῦ c
τι ἐγὼ ἄγροικον δοξάζων· ἀλλ' εὖ οἶδα ὅτι εἴ τισιν ἐντύχοις
οὓς ἡγοῖο σοφούς, μᾶλλον ἂν αὐτῶν φροντίζοις ἢ τῶν
πολλῶν. ἀλλὰ μὴ οὐχ οὗτοι ἡμεῖς ὦμεν (ἡμεῖς μὲν γὰρ
καὶ ἐκεῖ παρῆμεν καὶ ἦμεν τῶν πολλῶν), εἰ δὲ ἄλλοις 5
ἐντύχοις σοφοῖς, τάχ' ἂν αἰσχύνοιο αὐτούς, εἴ τι ἴσως
οἴοιο αἰσχρὸν ὂν ποιεῖν· ἢ πῶς λέγεις;'

'ἀληθῆ λέγεις,' φάναι.

'τοὺς δὲ πολλοὺς οὐκ ἂν αἰσχύνοιο εἴ τι οἴοιο αἰσχρὸν
10 ποιεῖν;'

d καὶ τὸν Φαῖδρον ἔφη ὑπολαβόντα εἰπεῖν 'ὦ φίλε
'Αγάθων, ἐὰν ἀποκρίνῃ Σωκράτει, οὐδὲν ἔτι διοίσει αὐτῷ
ὅπῃοῦν τῶν ἐνθάδε ὁτιοῦν γίγνεσθαι, ἐὰν μόνον ἔχῃ ὅτῳ
διαλέγηται, ἄλλως τε καὶ καλῷ.
5 Σωκράτους διαλεγομένου, ἀναγκαῖον δέ μοι ἐπιμεληθῆναι
τοῦ ἐγκωμίου τῷ Ἔρωτι καὶ ἀποδέξασθαι παρ' ἑνὸς ἑκάστου
ὑμῶν τὸν λόγον· ἀποδοὺς οὖν ἑκάτερος τῷ θεῷ οὕτως ἤδη
διαλεγέσθω.'

e 'ἀλλὰ καλῶς λέγεις, ὦ Φαῖδρε,' φάναι τὸν 'Αγάθωνα,
'καὶ οὐδέν με κωλύει λέγειν· Σωκράτει γὰρ καὶ αὖθις ἔσται
πολλάκις διαλέγεσθαι.

ἐγὼ δὲ δὴ βούλομαι πρῶτον μὲν εἰπεῖν ὡς χρή με εἰπεῖν,
5 ἔπειτα εἰπεῖν. δοκοῦσι γάρ μοι πάντες οἱ πρόσθεν εἰρηκότες
οὐ τὸν θεὸν ἐγκωμιάζειν ἀλλὰ τοὺς ἀνθρώπους εὐδαιμονίζειν
τῶν ἀγαθῶν ὧν ὁ θεὸς αὐτοῖς αἴτιος· ὁποῖος δέ τις αὐτὸς ὢν
195 ταῦτα ἐδωρήσατο, οὐδεὶς εἴρηκεν. εἷς δὲ τρόπος ὀρθὸς παντὸς
ἐπαίνου περὶ παντός, λόγῳ διελθεῖν οἷος οἵων αἴτιος ὢν
τυγχάνει περὶ οὗ ἂν ὁ λόγος ᾖ. οὕτω δὴ τὸν Ἔρωτα καὶ
ἡμᾶς δίκαιον ἐπαινέσαι πρῶτον αὐτὸν οἷός ἐστιν, ἔπειτα
5 τὰς δόσεις. φημὶ οὖν ἐγὼ πάντων θεῶν εὐδαιμόνων ὄντων
Ἔρωτα, εἰ θέμις καὶ ἀνεμέσητον εἰπεῖν, εὐδαιμονέστατον
εἶναι αὐτῶν, κάλλιστον ὄντα καὶ ἄριστον. ἔστι δὲ κάλλιστος
ὢν τοιόσδε. πρῶτον μὲν νεώτατος θεῶν, ὦ Φαῖδρε. μέγα
b δὲ τεκμήριον τῷ λόγῳ αὐτὸς παρέχεται; φεύγων φυγῇ τὸ
γῆρας, ταχὺ ὂν δῆλον ὅτι· θᾶττον γοῦν τοῦ δέοντος ἡμῖν
προσέρχεται. ὃ δὴ πέφυκεν Ἔρως μισεῖν καὶ οὐδ' ἐντὸς
πολλοῦ πλησιάζειν. μετὰ δὲ νέων ἀεὶ σύνεστί τε καί ἐστιν·
5 ὁ γὰρ παλαιὸς λόγος εὖ ἔχει, ὡς ὅμοιον ὁμοίῳ ἀεὶ πελάζει.
ἐγὼ δὲ Φαίδρῳ πολλὰ ἄλλα ὁμολογῶν τοῦτο οὐχ ὁμολογῶ,
ὡς Ἔρως Κρόνου καὶ 'Ιαπετοῦ ἀρχαιότερός ἐστιν, ἀλλὰ
c φημὶ νεώτατον αὐτὸν εἶναι θεῶν καὶ ἀεὶ νέον, τὰ δὲ παλαιὰ

a 2 οἷς (sic) οἵων m: οἷος ὢν m   b 4 ἔστιν] ἐστὶ νέος z: ἔσται z

πράγματα περὶ θεούς, ἃ Ἡσίοδος καὶ Παρμενίδης λέγουσιν,
Ἀνάγκῃ καὶ οὐκ Ἔρωτι γεγονέναι, εἰ ἐκεῖνοι ἀληθῆ ἔλεγον·
οὐ γὰρ ἂν ἐκτομαὶ οὐδὲ δεσμοὶ ἀλλήλων ἐγίγνοντο καὶ ἄλλα
πολλὰ καὶ βίαια, εἰ Ἔρως ἐν αὐτοῖς ἦν, ἀλλὰ φιλία καὶ 5
εἰρήνη, ὥσπερ νῦν, ἐξ οὗ Ἔρως τῶν θεῶν βασιλεύει. νέος
μὲν οὖν ἐστι, πρὸς δὲ τῷ νέῳ ἁπαλός· ποιητοῦ δ᾽ ἐστιν
ἐνδεὴς οἷος ἦν Ὅμηρος πρὸς τὸ ἐπιδεῖξαι θεοῦ ἁπαλότητα. d
Ὅμηρος γὰρ Ἄτην θεόν τέ φησιν εἶναι καὶ ἁπαλήν — τούς
γοῦν πόδας αὐτῆς ἁπαλοὺς εἶναι — λέγων

<blockquote>
τῆς μέν θ᾽ ἁπαλοὶ πόδες· οὐ γὰρ ἐπ᾽ οὔδεος
πίλναται, ἀλλ᾽ ἄρα ἥ γε κατ᾽ ἀνδρῶν κράατα βαίνει. 5
</blockquote>

καλῶ οὖν δοκεῖ μοι τεκμηρίῳ τὴν ἁπαλότητα ἀποφαίνειν,
ὅτι οὐκ ἐπὶ σκληροῦ βαίνει, ἀλλ᾽ ἐπὶ μαλθακοῦ. τῷ αὐτῷ
δὴ καὶ ἡμεῖς χρησόμεθα τεκμηρίῳ περὶ Ἔρωτα ὅτι ἁπαλός. e
οὐ γὰρ ἐπὶ γῆς βαίνει οὐδ᾽ ἐπὶ κρανίων, ἅ ἐστιν οὐ πάνυ
μαλακά, ἀλλ᾽ ἐν τοῖς μαλακωτάτοις τῶν ὄντων καὶ βαίνει
καὶ οἰκεῖ. ἐν γὰρ ἤθεσι καὶ ψυχαῖς θεῶν καὶ ἀνθρώπων τὴν
οἴκησιν ἵδρυται, καὶ οὐκ αὖ ἑξῆς ἐν πάσαις ταῖς ψυχαῖς, ἀλλ᾽ 5
ᾗτινι ἂν σκληρὸν ἦθος ἐχούσῃ ἐντύχῃ, ἀπέρχεται, ᾗ δ᾽ ἂν
μαλακόν, οἰκίζεται. ἁπτόμενον οὖν ἀεὶ καὶ ποσὶν καὶ πάντῃ
ἐν μαλακωτάτοις τῶν μαλακωτάτων, ἁπαλώτατον ἀνάγκη
εἶναι. νεώτατος μὲν δή ἐστι καὶ ἁπαλώτατος, πρὸς δὲ 196
τούτοις ὑγρὸς τὸ εἶδος. οὐ γὰρ ἂν οἷός τ᾽ ἦν πάντῃ περιπτύσσεσθαι οὐδὲ διὰ πάσης ψυχῆς καὶ εἰσιὼν τὸ πρῶτον
λανθάνειν καὶ ἐξιών, εἰ σκληρὸς ἦν. συμμέτρου δὲ καὶ
ὑγρᾶς ἰδέας μέγα τεκμήριον ἡ εὐσχημοσύνη, ὃ δὴ δια- 5
φερόντως ἐκ πάντων ὁμολογουμένως Ἔρως ἔχει· ἀσχημοσύνη
γὰρ καὶ Ἔρωτι πρὸς ἀλλήλους ἀεὶ πόλεμος. χρόας δὲ
κάλλος ἡ κατ᾽ ἄνθη δίαιτα τοῦ θεοῦ σημαίνει· ἀνανθεῖ γὰρ
καὶ ἀπηνθηκότι καὶ σώματι καὶ ψυχῇ καὶ ἄλλῳ ὁτῳοῦν οὐκ b
ἐνίζει Ἔρως, οὗ δ᾽ ἂν εὐανθής τε καὶ εὐώδης τόπος ᾖ,
ἐνταῦθα δὲ καὶ ἵζει καὶ μένει.

περὶ μὲν οὖν κάλλους τοῦ θεοῦ καὶ ταῦτα ἱκανὰ καὶ ἔτι

d 4 τῇ multi Homeri codices   οὔδει m Hom. codd.   b 3 δὲ c: om. m

5 πολλὰ λείπεται, περὶ δὲ ἀρετῆς Ἔρωτος μετὰ ταῦτα λεκτέον,
τὸ μὲν μέγιστον ὅτι Ἔρως οὔτ' ἀδικεῖ οὔτ' ἀδικεῖται οὔτε
ὑπὸ θεοῦ οὔτε θεόν, οὔτε ὑπ' ἀνθρώπου οὔτε ἄνθρωπον.
οὔτε γὰρ αὐτὸς βίᾳ πάσχει, εἴ τι πάσχει (βία γὰρ Ἔρωτος οὐχ
c ἅπτεται), οὔτε ποιῶν ποιεῖ· πᾶς γὰρ ἑκὼν Ἔρωτι πᾶν
ὑπηρετεῖ, ἃ δ' ἂν ἑκὼν ἑκόντι ὁμολογήσῃ, φασὶν "οἱ πόλεως
βασιλῆς νόμοι" δίκαια εἶναι. πρὸς δὲ τῇ δικαιοσύνῃ σωφροσύνης πλείστης μετέχει. εἶναι γὰρ ὁμολογεῖται σωφροσύνη
5 τὸ κρατεῖν ἡδονῶν καὶ ἐπιθυμιῶν, Ἔρωτος δὲ μηδεμίαν
ἡδονὴν κρείττω εἶναι· εἰ δὲ ἥττους, κρατοῖντ' ἂν ὑπὸ Ἔρωτος,
ὁ δὲ κρατοῖ, κρατῶν δὲ ἡδονῶν καὶ ἐπιθυμιῶν ὁ Ἔρως διαφερόντως ἂν σωφρονοῖ. καὶ μὴν εἴς γε ἀνδρείαν Ἔρωτι
d οὐδ' Ἄρης ἀνθίσταται. οὐ γὰρ ἔχει Ἔρωτα Ἄρης,
ἀλλ' Ἔρως Ἄρη — Ἀφροδίτης, ὡς λόγος — κρείττων δὲ ὁ ἔχων
τοῦ ἐχομένου· τοῦ δ' ἀνδρειοτάτου τῶν ἄλλων κρατῶν πάντων
ἂν ἀνδρειότατος εἴη. περὶ μὲν οὖν δικαιοσύνης καὶ σωφρο-
5 σύνης καὶ ἀνδρείας τοῦ θεοῦ εἴρηται, περὶ δὲ σοφίας λείπεται·
ὅσον οὖν δυνατόν, πειρατέον μὴ ἐλλείπειν. καὶ πρῶτον μέν,
ἵν' αὖ καὶ ἐγὼ τὴν ἡμετέραν τέχνην τιμήσω ὥσπερ Ἐρυξί-
e μαχος τὴν αὑτοῦ, ποιητὴς ὁ θεὸς σοφὸς οὕτως ὥστε καὶ
ἄλλον ποιῆσαι· πᾶς γοῦν ποιητὴς γίγνεται, κἂν ἄμουσος
ᾖ τὸ πρίν, οὗ ἂν Ἔρως ἅψηται. ᾧ δὴ πρέπει ἡμᾶς
μαρτυρίῳ χρῆσθαι, ὅτι ποιητὴς ὁ Ἔρως ἀγαθὸς ἐν κεφαλαίῳ
5 πᾶσαν ποίησιν τὴν κατὰ μουσικήν· ἃ γάρ τις ἢ μὴ ἔχει ἢ
μὴ οἶδεν, οὔτ' ἂν ἑτέρῳ δοίη οὔτ' ἂν ἄλλον διδάξειεν. καὶ
197 μὲν δὴ τήν γε τῶν ζῴων ποίησιν πάντων τίς ἐναντιώσεται
μὴ οὐχὶ Ἔρωτος εἶναι σοφίαν, ᾗ γίγνεταί τε καὶ φύεται
πάντα τὰ ζῷα; ἀλλὰ τὴν τῶν τεχνῶν δημιουργίαν οὐκ
ἴσμεν, ὅτι οὗ μὲν ἂν ὁ θεὸς οὗτος διδάσκαλος γένηται,
5 ἐλλόγιμος καὶ φανὸς ἀπέβη, οὗ δ' ἂν Ἔρως μὴ ἐφά-
ψηται, σκοτεινός; τοξικήν γε μὴν καὶ ἰατρικὴν καὶ μαντικὴν
Ἀπόλλων ἀνηῦρεν ἐπιθυμίας καὶ ἔρωτος ἡγεμονεύσαντος,
b ὥστε καὶ οὗτος Ἔρωτος ἂν εἴη μαθητής, καὶ Μοῦσαι
μουσικῆς καὶ Ἥφαιστος χαλκείας καὶ Ἀθηνᾶ ἱστουργίας
καὶ Ζεὺς κυβερνᾶν θεῶν τε καὶ ἀνθρώπων. ὅθεν δὴ

καὶ κατεσκευάσθη τῶν θεῶν τὰ πράγματα Ἔρωτος ἐγγενομένου, δῆλον ὅτι κάλλους — αἴσχει γὰρ οὐκ ἔπι ἔρως — πρὸ 5
τοῦ δέ, ὥσπερ ἐν ἀρχῇ εἶπον, πολλὰ καὶ δεινὰ θεοῖς ἐγίγνετο,
ὡς λέγεται, διὰ τὴν τῆς Ἀνάγκης βασιλείαν· ἐπειδὴ δ' ὁ
θεὸς οὗτος ἔφυ, ἐκ τοῦ ἐρᾶν τῶν καλῶν πάντ' ἀγαθὰ γέγονεν
καὶ θεοῖς καὶ ἀνθρώποις.

οὕτως ἐμοὶ δοκεῖ, ὦ Φαῖδρε, Ἔρως πρῶτος αὐτὸς ὢν c
κάλλιστος καὶ ἄριστος μετὰ τοῦτο ἄλλοις ἄλλων τοιούτων
αἴτιος εἶναι. ἐπέρχεται δέ μοι τι καὶ ἔμμετρον εἰπεῖν, ὅτι
οὗτός ἐστιν ὁ ποιῶν

εἰρήνην μὲν ἐν ἀνθρώποις, πελάγει δὲ γαλήνην 5
νηνεμίαν, ἀνέμων κοίτην ὕπνον τ' ἐνὶ κήδει.

οὗτος δὲ ἡμᾶς ἀλλοτριότητος μὲν κενοῖ, οἰκειότητος δὲ πληροῖ, d
τὰς τοιάσδε συνόδους μετ' ἀλλήλων πάσας τιθεὶς συνιέναι,
ἐν ἑορταῖς, ἐν χοροῖς, ἐν θυσίαισι γιγνόμενος ἡγεμών·
πρᾳότητα μὲν πορίζων, ἀγριότητα δ' ἐξορίζων· φιλόδωρος
εὐμενείας, ἄδωρος δυσμενείας· ἵλεως ἀγανός· θεατὸς σοφοῖς, 5
ἀγαστὸς θεοῖς· ζηλωτὸς ἀμοίροις, κτητὸς εὐμοίροις· τρυφῆς,
ἁβρότητος, χλιδῆς, χαρίτων, ἱμέρου, πόθου πατήρ· ἐπιμελὴς
ἀγαθῶν, ἀμελὴς κακῶν· ἐν πόνῳ, ἐν φόβῳ, ἐν πόθῳ, ἐν
λόγῳ κυβερνήτης, ἐπιβάτης, παραστάτης τε καὶ σωτὴρ e
ἄριστος, συμπάντων τε θεῶν καὶ ἀνθρώπων κόσμος, ἡγεμὼν
κάλλιστος καὶ ἄριστος, ᾧ χρὴ ἕπεσθαι πάντα ἄνδρα ἐφυμνοῦντα καλῶς, ᾠδῆς μετέχοντα ἣν ᾄδει θέλγων πάντων θεῶν
τε καὶ ἀνθρώπων νόημα. 5

οὗτος,' ἔφη, 'ὁ παρ' ἐμοῦ λόγος , ὦ Φαῖδρε, τῷ θεῷ
ἀνακείσθω, τὰ μὲν παιδιᾶς, τὰ δὲ σπουδῆς μετρίας, καθ'
ὅσον ἐγὼ δύναμαι, μετέχων.'

εἰπόντος δὲ τοῦ Ἀγάθωνος πάντας ἔφη ὁ Ἀριστόδημος 198
ἀναθορυβῆσαι τοὺς παρόντας, ὡς πρεπόντως τοῦ νεανίσκου
εἰρηκότος καὶ αὐτῷ καὶ τῷ θεῷ. τὸν οὖν Σωκράτη εἰπεῖν
βλέψαντα εἰς τὸν Ἐρυξίμαχον, 'ἆρά σοι δοκῶ,' φάναι, 'ὦ
παῖ Ἀκουμενοῦ, ἀδεὲς πάλαι δέος δεδιέναι, ἀλλ' οὐ μαντικῶς 5

b 5 ἔπι z: ἔνι m: ἔπεστιν m   c 1 πρῶτος m: πρὸ τῶν c
d 3 θυσίαισι m: εὐθυμίαις c   d 5 ἀγανός z: ἀγαθός m: ἀγαθοῖς c

ἃ νυνδὴ ἔλεγον εἰπεῖν, ὅτι ᾿Αγάθων θαυμαστῶς ἐροῖ, ἐγὼ δ᾽
ἀπορήσοιμι;᾽

'τὸ μὲν ἕτερον,᾽ φάναι τὸν ᾿Ερυξίμαχον, 'μαντικῶς μοι
δοκεῖς εἰρηκέναι, ὅτι ᾿Αγάθων εὖ ἐρεῖ· τὸ δὲ σὲ ἀπορήσειν,
10 οὐκ οἶμαι.᾽

b 'καὶ πῶς, ὦ μακάριε,᾽ εἰπεῖν τὸν Σωκράτη, 'οὐ μέλλω
ἀπορεῖν καὶ ἐγὼ καὶ ἄλλος ὁστισοῦν, μέλλων λέξειν μετὰ
καλὸν οὕτω καὶ παντοδαπὸν λόγον ῥηθέντα; καὶ τὰ μὲν ἄλλα
οὐχ ὁμοίως μὲν θαυμαστά· τὸ δὲ ἐπὶ τελευτῆς τοῦ κάλλους
5 τῶν ὀνομάτων καὶ ῥημάτων τίς οὐκ ἂν ἐξεπλάγη ἀκούων;
ἐπεὶ ἔγωγε ἐνθυμούμενος ὅτι αὐτὸς οὐχ οἷός τ᾽ ἔσομαι οὐδ᾽
ἐγγὺς τούτων οὐδὲν καλὸν εἰπεῖν, ὑπ᾽ αἰσχύνης ὀλίγου
c ἀποδρὰς ᾠχόμην, εἴ πη εἶχον. καὶ γάρ με Γοργίου ὁ λόγος
ἀνεμίμνησκεν, ὥστε ἀτεχνῶς τὸ τοῦ ῾Ομήρου ἐπεπόνθη·
ἐφοβούμην μή μοι τελευτῶν ὁ ᾿Αγάθων Γοργίου κεφαλὴν
δεινοῦ λέγειν ἐν τῷ λόγῳ ἐπὶ τὸν ἐμὸν λόγον πέμψας αὐτόν
5 με λίθον τῇ ἀφωνίᾳ ποιήσειεν. καὶ ἐνενόησα τότε ἄρα
καταγέλαστος ὤν, ἡνίκα ὑμῖν ὡμολόγουν ἐν τῷ μέρει μεθ᾽
d ὑμῶν ἐγκωμιάσεσθαι τὸν ῎Ερωτα καὶ ἔφην εἶναι δεινὸς τὰ
ἐρωτικά, οὐδὲν εἰδὼς ἄρα τοῦ πράγματος, ὡς ἔδει ἐγκωμιάζειν
ὁτιοῦν. ἐγὼ μὲν γὰρ ὑπ᾽ ἀβελτερίας ᾤμην δεῖν τἀληθῆ
λέγειν περὶ ἑκάστου τοῦ ἐγκωμιαζομένου, καὶ τοῦτο μὲν
5 ὑπάρχειν, ἐξ αὐτῶν δὲ τούτων τὰ κάλλιστα ἐκλεγομένους
ὡς εὐπρεπέστατα τιθέναι· καὶ πάνυ δὴ μέγα ἐφρόνουν ὡς εὖ
ἐρῶν, ὡς εἰδὼς τὴν ἀλήθειαν τοῦ ἐπαινεῖν ὁτιοῦν. τὸ δὲ ἄρα,
ὡς ἔοικεν, οὐ τοῦτο ἦν τὸ καλῶς ἐπαινεῖν ὁτιοῦν, ἀλλὰ τὸ ὡς
e μέγιστα ἀνατιθέναι τῷ πράγματι καὶ ὡς κάλλιστα, ἐάν τε ᾖ
οὕτως ἔχοντα ἐάν τε μή· εἰ δὲ ψευδῆ, οὐδὲν ἄρ᾽ ἦν πρᾶγμα.
προυρρήθη γάρ, ὡς ἔοικεν, ὅπως ἕκαστος ἡμῶν τὸν ῎Ερωτα
ἐγκωμιάζειν δόξει, οὐχ ὅπως ἐγκωμιάσεται. διὰ ταῦτα δὴ
5 οἶμαι πάντα λόγον κινοῦντες ἀνατίθετε τῷ ῎Ερωτι, καί
φατε αὐτὸν τοιοῦτόν τε εἶναι καὶ τοσούτων αἴτιον, ὅπως ἂν
199 φαίνηται ὡς κάλλιστος καὶ ἄριστος, δῆλον ὅτι τοῖς μὴ γιγνώ-
σκουσιν (οὐ γὰρ δήπου τοῖς γε εἰδόσιν) καὶ καλῶς γ᾽ ἔχει

a 2 δήπου z: ἂν που m: που m

καὶ σεμνῶς ὁ ἔπαινος. ἀλλὰ γὰρ ἐγὼ οὐκ ᾔδη ἄρα τὸν
τρόπον τοῦ ἐπαίνου, οὐ δ' εἰδὼς ὑμῖν ὡμολόγησα καὶ αὐτὸς
ἐν τῷ μέρει ἐπαινέσεσθαι. ἡ γλῶσσα οὖν ὑπέσχετο, ἡ δὲ 5
φρὴν οὔ· χαιρέτω δή. οὐ γὰρ ἔτι ἐγκωμιάζω τοῦτον τὸν
τρόπον (οὐ γὰρ ἂν δυναίμην), οὐ μέντοι ἀλλὰ τά γε ἀληθῆ,
εἰ βούλεσθε, ἐθέλω εἰπεῖν κατ' ἐμαυτόν, οὐ πρὸς τοὺς b
ὑμετέρους λόγους, ἵνα μὴ γέλωτα ὄφλω. ὅρα οὖν, ὦ Φαῖδρε,
εἴ τι καὶ τοιούτου λόγου δέῃ, περὶ Ἔρωτος τἀληθῆ λεγόμενα
ἀκούειν, ὀνόμασι δὲ καὶ θέσει ῥημάτων τοιαύτῃ ὁποία ἂν
τις τύχῃ ἐπελθοῦσα.' 5

τὸν οὖν Φαῖδρον ἔφη καὶ τοὺς ἄλλους κελεύειν λέγειν,
ὅπῃ αὐτὸς οἴοιτο δεῖν εἰπεῖν, ταύτῃ.

'ἔτι τοίνυν,' φάναι, 'ὦ Φαῖδρε, πάρες μοι Ἀγάθωνα σμίκρ'
ἄττα ἐρέσθαι, ἵνα ἀνομολογησάμενος παρ' αὐτοῦ οὕτως ἤδη
λέγω.' 10

'ἀλλὰ παρίημι,' φάναι τὸν Φαῖδρον, 'ἀλλ' ἐρώτα.' μετὰ c
ταῦτα δὴ τὸν Σωκράτη ἔφη ἐνθένδε ποθὲν ἄρξασθαι.

'καὶ μήν, ὦ φίλε Ἀγάθων, καλῶς μοι ἔδοξας καθηγήσασθαι τοῦ λόγου, λέγων ὅτι πρῶτον μὲν δέοι αὐτὸν ἐπιδεῖξαι
ὁποῖός τις ἐστιν ὁ Ἔρως, ὕστερον δὲ τὰ ἔργα αὐτοῦ. ταύτην 5
τὴν ἀρχὴν πάνυ ἄγαμαι. ἴθι οὖν μοι περὶ Ἔρωτος, ἐπειδὴ
καὶ τἆλλα καλῶς καὶ μεγαλοπρεπῶς διῆλθες οἷός ἐστι, καὶ
τόδε εἰπέ· πότερόν ἐστι τοιοῦτος οἷος εἶναί τινος ὁ Ἔρως d
ἔρως, ἢ οὐδενός; ἐρωτῶ δ' οὐκ εἰ μητρός τινος ἢ πατρός
ἐστιν (γελοῖον γὰρ ἂν εἴη τὸ ἐρώτημα εἰ Ἔρως ἐστὶν ἔρως
μητρὸς ἢ πατρός), ἀλλ' ὥσπερ ἂν εἰ αὐτὸ τοῦτο πατέρα
ἠρώτων, ἄρα ὁ πατήρ ἐστι πατήρ τινος ἢ οὔ; εἶπες ἂν 5
δήπου μοι, εἰ ἐβούλου καλῶς ἀποκρίνασθαι, ὅτι ἐστὶν ὑέος
γε ἢ θυγατρὸς ὁ πατὴρ πατήρ· ἢ οὔ; '

'πάνυ γε,' φάναι τὸν Ἀγάθωνα.

'οὐκοῦν καὶ ἡ μήτηρ ὡσαύτως; ' ὁμολογεῖσθαι καὶ τοῦτο.

'ἔτι τοίνυν,' εἰπεῖν τὸν Σωκράτη, 'ἀπόκριναι ὀλίγῳ πλείω, e
ἵνα μᾶλλον καταμάθῃς ὃ βούλομαι. εἰ γὰρ ἐροίμην, "τί

b 4 ὀνόμασει (sic) m   ἂν m: δ' ἂν m: δἂν z

δέ; ἀδελφός, αὐτὸ τοῦθ᾽ ὅπερ ἐστίν, ἐστί τινος ἀδελφὸς ἢ
οὔ;᾽᾽᾽ φάναι εἶναι.

5 ᾽οὐκοῦν ἀδελφοῦ ἢ ἀδελφῆς;᾽ ὁμολογεῖν.

᾽πειρῶ δή,᾽ φάναι, ᾽καὶ τὸν ἔρωτα εἰπεῖν. ὁ Ἔρως ἔρως
ἐστὶν οὐδενὸς ἢ τινος;᾽

᾽πάνυ μὲν οὖν ἐστιν.᾽

200 ᾽τοῦτο μὲν τοίνυν,᾽ εἰπεῖν τὸν Σωκράτη, ᾽φύλαξον παρὰ
σαυτῷ μεμνημένος ὅτου· τοσόνδε δὲ εἰπέ, πότερον ὁ Ἔρως
ἐκείνου οὗ ἐστιν ἔρως, ἐπιθυμεῖ αὐτοῦ ἢ οὔ;᾽

᾽πάνυ γε,᾽ φάναι.

5 ᾽πότερον ἔχων αὐτὸ οὗ ἐπιθυμεῖ τε καὶ ἐρᾷ, εἶτα ἐπιθυμεῖ
τε καὶ ἐρᾷ, ἢ οὐκ ἔχων;᾽

᾽οὐκ ἔχων, ὡς τὸ εἰκός γε,᾽ φάναι.

᾽σκόπει δή,᾽ εἰπεῖν τὸν Σωκράτη, ᾽ἀντὶ τοῦ εἰκότος εἰ
ἀνάγκη οὕτως, τὸ ἐπιθυμοῦν ἐπιθυμεῖν οὗ ἐνδεές ἐστιν, ἢ μὴ
b ἐπιθυμεῖν, ἐὰν μὴ ἐνδεὲς ᾖ; ἐμοὶ μὲν γὰρ θαυμαστῶς δοκεῖ,
ὦ Ἀγάθων, ὡς ἀνάγκη εἶναι· σοὶ δὲ πῶς;᾽

᾽κἀμοί,᾽ φάναι, ᾽δοκεῖ.᾽

᾽καλῶς λέγεις. ἆρ᾽ οὖν βούλοιτ᾽ ἄν τις μέγας ὢν μέγας
5 εἶναι, ἢ ἰσχυρὸς ὢν ἰσχυρός;᾽

᾽ἀδύνατον ἐκ τῶν ὡμολογημένων.᾽

᾽οὐ γάρ που ἐνδεὴς ἂν εἴη τούτων ὅ γε ὤν.᾽

᾽ἀληθῆ λέγεις.᾽

᾽εἰ γὰρ καὶ ἰσχυρὸς ὢν βούλοιτο ἰσχυρὸς εἶναι,᾽ φάναι τὸν
10 Σωκράτη, ᾽καὶ ταχὺς ὢν ταχύς, καὶ ὑγιὴς ὢν ὑγιής (ἴσως
γὰρ ἄν τις ταῦτα οἰηθείη καὶ πάντα τὰ τοιαῦτα τοὺς ὄντας
c τε τοιούτους καὶ ἔχοντας ταῦτα τούτων ἅπερ ἔχουσι καὶ
ἐπιθυμεῖν), ἵν᾽ οὖν μὴ ἐξαπατηθῶμεν, τούτου ἕνεκα λέγω.
τούτοις γάρ, ὦ Ἀγάθων, εἰ ἐννοεῖς, ἔχειν μὲν ἕκαστα
τούτων ἐν τῷ παρόντι ἀνάγκη ἃ ἔχουσιν, ἐάντε βούλωνται
5 ἐάντε μή, καὶ τούτου γε δήπου τίς ἂν ἐπιθυμήσειεν; ἀλλ᾽
ὅταν τις λέγῃ ὅτι ἐγὼ ὑγιαίνων βούλομαι καὶ ὑγιαίνειν,
καὶ πλουτῶν βούλομαι καὶ πλουτεῖν, καὶ ἐπιθυμῶ αὐτῶν
τούτων ἃ ἔχω, εἴποιμεν ἂν αὐτῷ ὅτι σύ, ὦ ἄνθρωπε,
d πλοῦτον κεκτημένος καὶ ὑγίειαν καὶ ἰσχὺν βούλει καὶ εἰς

τὸν ἔπειτα χρόνον ταῦτα κεκτῆσθαι, ἐπεὶ ἐν τῷ γε νῦν
παρόντι, εἴτε βούλει εἴτε μή, ἔχεις· σκόπει οὖν, ὅταν
τοῦτο λέγῃς, ὅτι ἐπιθυμῶ τῶν παρόντων, εἰ ἄλλο τι λέγεις
ἢ τόδε, ὅτι βούλομαι τὰ νῦν παρόντα καὶ εἰς τὸν ἔπειτα 5
χρόνον παρεῖναι. ἄλλο τι ὁμολογοῖ ἄν;' συμφάναι ἔφη τὸν
Ἀγάθωνα.

εἰπεῖν δὴ τὸν Σωκράτη, 'οὐκοῦν τοῦτό γ' ἐστὶν ἐκείνου
ἐρᾶν, ὃ οὔπω ἕτοιμον αὐτῷ ἐστιν οὐδὲ ἔχει, τὸ εἰς τὸν
ἔπειτα χρόνον ταῦτα εἶναι αὐτῷ σῳζόμενα καὶ παρόντα;'   10
'πάνυ γε,' φάναι.   e

'καὶ οὗτος ἄρα καὶ ἄλλος πᾶς ὁ ἐπιθυμῶν τοῦ μὴ ἑτοίμου
ἐπιθυμεῖ καὶ τοῦ μὴ παρόντος, καὶ ὃ μὴ ἔχει καὶ ὃ μή ἐστιν
αὐτὸς καὶ οὗ ἐνδεής ἐστι, τοιαῦτ' ἄττα ἐστὶν ὧν ἡ ἐπιθυμία
τε καὶ ὁ ἔρως ἐστίν;'   5
'πάνυ γ',' εἰπεῖν.

'ἴθι δή,' φάναι τὸν Σωκράτη, 'ἀνομολογησώμεθα τὰ εἰρημένα. ἄλλο τί ἐστιν ὁ Ἔρως πρῶτον μὲν τινῶν, ἔπειτα
τούτων ὧν ἂν ἔνδεια παρῇ αὐτῷ;'
'ναί,' φάναι.   201

'ἐπὶ δὴ τούτοις ἀναμνήσθητι τίνων ἔφησθα ἐν τῷ λόγῳ
εἶναι τὸν Ἔρωτα· εἰ δὲ βούλει, ἐγώ σε ἀναμνήσω. οἶμαι
γάρ σε οὑτωσί πως εἰπεῖν, ὅτι τοῖς θεοῖς κατεσκευάσθη τὰ
πράγματα δι' ἔρωτα καλῶν· αἰσχρῶν γὰρ οὐκ εἴη ἔρως. οὐχ 5
οὑτωσί πως ἔλεγες;'
'εἶπον γάρ,' φάναι τὸν Ἀγάθωνα.

'καὶ ἐπιεικῶς γε λέγεις, ὦ ἑταῖρε,' φάναι τὸν Σωκράτη·
'καὶ εἰ τοῦτο οὕτως ἔχει, ἄλλο τι ὁ Ἔρως κάλλους ἂν εἴη
ἔρως, αἴσχους δὲ οὔ;' ὡμολόγει.   10

'οὐκοῦν ὡμολόγηται, οὗ ἐνδεής ἐστι καὶ μὴ ἔχει, τούτου b
ἐρᾶν;'
'ναί,' εἰπεῖν.
'ἐνδεὴς ἄρ' ἐστὶ καὶ οὐκ ἔχει ὁ Ἔρως κάλλος.'
'ἀνάγκη,' φάναι.   5
'τί δέ; τὸ ἐνδεὲς κάλλους καὶ μηδαμῇ κεκτημένον κάλλος
ἄρα λέγεις σὺ καλὸν εἶναι;'

'οὐ δῆτα.'

'ἔτι οὖν ὁμολογεῖς Ἔρωτα καλὸν εἶναι, εἰ ταῦτα οὕτως
10 ἔχει;'

καὶ τὸν Ἀγάθωνα εἰπεῖν 'κινδυνεύω, ὦ Σώκρατες, οὐδὲν
εἰδέναι ὧν τότε εἶπον.'

c 'καὶ μὴν καλῶς γε εἶπας,' φάναι, 'ὦ Ἀγάθων. ἀλλὰ
σμικρὸν ἔτι εἰπέ· τἀγαθὰ οὐ καὶ καλὰ δοκεῖ σοι εἶναι;'
'ἔμοιγε.'

'εἰ ἄρα ὁ Ἔρως τῶν καλῶν ἐνδεής ἐστι, τὰ δὲ ἀγαθὰ
5 καλά, κἂν τῶν ἀγαθῶν ἐνδεὴς εἴη.'

'ἐγώ,' φάναι, 'ὦ Σώκρατες, σοὶ οὐκ ἂν δυναίμην ἀντιλέγειν, ἀλλ' οὕτως ἐχέτω ὡς σὺ λέγεις.'

'οὐ μὲν οὖν τῇ ἀληθείᾳ,' φάναι, 'ὦ φιλούμενε Ἀγάθων,
δύνασαι ἀντιλέγειν, ἐπεὶ Σωκράτει γε οὐδὲν χαλεπόν.

d καὶ σὲ μέν γε ἤδη ἐάσω· τὸν δὲ λόγον τὸν περὶ τοῦ
Ἔρωτος, ὅν ποτ' ἤκουσα γυναικὸς Μαντινικῆς Διοτίμας, ἣ
ταῦτά τε σοφὴ ἦν καὶ ἄλλα πολλά (καὶ Ἀθηναίοις ποτὲ
θυσαμένοις πρὸ τοῦ λοιμοῦ δέκα ἔτη ἀναβολὴν ἐποίησε τῆς
5 νόσου), ἣ δὴ καὶ ἐμὲ τὰ ἐρωτικὰ ἐδίδαξεν, ὃν οὖν ἐκείνη
ἔλεγε λόγον, πειράσομαι ὑμῖν διελθεῖν ἐκ τῶν ὡμολογημένων ἐμοὶ καὶ Ἀγάθωνι, αὐτὸς ἐπ' ἐμαυτοῦ, ὅπως ἂν
δύνωμαι. δεῖ δή, ὦ Ἀγάθων, ὥσπερ σὺ διηγήσω, διελθεῖν
e αὐτὸν πρῶτον, τίς ἐστιν ὁ Ἔρως καὶ ποῖός τις, ἔπειτα τὰ
ἔργα αὐτοῦ. δοκεῖ οὖν μοι ῥᾷστον εἶναι οὕτω διελθεῖν, ὡς
ποτέ με ἡ ξένη ἀνακρίνουσα διῄει. σχεδὸν γάρ τι καὶ ἐγὼ
πρὸς αὐτὴν ἕτερα τοιαῦτα ἔλεγον οἷάπερ νῦν πρὸς ἐμὲ
5 Ἀγάθων, ὡς εἴη ὁ Ἔρως μέγας θεός, εἴη δὲ τῶν καλῶν·
ἤλεγχε δή με τούτοις τοῖς λόγοις οἷσπερ ἐγὼ τοῦτον, ὡς
οὔτε καλὸς εἴη κατὰ τὸν ἐμὸν λόγον οὔτε ἀγαθός.

καὶ ἐγώ, "πῶς λέγεις," ἔφην, "ὦ Διοτίμα; αἰσχρὸς ἄρα ὁ
Ἔρως ἐστὶ καὶ κακός;"

10 καὶ ἥ, "οὐκ εὐφημήσεις;" ἔφη· "ἢ οἴει, ὅτι ἂν μὴ καλὸν
ᾖ, ἀναγκαῖον αὐτὸ εἶναι αἰσχρόν;"

202 "μάλιστά γε."

"ἦ καὶ ἂν μὴ σοφόν, ἀμαθές; ἢ οὐκ ᾔσθησαι ὅτι ἐστίν τι μεταξὺ σοφίας καὶ ἀμαθίας;"

"τί τοῦτο;"

"τὸ ὀρθὰ δοξάζειν καὶ ἄνευ τοῦ ἔχειν λόγον δοῦναι οὐκ 5 οἶσθ'," ἔφη, "ὅτι οὔτε ἐπίστασθαί ἐστιν (ἄλογον γὰρ πρᾶγμα πῶς ἂν εἴη ἐπιστήμη;) οὔτε ἀμαθία (τὸ γὰρ τοῦ ὄντος τυγχάνον πῶς ἂν εἴη ἀμαθία;); ἔστι δὲ δήπου τοιοῦτον ἡ ὀρθὴ δόξα, μεταξὺ φρονήσεως καὶ ἀμαθίας."

"ἀληθῆ," ἦν δ' ἐγώ, "λέγεις." 10

"μὴ τοίνυν ἀνάγκαζε ὃ μὴ καλόν ἐστιν αἰσχρὸν εἶναι, b μηδὲ ὃ μὴ ἀγαθόν, κακόν. οὕτω δὲ καὶ τὸν Ἔρωτα ἐπειδὴ αὐτὸς ὁμολογεῖς μὴ εἶναι ἀγαθὸν μηδὲ καλόν, μηδέν τι μᾶλλον οἴου δεῖν αὐτὸν αἰσχρὸν καὶ κακὸν εἶναι, ἀλλά τι μεταξύ," ἔφη, "τούτοιν." 5

"καὶ μήν," ἦν δ' ἐγώ, "ὁμολογεῖταί γε παρὰ πάντων μέγας θεὸς εἶναι."

"τῶν μὴ εἰδότων," ἔφη, "πάντων λέγεις, ἢ καὶ τῶν εἰδότων;"

"συμπάντων μὲν οὖν."

καὶ ἡ γελάσασα "καὶ πῶς ἄν," ἔφη, "ὦ Σώκρατες, 10 ὁμολογοῖτο μέγας θεὸς εἶναι παρὰ τούτων, οἳ φασιν αὐτὸν c οὐδὲ θεὸν εἶναι;"

"τίνες οὗτοι;" ἦν δ' ἐγώ.

"εἷς μέν," ἔφη, "σύ, μία δ' ἐγώ."

κἀγὼ εἶπον, "πῶς τοῦτο," ἔφην, "λέγεις;" 5

καὶ ἥ, "ῥᾳδίως," ἔφη. "λέγε γάρ μοι, οὐ πάντας θεοὺς φὴς εὐδαίμονας εἶναι καὶ καλούς; ἢ τολμήσαις ἄν τινα μὴ φάναι καλόν τε καὶ εὐδαίμονα θεῶν εἶναι;"

"μὰ Δί' οὐκ ἔγωγ'," ἔφην.

"εὐδαίμονας δὲ δὴ λέγεις οὐ τοὺς τἀγαθὰ καὶ τὰ καλὰ 10 κεκτημένους;"

"πάνυ γε."

"ἀλλὰ μὴν Ἔρωτά γε ὡμολόγηκας δι' ἔνδειαν τῶν d ἀγαθῶν καὶ καλῶν ἐπιθυμεῖν αὐτῶν τούτων ὧν ἐνδεής ἐστιν."

"ὡμολόγηκα γάρ."

5 "πῶς ἂν οὖν θεὸς εἴη ὅ γε τῶν καλῶν καὶ ἀγαθῶν ἄμοιρος;"
"οὐδαμῶς, ὥς γ' ἔοικεν."
"ὁρᾷς οὖν," ἔφη, "ὅτι καὶ σὺ Ἔρωτα οὐ θεὸν νομίζεις;"
"τί οὖν ἄν," ἔφην, "εἴη ὁ Ἔρως; θνητός;"
"ἥκιστά γε."
10 "ἀλλὰ τί μήν;"
"ὥσπερ τὰ πρότερα," ἔφη, "μεταξὺ θνητοῦ καὶ ἀθανάτου."
"τί οὖν, ὦ Διοτίμα;"
"δαίμων μέγας, ὦ Σώκρατες· καὶ γὰρ πᾶν τὸ δαιμόνιον
e μεταξύ ἐστι θεοῦ τε καὶ θνητοῦ."

"τίνα," ἦν δ' ἐγώ, "δύναμιν ἔχον;"
"ἑρμηνεῦον καὶ διαπορθμεῦον θεοῖς τὰ παρ' ἀνθρώπων
καὶ ἀνθρώποις τὰ παρὰ θεῶν, τῶν μὲν τὰς δεήσεις καὶ
5 θυσίας, τῶν δὲ τὰς ἐπιτάξεις τε καὶ ἀμοιβὰς τῶν θυσιῶν,
ἐν μέσῳ δὲ ὂν ἀμφοτέρων συμπληροῖ, ὥστε τὸ πᾶν αὐτὸ
αὑτῷ συνδεδέσθαι. διὰ τούτου καὶ ἡ μαντικὴ πᾶσα χωρεῖ
καὶ ἡ τῶν ἱερέων τέχνη τῶν τε περὶ τὰς θυσίας καὶ τελετὰς
203 καὶ τὰς ἐπῳδὰς καὶ τὴν μαντείαν πᾶσαν καὶ γοητείαν. θεὸς
δὲ ἀνθρώπῳ οὐ μείγνυται, ἀλλὰ διὰ τούτου πᾶσά ἐστιν ἡ
ὁμιλία καὶ ἡ διάλεκτος θεοῖς πρὸς ἀνθρώπους, καὶ ἐγρηγορόσι καὶ καθεύδουσι· καὶ ὁ μὲν περὶ τὰ τοιαῦτα σοφὸς
5 δαιμόνιος ἀνήρ, ὁ δὲ ἄλλο τι σοφὸς ὢν ἢ περὶ τέχνας
ἢ χειρουργίας τινὰς βάναυσος. οὗτοι δὴ οἱ δαίμονες
πολλοὶ καὶ παντοδαποί εἰσιν, εἷς δὲ τούτων ἐστὶ καὶ ὁ
Ἔρως."

"πατρὸς δέ," ἦν δ' ἐγώ, "τίνος ἐστὶ καὶ μητρός;"
b "μακρότερον μέν," ἔφη, "διηγήσασθαι· ὅμως δέ σοι ἐρῶ.
ὅτε γὰρ ἐγένετο ἡ Ἀφροδίτη, ἡστιῶντο οἱ θεοὶ οἵ τε ἄλλοι
καὶ ὁ τῆς Μήτιδος ὑὸς Πόρος. ἐπειδὴ δὲ ἐδείπνησαν,
προσαιτήσουσα οἷον δὴ εὐωχίας οὔσης ἀφίκετο ἡ Πενία, καὶ
5 ἦν περὶ τὰς θύρας. ὁ οὖν Πόρος μεθυσθεὶς τοῦ νέκταρος —
οἶνος γὰρ οὔπω ἦν — εἰς τὸν τοῦ Διὸς κῆπον εἰσελθὼν

a 1 [ ]ᾱ[ ]ειαν a : μαγγανείαν z : μαγείαν z
a 9 καὶ μητρός τίνος ἐστὶ a m   b 6 εξελθων a

ΣΥΜΠΟΣΙΟΝ 53

βεβαρημένος ηὗδεν. ἡ οὖν Πενία ἐπιβουλεύουσα διὰ τὴν
αὐτῆς ἀπορίαν παιδίον ποιήσασθαι ἐκ τοῦ Πόρου, κατα-
κλίνεταί τε παρ' αὐτῷ καὶ ἐκύησε τὸν Ἔρωτα. διὸ δὴ καὶ c
τῆς Ἀφροδίτης ἀκόλουθος καὶ θεράπων γέγονεν ὁ Ἔρως,
γεννηθεὶς ἐν τοῖς ἐκείνης γενεθλίοις, καὶ ἅμα φύσει ἐραστὴς ὢν περὶ τὸ καλὸν καὶ τῆς Ἀφροδίτης καλῆς οὔσης.
ἅτε οὖν Πόρου καὶ Πενίας ὑὸς ὢν ὁ Ἔρως ἐν τοιαύτῃ τύχῃ 5
καθέστηκεν. πρῶτον μὲν πένης ἀεί ἐστι, καὶ πολλοῦ δεῖ
ἁπαλός τε καὶ καλός, οἷον οἱ πολλοὶ οἴονται, ἀλλὰ σκληρὸς
καὶ αὐχμηρὸς καὶ ἀνυπόδητος καὶ ἄοικος, χαμαιπετὴς ἀεὶ d
ὢν καὶ ἄστρωτος, ἐπὶ θύραις καὶ ἐν ὁδοῖς ὑπαίθριος κοιμώ-
μενος, τὴν τῆς μητρὸς φύσιν ἔχων, ἀεὶ ἐνδείᾳ σύνοικος.
κατὰ δὲ αὖ τὸν πατέρα ἐπίβουλός ἐστι τοῖς καλοῖς καὶ τοῖς
ἀγαθοῖς, ἀνδρεῖος ὢν καὶ ἴτης καὶ σύντονος, θηρευτὴς 5
δεινός, ἀεί τινας πλέκων μηχανάς, καὶ φρονήσεως ἐπι-
θυμητὴς καὶ πόριμος, φιλοσοφῶν διὰ παντὸς τοῦ βίου,
δεινὸς γόης καὶ φαρμακεὺς καὶ σοφιστής· καὶ οὔτε ὡς
ἀθάνατος πέφυκεν οὔτε ὡς θνητός, ἀλλὰ τοτὲ μὲν τῆς αὐτῆς e
ἡμέρας θάλλει τε καὶ ζῇ, ὅταν εὐπορήσῃ, τοτὲ δὲ ἀποθνή-
σκει, πάλιν δὲ ἀναβιώσκεται διὰ τὴν τοῦ πατρὸς φύσιν, τὸ
δὲ ποριζόμενον ἀεὶ ὑπεκρεῖ, ὥστε οὔτε ἀπορεῖ Ἔρως ποτὲ
οὔτε πλουτεῖ, σοφίας τε αὖ καὶ ἀμαθίας ἐν μέσῳ ἐστίν. 5
ἔχει γὰρ ὧδε. θεῶν οὐδεὶς φιλοσοφεῖ οὐδ' ἐπιθυμεῖ σοφὸς 204
γενέσθαι — ἔστι γάρ — οὐδ' εἴ τις ἄλλος σοφός, οὐ φιλοσοφεῖ.
οὐδ' αὖ οἱ ἀμαθεῖς φιλοσοφοῦσιν οὐδ' ἐπιθυμοῦσι σοφοὶ
γενέσθαι· αὐτὸ γὰρ τοῦτό ἐστι χαλεπὸν ἀμαθία, τὸ μὴ
ὄντα καλὸν κἀγαθὸν μηδὲ φρόνιμον δοκεῖν αὑτῷ εἶναι 5
ἱκανόν. οὔκουν ἐπιθυμεῖ ὁ μὴ οἰόμενος ἐνδεὴς εἶναι οὗ ἂν
μὴ οἴηται ἐπιδεῖσθαι."

"τίνες οὖν," ἔφην ἐγώ, "ὦ Διοτίμα, οἱ φιλοσοφοῦντες, εἰ
μήτε οἱ σοφοὶ μήτε οἱ ἀμαθεῖς;"

"δῆλον δή," ἔφη, "τοῦτό γε ἤδη καὶ παιδί, ὅτι οἱ μεταξὺ b
τούτων ἀμφοτέρων, ὧν ἂν εἴη καὶ ὁ Ἔρως. ἔστιν γὰρ δὴ τῶν
καλλίστων ἡ σοφία, Ἔρως δ' ἐστὶν ἔρως περὶ τὸ καλόν,

e 2 ὅταν εὐπορήσῃ post ἀναβιώσκεται (e 3) transp. z

ὥστε ἀναγκαῖον Ἔρωτα φιλόσοφον εἶναι, φιλόσοφον δὲ
5 ὄντα μεταξὺ εἶναι σοφοῦ καὶ ἀμαθοῦς. αἰτία δὲ αὐτῷ καὶ
τούτων ἡ γένεσις· πατρὸς μὲν γὰρ σοφοῦ ἐστι καὶ εὐπόρου,
μητρὸς δὲ οὐ σοφῆς καὶ ἀπόρου. ἡ μὲν οὖν φύσις τοῦ
δαίμονος, ὦ φίλε Σώκρατες, αὕτη· ὃν δὲ σὺ ᾠήθης Ἔρωτα
c εἶναι, θαυμαστὸν οὐδὲν ἔπαθες. ᾠήθης δέ, ὡς ἐμοὶ δοκεῖ
τεκμαιρομένη ἐξ ὧν σὺ λέγεις, τὸ ἐρώμενον Ἔρωτα εἶναι,
οὐ τὸ ἐρῶν· διὰ ταῦτά σοι οἶμαι πάγκαλος ἐφαίνετο ὁ
Ἔρως. καὶ γάρ ἐστι τὸ ἐραστὸν τὸ τῷ ὄντι καλὸν καὶ
5 ἁβρὸν καὶ τέλεον καὶ μακαριστόν· τὸ δέ γε ἐρῶν ἄλλην
ἰδέαν τοιαύτην ἔχον, οἵαν ἐγὼ διῆλθον.''

   καὶ ἐγὼ εἶπον, ''εἶεν δή, ὦ ξένη, καλῶς γὰρ λέγεις·
τοιοῦτος ὢν ὁ Ἔρως τίνα χρείαν ἔχει τοῖς ἀνθρώποις;''
d ''τοῦτο δὴ μετὰ ταῦτ','' ἔφη, ''ὦ Σώκρατες, πειράσομαί σε
διδάξαι. ἔστι μὲν γὰρ δὴ τοιοῦτος καὶ οὕτω γεγονὼς ὁ
Ἔρως, ἔστι δὲ τῶν καλῶν, ὡς σὺ φής. εἰ δέ τις ἡμᾶς
ἔροιτο· 'τί τῶν καλῶν ἐστιν ὁ Ἔρως, ὦ Σώκρατές τε
5 καὶ Διοτίμα;' ὧδε δὲ σαφέστερον· ἐρᾷ ὁ ἐρῶν τῶν καλῶν·
τί ἐρᾷ;''

   καὶ ἐγὼ εἶπον ὅτι ''γενέσθαι αὐτῷ.''

   ''ἀλλ' ἔτι ποθεῖ,'' ἔφη, ''ἡ ἀπόκρισις ἐρώτησιν τοιάνδε· τί
ἔσται ἐκείνῳ ᾧ ἂν γένηται τὰ καλά;''
10 οὐ πάνυ ἔφην ἔτι ἔχειν ἐγὼ πρὸς ταύτην τὴν ἐρώτησιν
προχείρως ἀποκρίνασθαι.
e ''ἀλλ','' ἔφη, ''ὥσπερ ἂν εἴ τις μεταβαλὼν ἀντὶ τοῦ καλοῦ
τῷ ἀγαθῷ χρώμενος πυνθάνοιτο· 'φέρε, ὦ Σώκρατες, ἐρᾷ ὁ
ἐρῶν τῶν ἀγαθῶν· τί ἐρᾷ;'
   ''γενέσθαι,'' ἦν δ' ἐγώ, ''αὐτῷ.''
5 ''καὶ τί ἔσται ἐκείνῳ ᾧ ἂν γένηται τἀγαθά;''
   ''τοῦτ' εὐπορώτερον,'' ἦν δ' ἐγώ, ''ἔχω ἀποκρίνασθαι, ὅτι
εὐδαίμων ἔσται.''
205 ''κτήσει γάρ,'' ἔφη, ''ἀγαθῶν οἱ εὐδαίμονες εὐδαίμονες, καὶ
οὐκέτι προσδεῖ ἐρέσθαι 'ἵνα τί δὲ βούλεται εὐδαίμων εἶναι
ὁ βουλόμενος;' ἀλλὰ τέλος δοκεῖ ἔχειν ἡ ἀπόκρισις.''
   ''ἀληθῆ λέγεις,'' εἶπον ἐγώ.

"ταύτην δὴ τὴν βούλησιν καὶ τὸν ἔρωτα τοῦτον πότερα 5
κοινὸν οἴει εἶναι πάντων ἀνθρώπων, καὶ πάντας τἀγαθὰ
βούλεσθαι αὑτοῖς εἶναι ἀεί, ἢ πῶς λέγεις;"
"οὕτως," ἦν δ' ἐγώ· "κοινὸν εἶναι πάντων."
"τί δὴ οὖν," ἔφη, "ὦ Σώκρατες, οὐ πάντας ἐρᾶν φαμεν,
εἴπερ γε πάντες τῶν αὐτῶν ἐρῶσι καὶ ἀεί, ἀλλά τινάς φαμεν b
ἐρᾶν, τοὺς δ' οὔ;"
"θαυμάζω," ἦν δ' ἐγώ, "καὶ αὐτός."
"ἀλλὰ μὴ θαύμαζ'," ἔφη· "ἀφελόντες γὰρ ἄρα τοῦ ἔρωτός
τι εἶδος ὀνομάζομεν, τὸ τοῦ ὅλου ἐπιτιθέντες ὄνομα, ἔρωτα, 5
τὰ δὲ ἄλλα ἄλλοις καταχρώμεθα ὀνόμασιν."
"ὥσπερ τί;" ἦν δ' ἐγώ.
"ὥσπερ τόδε. οἶσθ' ὅτι ποίησίς ἐστί τι πολύ· ἡ γάρ
τοι ἐκ τοῦ μὴ ὄντος εἰς τὸ ὂν ἰόντι ὁτῳοῦν αἰτία πᾶσά ἐστι
ποίησις, ὥστε καὶ αἱ ὑπὸ πάσαις ταῖς τέχναις ἐργασίαι c
ποιήσεις εἰσὶ καὶ οἱ τούτων δημιουργοὶ πάντες ποιηταί."
"ἀληθῆ λέγεις."
"ἀλλ' ὅμως," ἦ δ' ἥ, "οἶσθ' ὅτι οὐ καλοῦνται ποιηταὶ ἀλλὰ
ἄλλα ἔχουσιν ὀνόματα, ἀπὸ δὲ πάσης τῆς ποιήσεως ἓν 5
μόριον ἀφορισθὲν τὸ περὶ τὴν μουσικὴν καὶ τὰ μέτρα τῷ
τοῦ ὅλου ὀνόματι προσαγορεύεται. ποίησις γὰρ τοῦτο
μόνον καλεῖται, καὶ οἱ ἔχοντες τοῦτο τὸ μόριον τῆς ποιήσεως
ποιηταί."
"ἀληθῆ λέγεις," ἔφην. 10
"οὕτω τοίνυν καὶ περὶ τὸν ἔρωτα. τὸ μὲν κεφάλαιόν ἐστι d
πᾶσα ἡ τῶν ἀγαθῶν ἐπιθυμία καὶ τοῦ εὐδαιμονεῖν ὁ μέ-
γιστός τε καὶ δολερὸς ἔρως παντί· ἀλλ' οἱ μὲν ἄλλη
τρεπόμενοι πολλαχῇ ἐπ' αὐτόν, ἢ κατὰ χρηματισμὸν ἢ κατὰ
φιλογυμναστίαν ἢ κατὰ φιλοσοφίαν, οὔτε ἐρᾶν καλοῦνται 5
οὔτε ἐρασταί, οἱ δὲ κατὰ ἕν τι εἶδος ἰόντες τε καὶ ἐσπου-
δακότες τὸ τοῦ ὅλου ὄνομα ἴσχουσιν, ἔρωτά τε καὶ ἐρᾶν καὶ
ἐρασταί."
"κινδυνεύεις ἀληθῆ," ἔφην ἐγώ, "λέγειν."
"καὶ λέγεται μέν γε τις," ἔφη, "λόγος, ὡς οἳ ἂν τὸ ἥμισυ 10

d 7 ἴσχουσιν m: εσχον a

e ἑαυτῶν ζητῶσιν, οὗτοι ἐρῶσιν· ὁ δ᾽ ἐμὸς λόγος οὔτε ἡμίσεός
φησιν εἶναι τὸν ἔρωτα οὔτε ὅλου, ἐὰν μὴ τυγχάνῃ γέ που,
ὦ ἑταῖρε, ἀγαθὸν ὄν, ἐπεὶ αὑτῶν γε καὶ πόδας καὶ χεῖρας
ἐθέλουσιν ἀποτέμνεσθαι οἱ ἄνθρωποι, ἐὰν αὑτοῖς δοκῇ τὰ
5 ἑαυτῶν πονηρὰ εἶναι. οὐ γὰρ τὸ ἑαυτῶν οἶμαι ἕκαστοι
ἀσπάζονται, εἰ μὴ εἴ τις τὸ μὲν ἀγαθὸν οἰκεῖον καλεῖ καὶ
ἑαυτοῦ, τὸ δὲ κακὸν ἀλλότριον· ὡς οὐδέν γε ἄλλο ἐστὶν οὗ
206 ἐρῶσιν ἄνθρωποι ἢ τοῦ ἀγαθοῦ. ἢ σοὶ δοκοῦσιν; ''
"μὰ Δί᾽ οὐκ ἔμοιγε,'' ἦν δ᾽ ἐγώ.
"ἆρ᾽ οὖν,'' ἦ δ᾽ ἥ, "οὕτως ἁπλοῦν ἐστι λέγειν ὅτι οἱ
ἄνθρωποι τἀγαθοῦ ἐρῶσιν; ''
5 "ναί,'' ἔφην.
"τί δέ; οὐ προσθετέον,'' ἔφη, "ὅτι καὶ εἶναι τὸ ἀγαθὸν
αὑτοῖς ἐρῶσιν; ''
"προσθετέον.''
"ἆρ᾽ οὖν,'' ἔφη, "καὶ οὐ μόνον εἶναι, ἀλλὰ καὶ ἀεὶ εἶναι; ''
10 "καὶ τοῦτο προσθετέον.''
"ἔστιν ἄρα συλλήβδην,'' ἔφη, "ὁ ἔρως τοῦ τὸ ἀγαθὸν αὑτῷ
εἶναι ἀεί.''
"ἀληθέστατα,'' ἔφην ἐγώ, "λέγεις.''
b "ὅτε δὴ τοῦτο ὁ ἔρως ἐστὶν ἀεί,'' ἦ δ᾽ ἥ, "τῶν τίνα τρόπον
διωκόντων αὐτὸ καὶ ἐν τίνι πράξει ἡ σπουδὴ καὶ ἡ σύντασις
ἔρως ἂν καλοῖτο; τί τοῦτο τυγχάνει ὂν τὸ ἔργον; ἔχεις
εἰπεῖν; ''
5 "οὐ μεντἂν σέ,'' ἔφην ἐγώ, "ὦ Διοτίμα, ἐθαύμαζον ἐπὶ
σοφίᾳ καὶ ἐφοίτων παρὰ σὲ αὐτὰ ταῦτα μαθησόμενος.''
"ἀλλὰ ἐγώ σοι,'' ἔφη, "ἐρῶ. ἔστι γὰρ τοῦτο τόκος ἐν
καλῷ καὶ κατὰ τὸ σῶμα καὶ κατὰ τὴν ψυχήν.''
"μαντείας,'' ἦν δ᾽ ἐγώ, "δεῖται ὅτι ποτε λέγεις, καὶ οὐ
10 μανθάνω.''
c "ἀλλ᾽ ἐγώ,'' ἦ δ᾽ ἥ, "σαφέστερον ἐρῶ. κυοῦσιν γάρ,'' ἔφη,
"ὦ Σώκρατες, πάντες ἄνθρωποι καὶ κατὰ τὸ σῶμα καὶ κατὰ
τὴν ψυχήν, καὶ ἐπειδὰν ἔν τινι ἡλικίᾳ γένωνται, τίκτειν
ἐπιθυμεῖ ἡμῶν ἡ φύσις. τίκτειν δὲ ἐν μὲν αἰσχρῷ οὐ

b 2 σύντασις a m: σύστασις m

δύναται, ἐν δὲ τῷ καλῷ. ἡ γὰρ ἀνδρὸς καὶ γυναικὸς 5
συνουσία τόκος ἐστίν. ἔστι δὲ τοῦτο θεῖον τὸ πρᾶγμα,
καὶ τοῦτο ἐν θνητῷ ὄντι τῷ ζῴῳ ἀθάνατον ἔνεστιν, ἡ κύησις
καὶ ἡ γέννησις. τὰ δὲ ἐν τῷ ἀναρμόστῳ ἀδύνατον γενέσθαι. ἀνάρμοστον δ' ἐστὶ τὸ αἰσχρὸν παντὶ τῷ θείῳ, τὸ d
δὲ καλὸν ἁρμόττον. Μοῖρα οὖν καὶ Εἰλείθυια ἡ Καλλονή
ἐστι τῇ γενέσει. διὰ ταῦτα ὅταν μὲν καλῷ προσπελάζῃ
τὸ κυοῦν, ἵλεών τε γίγνεται καὶ εὐφραινόμενον διαχεῖται
καὶ τίκτει τε καὶ γεννᾷ· ὅταν δὲ αἰσχρῷ, σκυθρωπόν τε 5
καὶ λυπούμενον συσπειρᾶται καὶ ἀποτρέπεται καὶ ἀνείλλεται
καὶ οὐ γεννᾷ, ἀλλὰ ἴσχον τὸ κύημα χαλεπῶς φέρει. ὅθεν δὴ
τῷ κυοῦντί τε καὶ ἤδη σπαργῶντι πολλὴ ἡ πτοίησις γέγονε
περὶ τὸ καλὸν διὰ τὸ μεγάλης ὠδῖνος ἀπολύειν τὸν ἔχοντα. e
ἔστιν γάρ, ὦ Σώκρατες," ἔφη, "οὐ τοῦ καλοῦ ὁ ἔρως, ὡς
σὺ οἴει."

"ἀλλὰ τί μήν;"

"τῆς γεννήσεως καὶ τοῦ τόκου ἐν τῷ καλῷ." 5

"εἶεν," ἦν δ' ἐγώ.

"πάνυ μὲν οὖν," ἔφη. "τί δὴ οὖν τῆς γεννήσεως; ὅτι
ἀειγενές ἐστι καὶ ἀθάνατον ὡς θνητῷ ἡ γέννησις. ἀθανασίας δὲ ἀναγκαῖον ἐπιθυμεῖν μετὰ ἀγαθοῦ ἐκ τῶν ὡμο- 207
λογημένων, εἴπερ τοῦ ἀγαθοῦ ἑαυτῷ εἶναι ἀεὶ ἔρως ἐστίν.
ἀναγκαῖον δὴ ἐκ τούτου τοῦ λόγου καὶ τῆς ἀθανασίας τὸν
ἔρωτα εἶναι."

ταῦτά τε οὖν πάντα ἐδίδασκέ με, ὁπότε περὶ τῶν ἐρω- 5
τικῶν λόγους ποιοῖτο, καί ποτε ἤρετο "τί οἴει, ὦ Σώκρατες,
αἴτιον εἶναι τούτου τοῦ ἔρωτος καὶ τῆς ἐπιθυμίας; ἢ οὐκ
αἰσθάνῃ ὡς δεινῶς διατίθεται πάντα τὰ θηρία ἐπειδὰν γεννᾶν ἐπιθυμήσῃ, καὶ τὰ πεζὰ καὶ τὰ πτηνά, νοσοῦντά τε
πάντα καὶ ἐρωτικῶς διατιθέμενα, πρῶτον μὲν περὶ τὸ συμ- b
μιγῆναι ἀλλήλοις, ἔπειτα περὶ τὴν τροφὴν τοῦ γενομένου,
καὶ ἕτοιμά ἐστιν ὑπὲρ τούτων καὶ διαμάχεσθαι τὰ ἀσθενέ-
στατα τοῖς ἰσχυροτάτοις καὶ ὑπεραποθνῄσκειν, καὶ αὐτὰ τῷ
λιμῷ παρατεινόμενα ὥστ' ἐκεῖνα ἐκτρέφειν, καὶ ἄλλο πᾶν 5

c 5 ἡ γάρ...6 ἐστίν del. z   d 1 θεῷ a m   e 7 γενεσεως a

58   ΠΛΑΤΩΝΟΣ

ποιοῦντα. τοὺς μὲν γὰρ ἀνθρώπους," ἔφη, "οἴοιτ᾽ ἄν τις ἐκ
λογισμοῦ ταῦτα ποιεῖν· τὰ δὲ θηρία τίς αἰτία οὕτως ἐρω-
c τικῶς διατίθεσθαι; ἔχεις λέγειν;"
   καὶ ἐγὼ αὖ ἔλεγον ὅτι οὐκ εἰδείην· ἡ δ᾽ εἶπεν, "διανοῇ
οὖν δεινός ποτε γενήσεσθαι τὰ ἐρωτικά, ἐὰν ταῦτα μὴ
ἐννοῇς;"
5 "ἀλλὰ διὰ ταῦτά τοι, ὦ Διοτίμα, ὅπερ νυνδὴ εἶπον, παρὰ
σὲ ἥκω, γνοὺς ὅτι διδασκάλων δέομαι. ἀλλά μοι λέγε
καὶ τούτων τὴν αἰτίαν καὶ τῶν ἄλλων τῶν περὶ τὰ ἐρωτικά."
   "εἰ τοίνυν," ἔφη, "πιστεύεις ἐκείνου εἶναι φύσει τὸν ἔρωτα,
οὗ πολλάκις ὡμολογήκαμεν, μὴ θαύμαζε. ἐνταῦθα γὰρ
d τὸν αὐτὸν ἐκείνῳ λόγον ἡ θνητὴ φύσις ζητεῖ κατὰ τὸ δυνατὸν
ἀεί τε εἶναι καὶ ἀθάνατος. δύναται δὲ ταύτῃ μόνον, τῇ
γενέσει, ὅτι ἀεὶ καταλείπει ἕτερον νέον ἀντὶ τοῦ παλαιοῦ,
ἐπεὶ καὶ ἐν ᾧ ἓν ἕκαστον τῶν ζῴων ζῆν καλεῖται καὶ εἶναι
5 τὸ αὐτό — οἷον ἐκ παιδαρίου ὁ αὐτὸς λέγεται ἕως ἂν πρε-
σβύτης γένηται· οὗτος μέντοι οὐδέποτε τὰ αὐτὰ ἔχων ἐν
αὑτῷ ὅμως ὁ αὐτὸς καλεῖται, ἀλλὰ νέος ἀεὶ γιγνόμενος, τὰ
δὲ ἀπολλύς, καὶ κατὰ τὰς τρίχας καὶ σάρκα καὶ ὀστᾶ καὶ
e αἷμα καὶ σύμπαν τὸ σῶμα. καὶ μὴ ὅτι κατὰ τὸ σῶμα,
ἀλλὰ καὶ κατὰ τὴν ψυχὴν οἱ τρόποι, τὰ ἤθη, δόξαι, ἐπιθυ-
μίαι, ἡδοναί, λῦπαι, φόβοι, τούτων ἕκαστα οὐδέποτε τὰ
αὐτὰ πάρεστιν ἑκάστῳ, ἀλλὰ τὰ μὲν γίγνεται, τὰ δὲ ἀπόλ-
5 λυται. πολὺ δὲ τούτων ἀτοπώτερον ἔτι, ὅτι καὶ αἱ ἐπιστῆμαι
208 μὴ ὅτι αἱ μὲν γίγνονται, αἱ δὲ ἀπόλλυνται ἡμῖν, καὶ οὐδέποτε οἱ αὐτοί ἐσμεν οὐδὲ κατὰ τὰς ἐπιστήμας, ἀλλὰ καὶ
μία ἑκάστη τῶν ἐπιστημῶν ταὐτὸν πάσχει. ὃ γὰρ καλεῖται
μελετᾶν, ὡς ἐξιούσης ἐστὶ τῆς ἐπιστήμης· λήθη γὰρ
5 ἐπιστήμης ἔξοδος, μελέτη δὲ πάλιν καινὴν ἐμποιοῦσα ἀντὶ
τῆς ἀπιούσης μνήμην σῴζει τὴν ἐπιστήμην, ὥστε τὴν
αὐτὴν δοκεῖν εἶναι. τούτῳ γὰρ τῷ τρόπῳ πᾶν τὸ θνητὸν
σῴζεται, οὐ τῷ παντάπασιν τὸ αὐτὸ ἀεὶ εἶναι ὥσπερ τὸ
b θεῖον, ἀλλὰ τῷ τὸ ἀπιὸν καὶ παλαιούμενον ἕτερον νέον
ἐγκαταλείπειν οἷον αὐτὸ ἦν. ταύτῃ τῇ μηχανῇ, ὦ Σώ-

        c 2 τόποι m   a 6 μνημη a

κρατες," ἔφη, "θνητὸν ἀθανασίας μετέχει, καὶ σῶμα καὶ τἆλλα
πάντα· ἀθάνατον δὲ ἄλλη. μὴ οὖν θαύμαζε εἰ τὸ αὑτοῦ
ἀποβλάστημα φύσει πᾶν τιμᾷ· ἀθανασίας γὰρ χάριν παντὶ 5
αὕτη ἡ σπουδὴ καὶ ὁ ἔρως ἕπεται."

καὶ ἐγὼ ἀκούσας τὸν λόγον ἐθαύμασά τε καὶ εἶπον
"εἶεν," ἦν δ᾽ ἐγώ, "ὦ σοφωτάτη Διοτίμα, ταῦτα ὡς ἀληθῶς
οὕτως ἔχει;"

καὶ ἥ, ὥσπερ οἱ τέλεοι σοφισταί, "εὖ ἴσθι," ἔφη, "ὦ c
Σώκρατες· ἐπεί γε καὶ τῶν ἀνθρώπων εἰ ἐθέλεις εἰς τὴν
φιλοτιμίαν βλέψαι, θαυμάζοις ἂν τῆς ἀλογίας περὶ ἃ ἐγὼ
εἴρηκα εἰ μὴ ἐννοεῖς, ἐνθυμηθεὶς ὡς δεινῶς διάκεινται ἔρωτι
τοῦ ὀνομαστοὶ γενέσθαι καὶ κλέος ἐς τὸν ἀεὶ χρόνον 5
ἀθάνατον καταθέσθαι, καὶ ὑπὲρ τούτου κινδύνους τε
κινδυνεύειν ἕτοιμοί εἰσι πάντας ἔτι μᾶλλον ἢ ὑπὲρ τῶν
παίδων, καὶ χρήματα ἀναλίσκειν καὶ πόνους πονεῖν ˏοὕσ- d
τινασοῦν, καὶ ὑπεραποθνήσκειν. ἐπεὶ οἴει σύ," ἔφη, "Ἄλκηστιν
ὑπὲρ Ἀδμήτου ἀποθανεῖν ἄν, ἢ Ἀχιλλέα Πατρόκλῳ ἐπαποθανεῖν, ἢ προαποθανεῖν τὸν ὑμέτερον Κόδρον ὑπὲρ τῆς
βασιλείας τῶν παίδων, μὴ οἰομένους ἀθάνατον μνήμην 5
ἀρετῆς πέρι ἑαυτῶν ἔσεσθαι, ἣν νῦν ἡμεῖς ἔχομεν; πολλοῦ
γε δεῖ," ἔφη, "ἀλλ᾽ οἶμαι ὑπὲρ ἀρετῆς ἀθανάτου καὶ τοιαύτης
δόξης εὐκλεοῦς πάντες πάντα ποιοῦσιν, ὅσῳ ἂν ἀμείνους
ὦσι, τοσούτῳ μᾶλλον· τοῦ γὰρ ἀθανάτου ἐρῶσιν. οἱ μὲν e
οὖν ἐγκύμονες," ἔφη, "κατὰ τὰ σώματα ὄντες πρὸς τὰς γυναῖκας
μᾶλλον τρέπονται καὶ ταύτῃ ἐρωτικοί εἰσιν, διὰ παιδογονίας
ἀθανασίαν καὶ μνήμην καὶ εὐδαιμονίαν, ὡς οἴονται, αὑτοῖς
εἰς τὸν ἔπειτα χρόνον πάντα ποριζόμενοι· οἱ δὲ κατὰ τὴν 5
ψυχήν — εἰσὶ γὰρ οὖν," ἔφη, "οἳ ἐν ταῖς ψυχαῖς κυοῦσιν ἔτι 209
μᾶλλον ἢ ἐν τοῖς σώμασιν, ἃ ψυχῇ προσήκει καὶ κυῆσαι
καὶ τεκεῖν. τί οὖν προσήκει; φρόνησίν τε καὶ τὴν ἄλλην
ἀρετήν· ὧν δή εἰσι καὶ οἱ ποιηταὶ πάντες γεννήτορες καὶ
τῶν δημιουργῶν ὅσοι λέγονται εὑρετικοὶ εἶναι. πολὺ δὲ 5
μεγίστη," ἔφη, "καὶ καλλίστη τῆς φρονήσεως ἡ περὶ τὰ τῶν

b 4 ἀδύνατον z   d 6 πέρι z: περι a: περὶ m   a 3 τεκεῖν a:
κυεῖν m   a 6 τὰ z: τὰς a m

πόλεών τε καὶ οἰκήσεων διακόσμησις, ᾗ δὴ ὄνομά ἐστι
σωφροσύνη τε καὶ δικαιοσύνη. τούτων δ' αὖ ὅταν τις ἐκ
b νέου ἐγκύμων ᾖ τὴν ψυχήν, ἤθεος ὢν καὶ ἡκούσης τῆς
ἡλικίας τίκτειν τε καὶ γεννᾶν ἤδη ἐπιθυμεῖ. ζητεῖ δὴ
οἶμαι καὶ οὗτος περιιὼν τὸ καλὸν ἐν ᾧ ἂν γεννήσειεν· ἐν
τῷ γὰρ αἰσχρῷ οὐδέποτε γεννήσει. τά τε οὖν σώματα τὰ
5 καλὰ μᾶλλον ἢ τὰ αἰσχρὰ ἀσπάζεται ἅτε κυῶν, καὶ ἂν
ἐντύχῃ ψυχῇ καλῇ καὶ γενναίᾳ καὶ εὐφυεῖ, πάνυ δὴ ἀσπάζεται τὸ συναμφότερον, καὶ πρὸς τοῦτον τὸν ἄνθρωπον
εὐθὺς εὐπορεῖ λόγων περὶ ἀρετῆς καὶ περὶ οἷον χρὴ εἶναι
c τὸν ἄνδρα τὸν ἀγαθὸν καὶ ἃ ἐπιτηδεύειν, καὶ ἐπιχειρεῖ
παιδεύειν. ἁπτόμενος γὰρ οἶμαι τοῦ καλοῦ καὶ ὁμιλῶν
αὐτῷ, ἃ πάλαι ἐκύει τίκτει καὶ γεννᾷ, καὶ παρὼν καὶ ἀπὼν
μεμνημένος, καὶ τὸ γεννηθὲν συνεκτρέφει κοινῇ μετ' ἐκείνου,
5 ὥστε πολὺ μείζω κοινωνίαν τῆς τῶν παίδων πρὸς ἀλλήλους
οἱ τοιοῦτοι ἴσχουσι καὶ φιλίαν βεβαιοτέραν, ἅτε καλλιόνων
καὶ ἀθανατωτέρων παίδων κεκοινωνηκότες. καὶ πᾶς ἂν
δέξαιτο ἑαυτῷ τοιούτους παῖδας μᾶλλον γεγονέναι ἢ τοὺς
d ἀνθρωπίνους, καὶ εἰς Ὅμηρον ἀποβλέψας καὶ Ἡσίοδον καὶ
τοὺς ἄλλους ποιητὰς τοὺς ἀγαθοὺς ζηλῶν, οἷα ἔκγονα ἑαυτῶν
καταλείπουσιν, ἃ ἐκείνοις ἀθάνατον κλέος καὶ μνήμην παρέχεται αὐτὰ τοιαῦτα ὄντα· εἰ δὲ βούλει," ἔφη, "οἵους Λυκοῦργος
5 παῖδας κατελίπετο ἐν Λακεδαίμονι σωτῆρας τῆς Λακεδαί-
μονος καὶ ὡς ἔπος εἰπεῖν τῆς Ἑλλάδος. τίμιος δὲ παρ'
ὑμῖν καὶ Σόλων διὰ τὴν τῶν νόμων γέννησιν, καὶ ἄλλοι
e ἄλλοθι πολλαχοῦ ἄνδρες, καὶ ἐν Ἕλλησι καὶ ἐν βαρβάροις,
πολλὰ καὶ καλὰ ἀποφηνάμενοι ἔργα, γεννήσαντες παντοίαν
ἀρετήν· ὧν καὶ ἱερὰ πολλὰ ἤδη γέγονε διὰ τοὺς τοιούτους
παῖδας, διὰ δὲ τοὺς ἀνθρωπίνους οὐδενός πω.
5 ταῦτα μὲν οὖν τὰ ἐρωτικὰ ἴσως, ὦ Σώκρατες, κἂν σὺ
210 μυηθείης· τὰ δὲ τέλεα καὶ ἐποπτικά, ὧν ἕνεκα καὶ ταῦτα
ἔστιν, ἐάν τις ὀρθῶς μετίῃ, οὐκ οἶδ' εἰ οἷός τ' ἂν εἴης.
ἐρῶ μὲν οὖν," ἔφη, "ἐγὼ καὶ προθυμίας οὐδὲν ἀπολείψω·

a 7 διακοσμήσεις m   b 1 ἤθεος z: θεῖος am   b 2 επιθυμη a
e 2 καλὰ m: αλλα a

πειρῶ δὲ ἕπεσθαι, ἂν οἷός τε ᾖς.   δεῖ γάρ," ἔφη, "τὸν ὀρθῶς
ἰόντα ἐπὶ τοῦτο τὸ πρᾶγμα ἄρχεσθαι μὲν νέον ὄντα ἰέναι 5
ἐπὶ τὰ καλὰ σώματα, καὶ πρῶτον μέν, ἐὰν ὀρθῶς ἡγῆται
ὁ ἡγούμενος, ἑνὸς αὐτὸν σώματος ἐρᾶν καὶ ἐνταῦθα γεννᾶν
λόγους καλούς, ἔπειτα δὲ αὐτὸν κατανοῆσαι ὅτι τὸ κάλλος
τὸ ἐπὶ ὅτῳοῦν σώματι τῷ ἐπὶ ἑτέρῳ σώματι ἀδελφόν ἐστι, b
καὶ εἰ δεῖ διώκειν τὸ ἐπ' εἴδει καλόν, πολλὴ ἄνοια μὴ οὐχ
ἕν τε καὶ ταὐτὸν ἡγεῖσθαι τὸ ἐπὶ πᾶσιν τοῖς σώμασι κάλλος·
τοῦτο δ' ἐννοήσαντα καταστῆναι πάντων τῶν καλῶν σωμάτων
ἐραστήν, ἑνὸς δὲ τὸ σφόδρα τοῦτο χαλάσαι καταφρονή- 5
σαντα καὶ σμικρὸν ἡγησάμενον· μετὰ δὲ ταῦτα τὸ ἐν ταῖς
ψυχαῖς κάλλος τιμιώτερον ἡγήσασθαι τοῦ ἐν τῷ σώματι,
ὥστε καὶ ἐὰν ἐπιεικὴς ὢν τὴν ψυχήν τις κἂν σμικρὸν ἄνθος
ἔχῃ, ἐξαρκεῖν αὐτῷ καὶ ἐρᾶν καὶ κήδεσθαι καὶ τίκτειν λόγους c
τοιούτους [καὶ ζητεῖν] οἵτινες ποιήσουσι βελτίους τοὺς
νέους, ἵνα ἀναγκασθῇ αὖ θεάσασθαι τὸ ἐν τοῖς ἐπιτηδεύμασι
καὶ τοῖς νόμοις καλὸν καὶ τοῦτ' ἰδεῖν ὅτι πᾶν αὐτὸ αὑτῷ
συγγενές ἐστιν, ἵνα τὸ περὶ τὸ σῶμα καλὸν σμικρόν τι 5
ἡγήσηται εἶναι· μετὰ δὲ τὰ ἐπιτηδεύματα ἐπὶ τὰς ἐπιστήμας
ἀγαγεῖν, ἵνα ἴδῃ αὖ ἐπιστημῶν κάλλος, καὶ βλέπων πρὸς
πολὺ ἤδη τὸ καλὸν μηκέτι τὸ παρ' ἑνί, ὥσπερ οἰκέτης, d
ἀγαπῶν παιδαρίου κάλλος ἢ ἀνθρώπου τινὸς ἢ ἐπιτηδεύ-
ματος ἑνός, δουλεύων φαῦλος ᾖ καὶ σμικρολόγος, ἀλλ' ἐπὶ
τὸ πολὺ πέλαγος τετραμμένος τοῦ καλοῦ καὶ θεωρῶν πολλοὺς καὶ καλοὺς λόγους καὶ μεγαλοπρεπεῖς τίκτῃ καὶ διανοή- 5
ματα ἐν φιλοσοφίᾳ ἀφθόνῳ, ἕως ἂν ἐνταῦθα ῥωσθεὶς καὶ
αὐξηθεὶς κατίδῃ τινὰ ἐπιστήμην μίαν τοιαύτην, ἥ ἐστι καλοῦ
τοιοῦδε.   πειρῶ δέ μοι," ἔφη, "τὸν νοῦν προσέχειν ὡς οἷόν e
τε μάλιστα.   ὃς γὰρ ἂν μέχρι ἐνταῦθα πρὸς τὰ ἐρωτικὰ
παιδαγωγηθῇ, θεώμενος ἐφεξῆς τε καὶ ὀρθῶς τὰ καλά, πρὸς
τέλος ἤδη ἰὼν τῶν ἐρωτικῶν ἐξαίφνης κατόψεταί τι θαυμαστὸν τὴν φύσιν καλόν, τοῦτο ἐκεῖνο, ὦ Σώκρατες, οὗ δὴ 5
ἕνεκεν καὶ οἱ ἔμπροσθεν πάντες πόνοι ἦσαν, πρῶτον μὲν
ἀεὶ ὂν καὶ οὔτε γιγνόμενον οὔτε ἀπολλύμενον, οὔτε αὐξανό- 211

a 4 πειρω δε και συ επεσθαι a   c 2 καὶ ζητεῖν del. z

μενον οὔτε φθίνον, ἔπειτα οὐ τῇ μὲν καλόν, τῇ δ᾽ αἰσχρόν,
οὐδὲ τοτὲ μέν, τοτὲ δὲ οὔ, οὐδὲ πρὸς μὲν τὸ καλόν, πρὸς
δὲ τὸ αἰσχρόν, οὐδ᾽ ἔνθα μὲν καλόν, ἔνθα δὲ αἰσχρόν, ὡς
5 τισὶ μὲν ὂν καλόν, τισὶ δὲ αἰσχρόν· οὐδ᾽ αὖ φαντασθήσεται
αὐτῷ τὸ καλὸν οἷον πρόσωπόν τι οὐδὲ χεῖρες οὐδὲ ἄλλο
οὐδὲν ὧν σῶμα μετέχει, οὐδέ τις λόγος οὐδέ τις ἐπιστήμη,
οὐδέ που ὂν ἐν ἑτέρῳ τινί, οἷον ἐν ζῴῳ ἢ ἐν γῇ ἢ ἐν οὐρανῷ
b ἢ ἔν τῳ ἄλλῳ, ἀλλ᾽ αὐτὸ καθ᾽ αὑτὸ μεθ᾽ αὑτοῦ μονοειδὲς ἀεὶ
ὄν, τὰ δὲ ἄλλα πάντα καλὰ ἐκείνου μετέχοντα τρόπον τινὰ
τοιοῦτον, οἷον γιγνομένων τε τῶν ἄλλων καὶ ἀπολλυμένων
μηδὲν ἐκεῖνο μήτε τι πλέον μήτε ἔλαττον γίγνεσθαι μηδὲ
5 πάσχειν μηδέν. ὅταν δή τις ἀπὸ τῶνδε διὰ τὸ ὀρθῶς παιδεραστεῖν ἐπανιὼν ἐκεῖνο τὸ καλὸν ἄρχηται καθορᾶν, σχεδὸν
ἄν τι ἅπτοιτο τοῦ τέλους. τοῦτο γὰρ δή ἐστι τὸ ὀρθῶς ἐπὶ
c τὰ ἐρωτικὰ ἰέναι ἢ ὑπ᾽ ἄλλου ἄγεσθαι, ἀρχόμενον ἀπὸ
τῶνδε τῶν καλῶν ἐκείνου ἕνεκα τοῦ καλοῦ ἀεὶ ἐπανιέναι,
ὥσπερ ἐπαναβασμοῖς χρώμενον, ἀπὸ ἑνὸς ἐπὶ δύο καὶ ἀπὸ
δυοῖν ἐπὶ πάντα τὰ καλὰ σώματα, καὶ ἀπὸ τῶν καλῶν
5 σωμάτων ἐπὶ τὰ καλὰ ἐπιτηδεύματα, καὶ ἀπὸ τῶν ἐπιτηδευμάτων ἐπὶ τὰ καλὰ μαθήματα, καὶ ἀπὸ τῶν μαθημάτων ἐπ᾽
ἐκεῖνο τὸ μάθημα τελευτῆσαι, ὅ ἐστιν οὐκ ἄλλου ἢ αὐτοῦ
ἐκείνου τοῦ καλοῦ μάθημα, ἵνα γνῷ αὐτὸ τελευτῶν ὅ ἐστι
d καλόν. ἐνταῦθα τοῦ βίου, ὦ φίλε Σώκρατες,᾽᾽ ἔφη ἡ Μαντινικὴ ξένη, ᾽᾽εἴπερ που ἄλλοθι, βιωτὸν ἀνθρώπῳ, θεωμένῳ
αὐτὸ τὸ καλόν. ὃ ἐάν ποτε ἴδῃς, οὐ κατὰ χρυσίον τε καὶ
ἐσθῆτα καὶ τοὺς καλοὺς παῖδάς τε καὶ νεανίσκους δόξει σοι
5 εἶναι, οὓς νῦν ὁρῶν ἐκπέπληξαι καὶ ἕτοιμος εἶ καὶ σὺ καὶ
ἄλλοι πολλοί, ὁρῶντες τὰ παιδικὰ καὶ συνόντες ἀεὶ αὐτοῖς,
εἴ πως οἷόν τ᾽ ἦν, μήτ᾽ ἐσθίειν μήτε πίνειν, ἀλλὰ θεᾶσθαι
μόνον καὶ συνεῖναι. τί δῆτα,᾽᾽ ἔφη, ᾽᾽οἰόμεθα, εἴ τῳ γένοιτο
e αὐτὸ τὸ καλὸν ἰδεῖν εἰλικρινές, καθαρόν, ἄμεικτον, ἀλλὰ
μὴ ἀνάπλεων σαρκῶν τε ἀνθρωπίνων καὶ χρωμάτων καὶ
ἄλλης πολλῆς φλυαρίας θνητῆς, ἀλλ᾽ αὐτὸ τὸ θεῖον καλὸν

c 6 καί...7 τελευτῆσαι...8 ἵνα γνῷ z: καί...τελευτήσῃ...καὶ γνῷ
a m: ἵνα (vel ἕως ἄν)...τελευτήσῃ...καὶ γνῷ z

δύναιτο μονοειδὲς κατιδεῖν; ἆρ' οἴει," ἔφη, "φαῦλον βίον
γίγνεσθαι ἐκεῖσε βλέποντος ἀνθρώπου καὶ ἐκεῖνο ᾧ δεῖ 212
θεωμένου καὶ συνόντος αὐτῷ; ἢ οὐκ ἐνθυμῇ," ἔφη, "ὅτι ἐνταῦθα
αὐτῷ μοναχοῦ γενήσεται, ὁρῶντι ᾧ ὁρατὸν τὸ καλόν, τίκτειν
οὐκ εἴδωλα ἀρετῆς, ἅτε οὐκ εἰδώλου ἐφαπτομένῳ, ἀλλὰ
ἀληθῆ, ἅτε τοῦ ἀληθοῦς ἐφαπτομένῳ· τεκόντι δὲ ἀρετὴν 5
ἀληθῆ καὶ θρεψαμένῳ ὑπάρχει θεοφιλεῖ γενέσθαι, καὶ εἴπερ
τῳ ἄλλῳ ἀνθρώπων ἀθανάτῳ καὶ ἐκείνῳ;"

ταῦτα δή, ὦ Φαῖδρέ τε καὶ οἱ ἄλλοι, ἔφη μὲν Διοτίμα, b
πέπεισμαι δ' ἐγώ· πεπεισμένος δὲ πειρῶμαι καὶ τοὺς ἄλλους
πείθειν ὅτι τούτου τοῦ κτήματος τῇ ἀνθρωπείᾳ φύσει συνεργὸν ἀμείνω Ἔρωτος οὐκ ἄν τις ῥᾳδίως λάβοι. διὸ δὴ
ἔγωγέ φημι χρῆναι πάντα ἄνδρα τὸν Ἔρωτα τιμᾶν, καὶ 5
αὐτὸς τιμῶ τὰ ἐρωτικὰ καὶ διαφερόντως ἀσκῶ, καὶ τοῖς
ἄλλοις παρακελεύομαι, καὶ νῦν τε καὶ ἀεὶ ἐγκωμιάζω τὴν
δύναμιν καὶ ἀνδρείαν τοῦ Ἔρωτος καθ' ὅσον οἷός τ' εἰμί. τοῦτον οὖν τὸν λόγον, ὦ Φαῖδρε, εἰ μὲν βούλει, ὡς ἐγκώμιον εἰς c
Ἔρωτα νόμισον εἰρῆσθαι, εἰ δέ, ὅτι καὶ ὅπῃ χαίρεις ὀνομάζων,
τοῦτο ὀνόμαζε.'

εἰπόντος δὲ ταῦτα τοῦ Σωκράτους τοὺς μὲν ἐπαινεῖν, τὸν
δὲ Ἀριστοφάνη λέγειν τι ἐπιχειρεῖν, ὅτι ἐμνήσθη αὐτοῦ 5
λέγων ὁ Σωκράτης περὶ τοῦ λόγου· καὶ ἐξαίφνης τὴν αὔλειον
θύραν κρουομένην πολὺν ψόφον παρασχεῖν ὡς κωμαστῶν, καὶ
αὐλητρίδος φωνὴν ἀκούειν. τὸν οὖν Ἀγάθωνα, 'παῖδες,' φάναι,
'οὐ σκέψεσθε; καὶ ἐὰν μέν τις τῶν ἐπιτηδείων ᾖ, καλεῖτε· d
εἰ δὲ μή, λέγετε ὅτι οὐ πίνομεν ἀλλ' ἀναπαυόμεθα ἤδη.'

καὶ οὐ πολὺ ὕστερον Ἀλκιβιάδου τὴν φωνὴν ἀκούειν ἐν
τῇ αὐλῇ σφόδρα μεθύοντος καὶ μέγα βοῶντος, ἐρωτῶντος
ὅπου Ἀγάθων καὶ κελεύοντος ἄγειν παρ' Ἀγάθωνα. ἄγειν 5
οὖν αὐτὸν παρὰ σφᾶς τήν τε αὐλητρίδα ὑπολαβοῦσαν καὶ
ἄλλους τινὰς τῶν ἀκολούθων, καὶ ἐπιστῆναι ἐπὶ τὰς θύρας
ἐστεφανωμένον αὐτὸν κιττοῦ τέ τινι στεφάνῳ δασεῖ καὶ e
ἴων, καὶ ταινίας ἔχοντα ἐπὶ τῆς κεφαλῆς πάνυ πολλάς, καὶ

a 1 ᾧ δεῖ z: ὦ (sic) δεῖ m: ὡδὶ m: ὃ δεῖ m [a]   c 7 κροτουμένην m
d 2 αλλα παυο[a

εἰπεῖν· 'ἄνδρες, χαίρετε· μεθύοντα ἄνδρα πάνυ σφόδρα
δέξεσθε συμπότην, ἢ ἀπίωμεν ἀναδήσαντες μόνον 'Αγάθωνα,
5 ἐφ' ᾧπερ ἤλθομεν; ἐγὼ γάρ τοι,' φάναι, 'χθὲς μὲν οὐχ
οἷός τ' ἐγενόμην ἀφικέσθαι, νῦν δὲ ἥκω ἐπὶ τῇ κεφαλῇ
ἔχων τὰς ταινίας, ἵνα ἀπὸ τῆς ἐμῆς κεφαλῆς τὴν τοῦ σοφωτάτου καὶ καλλίστου κεφαλήν, ἀνειπὼν οὑτωσί, ἀναδήσω.
ἆρα καταγελάσεσθέ μου ὡς μεθύοντος; ἐγὼ δέ, κἂν ὑμεῖς
213 γελᾶτε, ὅμως εὖ οἶδ' ὅτι ἀληθῆ λέγω. ἀλλά μοι λέγετε
αὐτόθεν, ἐπὶ ῥητοῖς εἰσίω ἢ μή; συμπίεσθε ἢ οὔ;'

πάντας οὖν ἀναθορυβῆσαι καὶ κελεύειν εἰσιέναι καὶ
κατακλίνεσθαι, καὶ τὸν 'Αγάθωνα καλεῖν αὐτόν. καὶ τὸν
5 ἰέναι ἀγόμενον ὑπὸ τῶν ἀνθρώπων, καὶ περιαιρούμενον ἅμα
τὰς ταινίας ὡς ἀναδήσοντα, ἐπίπροσθε τῶν ὀφθαλμῶν ἔχοντα
οὐ κατιδεῖν τὸν Σωκράτη, ἀλλὰ καθίζεσθαι παρὰ τὸν 'Αγά-
b θωνα ἐν μέσῳ Σωκράτους τε καὶ ἐκείνου· παραχωρῆσαι
γὰρ τὸν Σωκράτη ὡς ἐκεῖνον κατιδεῖν. παρακαθεζόμενον
δὲ αὐτὸν ἀσπάζεσθαί τε τὸν 'Αγάθωνα καὶ ἀναδεῖν.

εἰπεῖν οὖν τὸν 'Αγάθωνα 'ὑπολύετε, παῖδες, 'Αλκιβιάδην,
5 ἵνα ἐκ τρίτων κατακέηται.'

'πάνυ γε,' εἰπεῖν τὸν 'Αλκιβιάδην· 'ἀλλὰ τίς ἡμῖν ὅδε
τρίτος συμπότης;' καὶ ἅμα μεταστρεφόμενον αὐτὸν ὁρᾶν
τὸν Σωκράτη, ἰδόντα δὲ ἀναπηδῆσαι καὶ εἰπεῖν· 'ὦ Ἡράκλεις,
τουτὶ τί ἦν; Σωκράτης οὗτος; ἐλλοχῶν αὖ με ἐνταῦθα κατέ-
c κεισο, ὥσπερ εἰώθεις ἐξαίφνης ἀναφαίνεσθαι ὅπου ἐγὼ ᾤμην
ἥκιστά σε ἔσεσθαι. καὶ νῦν τί ἥκεις; καὶ τί αὖ ἐνταῦθα
κατεκλίνης; ὡς οὐ παρὰ 'Αριστοφάνει οὐδὲ εἴ τις ἄλλος
γελοῖός ἐστί τε καὶ βούλεται, ἀλλὰ διεμηχανήσω ὅπως παρὰ
5 τῷ καλλίστῳ τῶν ἔνδον κατακείσῃ.'

καὶ τὸν Σωκράτη, ''Αγάθων,' φάναι, 'ὅρα εἴ μοι ἐπαμυνεῖς·
ὡς ἐμοὶ ὁ τούτου ἔρως τοῦ ἀνθρώπου οὐ φαῦλον πρᾶγμα
γέγονεν. ἀπ' ἐκείνου γὰρ τοῦ χρόνου, ἀφ' οὗ τούτου
d ἠράσθην, οὐκέτι ἔξεστίν μοι οὔτε προσβλέψαι οὔτε δια-
λεχθῆναι καλῷ οὐδ' ἑνί, ἢ οὑτοσὶ ζηλοτυπῶν με καὶ φθονῶν

θαυμαστὰ ἐργάζεται καὶ λοιδορεῖταί τε καὶ τὼ χεῖρε μόγις
ἀπέχεται. ὅρα οὖν μή τι καὶ νῦν ἐργάσηται, ἀλλὰ διάλ-
λαξον ἡμᾶς, ἢ ἐὰν ἐπιχειρῇ βιάζεσθαι, ἐπάμυνε, ὡς ἐγὼ 5
τὴν τούτου μανίαν τε καὶ φιλεραστίαν πάνυ ὀρρωδῶ.'
'ἀλλ' οὐκ ἔστι,' φάναι τὸν Ἀλκιβιάδην, 'ἐμοὶ καὶ σοὶ διαλ-
λαγή. ἀλλὰ τούτων μὲν εἰς αὖθίς σε τιμωρήσομαι· νῦν
δέ μοι, Ἀγάθων,' φάναι, 'μετάδος τῶν ταινιῶν, ἵνα ἀναδήσω e
καὶ τὴν τούτου ταυτηνὶ τὴν θαυμαστὴν κεφαλήν, καὶ μή μοι
μέμφηται ὅτι σὲ μὲν ἀνέδησα, αὐτὸν δὲ νικῶντα ἐν λόγοις
πάντας ἀνθρώπους, οὐ μόνον πρώην ὥσπερ σύ, ἀλλ' ἀεί,
ἔπειτα οὐκ ἀνέδησα.' καὶ ἅμ' αὐτὸν λαβόντα τῶν ταινιῶν 5
ἀναδεῖν τὸν Σωκράτη καὶ κατακλίνεσθαι.
    ἐπειδὴ δὲ κατεκλίνη, εἰπεῖν· 'εἶεν δή, ἄνδρες· δοκεῖτε
γάρ μοι νήφειν. οὐκ ἐπιτρεπτέον οὖν ὑμῖν, ἀλλὰ ποτέον·
ὡμολόγηται γὰρ ταῦθ' ἡμῖν. ἄρχοντα οὖν αἱροῦμαι τῆς
πόσεως, ἕως ἂν ὑμεῖς ἱκανῶς πίητε, ἐμαυτόν. ἀλλὰ φερέτω, 10
Ἀγάθων, εἴ τι ἐστὶν ἔκπωμα μέγα. μᾶλλον δὲ οὐδὲν δεῖ,
ἀλλὰ φέρε, παῖ,' φάναι, 'τὸν ψυκτῆρα ἐκεῖνον,' ἰδόντα αὐτὸν
πλέον ἢ ὀκτὼ κοτύλας χωροῦντα. τοῦτον ἐμπλησάμενον 214
πρῶτον μὲν αὐτὸν ἐκπιεῖν, ἔπειτα τῷ Σωκράτει κελεύειν
ἐγχεῖν καὶ ἅμα εἰπεῖν· 'πρὸς μὲν Σωκράτη, ὦ ἄνδρες, τὸ
σόφισμά μοι οὐδέν· ὁπόσον γὰρ ἂν κελεύῃ τις, τοσοῦτον
ἐκπιὼν οὐδὲν μᾶλλον μή ποτε μεθυσθῇ.' 5
    τὸν μὲν οὖν Σωκράτη ἐγχέαντος τοῦ παιδὸς πίνειν· τὸν
δ' Ἐρυξίμαχον 'πῶς οὖν,' φάναι, 'ὦ Ἀλκιβιάδη, ποιοῦμεν;
οὕτως οὔτε τι λέγομεν ἐπὶ τῇ κύλικι οὔτε τι ᾄδομεν, ἀλλ' b
ἀτεχνῶς ὥσπερ οἱ διψῶντες πιόμεθα;'
    τὸν οὖν Ἀλκιβιάδην εἰπεῖν· 'ὦ Ἐρυξίμαχε, βέλτιστε
βελτίστου πατρὸς καὶ σωφρονεστάτου, χαῖρε.'
    'καὶ γὰρ σύ,' φάναι τὸν Ἐρυξίμαχον· 'ἀλλὰ τί ποιῶμεν;' 5
'ὅτι ἂν σὺ κελεύῃς. δεῖ γάρ σοι πείθεσθαι·
        ἰητρὸς γὰρ ἀνὴρ πολλῶν ἀντάξιος ἄλλων·
ἐπίτατte οὖν ὅτι βούλει.'
    'ἄκουσον δή,' εἰπεῖν τὸν Ἐρυξίμαχον. 'ἡμῖν πρὶν σὲ
    d 3 θαυμάσια m   b 1 οὔτ' ἐπᾴδομεν m [a]

10 εἰσελθεῖν ἔδοξε χρῆναι ἐπὶ δεξιὰ ἕκαστον ἐν μέρει λόγον
c περὶ Ἔρωτος εἰπεῖν ὡς δύναιτο κάλλιστον, καὶ ἐγκωμιάσαι.

οἱ μὲν οὖν ἄλλοι πάντες ἡμεῖς εἰρήκαμεν· σὺ δ᾽ ἐπειδὴ οὐκ
εἴρηκας καὶ ἐκπέπωκας, δίκαιος εἶ εἰπεῖν, εἰπὼν δὲ ἐπιτάξαι
Σωκράτει ὅτι ἂν βούλῃ, καὶ τοῦτον τῷ ἐπὶ δεξιὰ καὶ οὕτω
5 τοὺς ἄλλους.᾽

'ἀλλά,᾽ φάναι, 'ὦ Ἐρυξίμαχε,᾽ τὸν Ἀλκιβιάδην, 'καλῶς μὲν
λέγεις, μεθύοντα δὲ ἄνδρα παρὰ νηφόντων λόγους παρα-
βάλλειν μὴ οὐκ ἐξ ἴσου ᾖ. καὶ ἅμα, ὦ μακάριε, πείθει τί
d σε Σωκράτης ὧν ἄρτι εἶπεν; ἢ οἶσθα ὅτι τοὐναντίον ἐστὶ
πᾶν ἢ ὃ ἔλεγεν; οὗτος γάρ, ἐάν τινα ἐγὼ ἐπαινέσω τούτου
παρόντος ἢ θεὸν ἢ ἄνθρωπον ἄλλον ἢ τοῦτον, οὐκ ἀφέξεταί
μου τὼ χεῖρε.᾽

5 'οὐκ εὐφημήσεις;᾽ φάναι τὸν Σωκράτη.

'μὰ τὸν Ποσειδῶ,᾽ εἰπεῖν τὸν Ἀλκιβιάδην, 'μηδὲν λέγε
πρὸς ταῦτα, ὡς ἐγὼ οὐδ᾽ ἂν ἕνα ἄλλον ἐπαινέσαιμι σοῦ
παρόντος.᾽

'ἀλλ᾽ οὕτω ποίει,᾽ φάναι τὸν Ἐρυξίμαχον, 'εἰ βούλει·
10 Σωκράτη ἐπαίνεσον.᾽

e 'πῶς λέγεις;᾽ εἰπεῖν τὸν Ἀλκιβιάδην· 'δοκεῖ χρῆναι, ὦ
Ἐρυξίμαχε; ἐπιθῶμαι τῷ ἀνδρὶ καὶ τιμωρήσωμαι ὑμῶν
ἐναντίον;᾽

'οὗτος,᾽ φάναι τὸν Σωκράτη, 'τί ἐν νῷ ἔχεις; ἐπὶ τὰ
5 γελοιότερά με ἐπαινέσεις; ἢ τί ποιήσεις;᾽

'τἀληθῆ ἐρῶ. ἀλλ᾽ ὅρα εἰ παρίῃς.᾽

'ἀλλὰ μέντοι,᾽ φάναι, 'τά γε ἀληθῆ παρίημι καὶ κελεύω
λέγειν.᾽

7 'οὐκ ἂν φθάνοιμι,᾽ εἰπεῖν τὸν Ἀλκιβιάδην. 'καὶ μέντοι
10 οὑτωσὶ ποίησον. ἐάν τι μὴ ἀληθὲς λέγω, μεταξὺ ἐπιλαβοῦ,
ἂν βούλῃ, καὶ εἰπὲ ὅτι τοῦτο ψεύδομαι· ἑκὼν γὰρ εἶναι οὐδὲν
215 ψεύσομαι. ἐὰν μέντοι ἀναμιμνῃσκόμενος ἄλλο ἄλλοθεν
λέγω, μηδὲν θαυμάσῃς· οὐ γάρ τι ῥᾴδιον τὴν σὴν ἀτοπίαν
ὧδ᾽ ἔχοντι εὐπόρως καὶ ἐφεξῆς καταριθμῆσαι.

Σωκράτη δ᾽ ἐγὼ ἐπαινεῖν, ὦ ἄνδρες, οὕτως ἐπιχειρήσω,

e 5 ἐπαινέσει vel ἐπαινέσαι z [a]

δι' εἰκόνων. οὗτος μὲν οὖν ἴσως οἰήσεται ἐπὶ τὰ γελοιότερα, 5
ἔσται δ' ἡ εἰκὼν τοῦ ἀληθοῦς ἕνεκα, οὐ τοῦ γελοίου. φημὶ
γὰρ δὴ ὁμοιότατον αὐτὸν εἶναι τοῖς σιληνοῖς τούτοις τοῖς
ἐν τοῖς ἑρμογλυφείοις καθημένοις, οὕστινας ἐργάζονται οἱ b
δημιουργοὶ σύριγγας ἢ αὐλοὺς ἔχοντας, οἳ διχάδε διοιχθέντες
φαίνονται ἔνδοθεν ἀγάλματα ἔχοντες θεῶν. καὶ φημὶ αὖ
ἐοικέναι αὐτὸν τῷ σατύρῳ τῷ Μαρσύᾳ. ὅτι μὲν οὖν τό γε
εἶδος ὅμοιος εἶ τούτοις, ὦ Σώκρατες, οὐδ' αὐτὸς ἄν που 5
ἀμφισβητήσαις· ὡς δὲ καὶ τἆλλα ἔοικας, μετὰ τοῦτο ἄκουε.
ὑβριστὴς εἶ· ἢ οὔ; ἐὰν γὰρ μὴ ὁμολογῇς, μάρτυρας παρ-
έξομαι. ἀλλ' οὐκ αὐλητής; πολύ γε θαυμασιώτερος ἐκείνου.
ὁ μέν γε δι' ὀργάνων ἐκήλει τοὺς ἀνθρώπους τῇ ἀπὸ τοῦ c
στόματος δυνάμει, καὶ ἔτι νυνὶ ὃς ἂν τὰ ἐκείνου αὐλῇ (ἃ γὰρ
Ὄλυμπος ηὔλει, Μαρσύου λέγω, τούτου διδάξαντος)· τὰ οὖν
ἐκείνου ἐάντε ἀγαθὸς αὐλητὴς αὐλῇ ἐάντε φαύλη αὐλητρίς,
μόνα κατέχεσθαι ποιεῖ καὶ δηλοῖ τοὺς τῶν θεῶν τε καὶ 5
τελετῶν δεομένους διὰ τὸ θεῖα εἶναι. σὺ δ' ἐκείνου τοσοῦτον
μόνον διαφέρεις, ὅτι ἄνευ ὀργάνων ψιλοῖς λόγοις ταὐτὸν
τοῦτο ποιεῖς. ἡμεῖς γοῦν ὅταν μέν του ἄλλου ἀκούωμεν d
λέγοντος καὶ πάνυ ἀγαθοῦ ῥήτορος ἄλλους λόγους, οὐδὲν
μέλει ὡς ἔπος εἰπεῖν οὐδενί· ἐπειδὰν δὲ σοῦ τις ἀκούῃ ἢ τῶν
σῶν λόγων ἄλλου λέγοντος, κἂν πάνυ φαῦλος ᾖ ὁ λέγων,
ἐάντε γυνὴ ἀκούῃ ἐάντε ἀνὴρ ἐάντε μειράκιον, ἐκπεπλη- 5
γμένοι ἐσμὲν καὶ κατεχόμεθα. ἐγὼ γοῦν, ὦ ἄνδρες, εἰ μὴ
ἔμελλον κομιδῇ δόξειν μεθύειν, εἶπον ὀμόσας ἂν ὑμῖν οἷα δὴ
πέπονθα αὐτὸς ὑπὸ τῶν τούτου λόγων καὶ πάσχω ἔτι καὶ
νυνί. ὅταν γὰρ ἀκούω, πολύ μοι μᾶλλον ἢ τῶν κορυβαν- e
τιώντων ἥ τε καρδία πηδᾷ καὶ δάκρυα ἐκχεῖται ὑπὸ τῶν
λόγων τῶν τούτου, ὁρῶ δὲ καὶ ἄλλους παμπόλλους τὰ
αὐτὰ πάσχοντας· Περικλέους δὲ ἀκούων καὶ ἄλλων ἀγαθῶν
ῥητόρων εὖ μὲν ἡγούμην λέγειν, τοιοῦτον δ' οὐδὲν ἔπασχον, 5
οὐδ' ἐτεθορύβητό μου ἡ ψυχὴ οὐδ' ἠγανάκτει ὡς ἀνδραποδωδῶς διακειμένου, ἀλλ' ὑπὸ τουτουΐ τοῦ Μαρσύου πολλάκις δὴ
οὕτω διετέθην ὥστε μοι δόξαι μὴ βιωτὸν εἶναι ἔχοντι ὡς 216

b 5 ἂν z: δή m [a]

ἔχω. καὶ ταῦτα, ὦ Σώκρατες, οὐκ ἐρεῖς ὡς οὐκ ἀληθῆ. καὶ
ἔτι γε νῦν σύνοιδ᾽ ἐμαυτῷ ὅτι εἰ ἐθέλοιμι παρέχειν τὰ ὦτα,
οὐκ ἂν καρτερήσαιμι ἀλλὰ ταὐτὰ ἂν πάσχοιμι. ἀναγκάζει
5 γάρ με ὁμολογεῖν ὅτι πολλοῦ ἐνδεὴς ὢν αὐτὸς ἔτι ἐμαυτοῦ
μὲν ἀμελῶ, τὰ δ᾽ Ἀθηναίων πράττω. βίᾳ οὖν ὥσπερ ἀπὸ
τῶν Σειρήνων ἐπισχόμενος τὰ ὦτα οἴχομαι φεύγων, ἵνα μὴ
αὐτοῦ καθήμενος παρὰ τούτῳ καταγηράσω. πέπονθα δὲ
b πρὸς τοῦτον μόνον ἀνθρώπων, ὃ οὐκ ἄν τις οἴοιτο ἐν ἐμοὶ
ἐνεῖναι, τὸ αἰσχύνεσθαι ὁντινοῦν· ἐγὼ δὲ τοῦτον μόνον
αἰσχύνομαι. σύνοιδα γὰρ ἐμαυτῷ ἀντιλέγειν μὲν οὐ δυνα-
μένῳ ὡς οὐ δεῖ ποιεῖν ἃ οὗτος κελεύει, ἐπειδὰν δὲ ἀπέλθω,
5 ἡττημένῳ τῆς τιμῆς τῆς ὑπὸ τῶν πολλῶν. δραπετεύω οὖν
αὐτὸν καὶ φεύγω, καὶ ὅταν ἴδω, αἰσχύνομαι τὰ ὡμολογημένα.
c καὶ πολλάκις μὲν ἡδέως ἂν ἴδοιμι αὐτὸν μὴ ὄντα ἐν ἀνθρώποις·
εἰ δ᾽ αὖ τοῦτο γένοιτο, εὖ οἶδα ὅτι πολὺ μεῖζον ἂν ἀχθοίμην,
ὥστε οὐκ ἔχω ὅτι χρήσωμαι τούτῳ τῷ ἀνθρώπῳ.
   καὶ ὑπὸ μὲν δὴ τῶν αὐλημάτων καὶ ἐγὼ καὶ ἄλλοι πολλοὶ
5 τοιαῦτα πεπόνθασιν ὑπὸ τοῦδε τοῦ σατύρου· ἀλλὰ δὲ ἐμοῦ
ἀκούσατε ὡς ὅμοιός τ᾽ ἐστὶν οἷς ἐγὼ ᾔκασα αὐτὸν καὶ τὴν
δύναμιν ὡς θαυμασίαν ἔχει. εὖ γὰρ ἴστε ὅτι οὐδεὶς ὑμῶν
d τοῦτον γιγνώσκει· ἀλλὰ ἐγὼ δηλώσω, ἐπείπερ ἠρξάμην.
ὁρᾶτε γὰρ ὅτι Σωκράτης ἐρωτικῶς διάκειται τῶν καλῶν καὶ
ἀεὶ περὶ τούτους ἐστὶ καὶ ἐκπέπληκται, καὶ αὖ ἀγνοεῖ πάντα
καὶ οὐδὲν οἶδεν, ὡς τὸ σχῆμα αὐτοῦ τοῦτο οὐ σιληνῶδες;
5 σφόδρα γε. τοῦτο γὰρ οὗτος ἔξωθεν περιβέβληται, ὥσπερ
ὁ γεγλυμμένος σιληνός· ἔνδοθεν δὲ ἀνοιχθεὶς πόσης οἴεσθε
γέμει, ὦ ἄνδρες συμπόται, σωφροσύνης; ἴστε ὅτι οὔτε εἴ τις
καλός ἐστι μέλει αὐτῷ οὐδέν, ἀλλὰ καταφρονεῖ τοσοῦτον
e ὅσον οὐδ᾽ ἂν εἷς οἰηθείη, οὔτ᾽ εἴ τις πλούσιος, οὔτ᾽ εἰ ἄλλην
τινὰ τιμὴν ἔχων τῶν ὑπὸ πλήθους μακαριζομένων· ἡγεῖται
δὲ πάντα ταῦτα τὰ κτήματα οὐδενὸς ἄξια καὶ ἡμᾶς οὐδὲν
εἶναι — λέγω ὑμῖν — εἰρωνευόμενος δὲ καὶ παίζων πάντα τὸν
5 βίον πρὸς τοὺς ἀνθρώπους διατελεῖ. σπουδάσαντος δὲ αὐτοῦ
καὶ ἀνοιχθέντος οὐκ οἶδα εἴ τις ἑώρακεν τὰ ἐντὸς ἀγάλματα·
ἀλλ᾽ ἐγὼ ἤδη ποτ᾽ εἶδον, καί μοι ἔδοξεν οὕτω θεῖα καὶ

ΣΥΜΠΟΣΙΟΝ

ΣΥΜΠΟΣΙΟΝ   69

χρυσᾶ εἶναι καὶ πάγκαλα καὶ θαυμαστά, ὥστε ποιητέον εἶναι 217
ἔμβραχυ ὅτι κελεύοι Σωκράτης. ἡγούμενος δὲ αὐτὸν ἐσπουδακέναι ἐπὶ τῇ ἐμῇ ὥρᾳ ἕρμαιον ἡγησάμην εἶναι καὶ εὐτύχημα
ἐμὸν θαυμαστόν, ὡς ὑπάρχον μοι χαρισαμένῳ Σωκράτει πάντ᾽
ἀκοῦσαι ὅσαπερ οὗτος ᾔδει· ἐφρόνουν γὰρ δὴ ἐπὶ τῇ ὥρᾳ 5
θαυμάσιον ὅσον. ταῦτα οὖν διανοηθείς, πρὸ τοῦ οὐκ εἰωθὼς
ἄνευ ἀκολούθου μόνος μετ᾽ αὐτοῦ γίγνεσθαι, τότε ἀποπέμπων
τὸν ἀκόλουθον μόνος συνεγιγνόμην (δεῖ γὰρ πρὸς ὑμᾶς πάντα b
τἀληθῆ εἰπεῖν· ἀλλὰ προσέχετε τὸν νοῦν, καὶ εἰ ψεύδομαι,
Σώκρατες, ἐξέλεγχε)· συνεγιγνόμην γάρ, ὦ ἄνδρες, μόνος
μόνῳ, καὶ ᾤμην αὐτίκα διαλέξεσθαι αὐτόν μοι ἅπερ ἂν
ἐραστὴς παιδικοῖς ἐν ἐρημίᾳ διαλεχθείη, καὶ ἔχαιρον. τούτων 5
δ᾽ οὐ μάλα ἐγίγνετο οὐδέν, ἀλλ᾽ ὥσπερ εἰώθει διαλεχθεὶς ἄν
μοι καὶ συνημερεύσας ᾤχετο ἀπιών. μετὰ ταῦτα συγγυμνά-
ζεσθαι προυκαλούμην αὐτὸν καὶ συνεγυμναζόμην, ὥς τι c
ἐνταῦθα περανῶν. συνεγυμνάζετο οὖν μοι καὶ προσεπάλαιεν
πολλάκις οὐδενὸς παρόντος. καὶ τί δεῖ λέγειν; οὐδὲν γάρ
μοι πλέον ἦν. ἐπειδὴ δὲ οὐδαμῇ ταύτῃ ἤνυτον, ἔδοξέ μοι
ἐπιθετέον εἶναι τῷ ἀνδρὶ κατὰ τὸ καρτερὸν καὶ οὐκ ἀνετέον, 5
ἐπειδήπερ ἐνεκεχειρήκη, ἀλλὰ ἰστέον ἤδη τί ἐστι τὸ πρᾶγμα.
προκαλοῦμαι δὴ αὐτὸν πρὸς τὸ συνδειπνεῖν, ἀτεχνῶς ὥσπερ
ἐραστὴς παιδικοῖς ἐπιβουλεύων. καί μοι οὐδὲ τοῦτο ταχὺ
ὑπήκουσεν, ὅμως δ᾽ οὖν χρόνῳ ἐπείσθη. ἐπειδὴ δὲ ἀφίκετο d
τὸ πρῶτον, δειπνήσας ἀπιέναι ἐβούλετο. καὶ τότε μὲν
αἰσχυνόμενος ἀφῆκα αὐτόν· αὖθις δ᾽ ἐπιβουλεύσας, ἐπειδὴ
ἐδεδειπνήκεμεν διελεγόμην ἀεὶ πόρρω τῶν νυκτῶν, καὶ ἐπειδὴ
ἐβούλετο ἀπιέναι, σκηπτόμενος ὅτι ὀψὲ εἴη, προσηνάγκασα 5
αὐτὸν μένειν. ἀνεπαύετο οὖν ἐν τῇ ἐχομένῃ ἐμοῦ κλίνῃ, ἐν
ᾗπερ ἐδείπνει, καὶ οὐδεὶς ἐν τῷ οἰκήματι ἄλλος καθηῦδεν ἢ
ἡμεῖς. μέχρι μὲν οὖν δὴ δεῦρο τοῦ λόγου καλῶς ἂν ἔχοι e
καὶ πρὸς ὁντινοῦν λέγειν· τὸ δ᾽ ἐντεῦθεν οὐκ ἄν μου ἠκούσατε
λέγοντος, εἰ μὴ πρῶτον μέν, τὸ λεγόμενον, οἶνος ἄνευ τε
παίδων καὶ μετὰ παίδων ἦν ἀληθής, ἔπειτα ἀφανίσαι Σω-

---

a 2 ἔμβραχυ z: ἐν βραχεῖ m [a]   d 4 ἐδεδειπνήκεμεν z: δεδειπνή-
καμεν c: ἐδεδειπνήκει a m   ἀεὶ c: om. a m

5 κράτους ἔργον ὑπερήφανον εἰς ἔπαινον ἐλθόντα ἄδικόν μοι
φαίνεται. ἔτι δὲ τὸ τοῦ δηχθέντος ὑπὸ τοῦ ἔχεως πάθος
κἄμ' ἔχει. φασὶ γάρ που τινὰ τοῦτο παθόντα οὐκ ἐθέλειν
λέγειν οἷον ἦν πλὴν τοῖς δεδηγμένοις, ὡς μόνοις γνωσομένοις
218 τε καὶ συγγνωσομένοις εἰ πᾶν ἐτόλμα δρᾶν τε καὶ λέγειν
ὑπὸ τῆς ὀδύνης. ἐγὼ οὖν δεδηγμένος τε ὑπὸ ἀλγεινοτέρου
καὶ τὸ ἀλγεινότατον ὧν ἄν τις δηχθείη (τὴν καρδίαν γὰρ
ἢ ψυχὴν ἢ ὅτι δεῖ αὐτὸ ὀνομάσαι πληγείς τε καὶ δηχθεὶς
5 ὑπὸ τῶν ἐν φιλοσοφίᾳ λόγων, οἳ ἔχονται ἐχίδνης ἀγριώτερον,
νέου ψυχῆς μὴ ἀφυοῦς ὅταν λάβωνται, καὶ ποιοῦσι δρᾶν
τε καὶ λέγειν ὁτιοῦν), καὶ ὁρῶν αὖ Φαίδρους, Ἀγάθωνας,
b Ἐρυξιμάχους, Παυσανίας, Ἀριστοδήμους τε καὶ Ἀριστο-
φάνας — Σωκράτη δὲ αὐτὸν τί δεῖ λέγειν, καὶ ὅσοι ἄλλοι;
πάντες γὰρ κεκοινωνήκατε τῆς φιλοσόφου μανίας τε καὶ
βακχείας. διὸ πάντες ἀκούσεσθε· συγγνώσεσθε γὰρ τοῖς τε
5 τότε πραχθεῖσι καὶ τοῖς νῦν λεγομένοις. οἱ δὲ οἰκέται, καὶ
εἴ τις ἄλλος ἐστὶν βέβηλός τε καὶ ἄγροικος, πύλας πάνυ
μεγάλας τοῖς ὠσὶν ἐπίθεσθε.
ἐπειδὴ γὰρ οὖν, ὦ ἄνδρες, ὅ τε λύχνος ἀπεσβήκει καὶ
c οἱ παῖδες ἔξω ἦσαν, ἔδοξέ μοι χρῆναι μηδὲν ποικίλλειν πρὸς
αὐτόν, ἀλλ' ἐλευθέρως εἰπεῖν ἅ μοι ἐδόκει· καὶ εἶπον κινήσας
αὐτόν, "Σώκρατες, καθεύδεις;"
"οὐ δῆτα," ἦ δ' ὅς.
5 "οἶσθα οὖν ἅ μοι δέδοκται;"
"τί μάλιστα;" ἔφη.
"σὺ ἐμοὶ δοκεῖς," ἦν δ' ἐγώ, "ἐμοῦ ἐραστὴς ἄξιος γεγονέναι
μόνος, καί μοι φαίνῃ ὀκνεῖν μνησθῆναι πρός με. ἐγὼ δὲ
οὑτωσὶ ἔχω· πάνυ ἀνόητον ἡγοῦμαι εἶναι σοὶ μὴ οὐ καὶ
10 τοῦτο χαρίζεσθαι καὶ εἴ τι ἄλλο ἢ τῆς οὐσίας τῆς ἐμῆς
d δέοιο ἢ τῶν φίλων τῶν ἐμῶν. ἐμοὶ μὲν γὰρ οὐδέν ἐστι
πρεσβύτερον τοῦ ὡς ὅτι βέλτιστον ἐμὲ γενέσθαι, τούτου δὲ
οἶμαί μοι συλλήπτορα οὐδένα κυριώτερον εἶναι σοῦ. ἐγὼ δὴ
τοιούτῳ ἀνδρὶ πολὺ μᾶλλον ἂν μὴ χαριζόμενος αἰσχυνοίμην
5 τοὺς φρονίμους, ἢ χαριζόμενος τούς τε πολλοὺς καὶ ἄφρονας."

d 3 μοι m: [ ]ı a: μου m

καὶ οὗτος ἀκούσας μάλα εἰρωνικῶς καὶ σφόδρα ἑαυτοῦ τε
καὶ εἰωθότως ἔλεξεν· "ὦ φίλε Ἀλκιβιάδη, κινδυνεύεις τῷ
ὄντι οὐ φαῦλος εἶναι, εἴπερ ἀληθῆ τυγχάνει ὄντα ἃ λέγεις
περὶ ἐμοῦ, καί τις ἔστ' ἐν ἐμοὶ δύναμις δι' ἧς ἂν σὺ γένοιο e
ἀμείνων· ἀμήχανόν τοι κάλλος ὁρῴης ἂν ἐν ἐμοὶ καὶ τῆς
παρὰ σοὶ εὐμορφίας πάμπολυ διαφέρον. εἰ δὴ καθορῶν
αὐτὸ κοινώσασθαί τέ μοι ἐπιχειρεῖς καὶ ἀλλάξασθαι κάλλος
ἀντὶ κάλλους, οὐκ ὀλίγῳ μου πλεονεκτεῖν διανοῇ. ἀλλ' 5
ἀντὶ δόξης ἀλήθειαν καλῶν κτᾶσθαι ἐπιχειρεῖς καὶ τῷ
ὄντι χρύσεα χαλκείων διαμείβεσθαι νοεῖς. ἀλλ', ὦ 219
μακάριε, ἄμεινον σκόπει, μή σε λανθάνω οὐδὲν ὤν. ἤ τοι
τῆς διανοίας ὄψις ἄρχεται ὀξὺ βλέπειν ὅταν ἡ τῶν ὀμμάτων
τῆς ἀκμῆς †λήγειν ἐπιχειρῇ†· σὺ δὲ τούτων ἔτι πόρρω."
κἀγὼ ἀκούσας, "τὰ μὲν παρ' ἐμοῦ," ἔφην, "ταῦτά ἐστιν, ὧν 5
οὐδὲν ἄλλως εἴρηται ἢ ὡς διανοοῦμαι· σὺ δὲ αὐτὸς οὕτω
βουλεύου ὅτι σοί τε ἄριστον καὶ ἐμοὶ ἡγῇ."
"ἀλλ'," ἔφη, "τοῦτό γ' εὖ λέγεις· ἐν γὰρ τῷ ἐπιόντι χρόνῳ
βουλευόμενοι πράξομεν ὃ ἂν φαίνηται νῷν περί τε τούτων b
καὶ περὶ τῶν ἄλλων ἄριστον."
ἐγὼ μὲν δὴ ταῦτα ἀκούσας τε καὶ εἰπών, καὶ ἀφεὶς
ὥσπερ βέλη, τετρῶσθαι αὐτὸν ᾤμην· καὶ ἀναστάς γε, οὐδ'
ἐπιτρέψας τούτῳ εἰπεῖν οὐδὲν ἔτι, ἀμφιέσας τὸ ἱμάτιον 5
τὸ ἐμαυτοῦ τοῦτον (καὶ γὰρ ἦν χειμών) ὑπὸ τὸν τρίβωνα
κατακλινεὶς τὸν τουτουί, περιβαλὼν τὼ χεῖρε τούτῳ τῷ
δαιμονίῳ ὡς ἀληθῶς καὶ θαυμαστῷ, κατεκείμην τὴν νύκτα c
ὅλην. καὶ οὐδὲ ταῦτα αὖ, ὦ Σώκρατες, ἐρεῖς ὅτι ψεύδομαι.
ποιήσαντος δὲ δὴ ταῦτα ἐμοῦ οὗτος τοσοῦτον περιεγένετό
τε καὶ κατεφρόνησεν καὶ κατεγέλασεν τῆς ἐμῆς ὥρας καὶ
ὕβρισεν. καὶ περὶ ἐκεῖνό γε ᾤμην τι εἶναι, ὦ ἄνδρες δικασταί· 5
δικασταὶ γάρ ἐστε τῆς Σωκράτους ὑπερηφανίας. εὖ γὰρ
ἴστε μὰ θεούς, μὰ θεάς, οὐδὲν περιττότερον καταδεδαρθηκὼς
ἀνέστην μετὰ Σωκράτους, ἢ εἰ μετὰ πατρὸς καθηῦδον ἢ d
ἀδελφοῦ πρεσβυτέρου.
τὸ δὴ μετὰ τοῦτο τίνα οἴεσθέ με διάνοιαν ἔχειν, ἡγού-

μενον μὲν ἠτιμάσθαι, ἀγάμενον δὲ τὴν τούτου φύσιν τε καὶ
5 σωφροσύνην καὶ ἀνδρείαν, ἐντετυχηκότα ἀνθρώπῳ τοιούτῳ
οἵῳ ἐγὼ οὐκ ἂν ᾤμην ποτ' ἐντυχεῖν εἰς φρόνησιν καὶ εἰς
καρτερίαν; ὥστε οὔθ' ὅπως οὖν ὀργιζοίμην εἶχον καὶ ἀπο-
στερηθείην τῆς τούτου συνουσίας, οὔτε ὅπῃ προσαγαγοίμην
e αὐτὸν ηὐπόρουν.   εὖ γὰρ ἤδη ὅτι χρήμασί γε πολὺ μᾶλλον
ἄτρωτος ἦν πανταχῇ ἢ σιδήρῳ ὁ Αἴας, ᾧ τε ᾤμην αὐτὸν
μόνῳ ἁλώσεσθαι, διεπεφεύγει με.   ἠπόρουν δή, καταδε-
δουλωμένος τε ὑπὸ τοῦ ἀνθρώπου ὡς οὐδεὶς ὑπ' οὐδενὸς
5 ἄλλου περιῇα.   ταῦτά τε γάρ μοι ἅπαντα προυγεγόνει, καὶ
μετὰ ταῦτα στρατεία ἡμῖν εἰς Ποτείδαιαν ἐγένετο κοινὴ
καὶ συνεσιτοῦμεν ἐκεῖ.   πρῶτον μὲν οὖν τοῖς πόνοις οὐ
μόνον ἐμοῦ περιῆν, ἀλλὰ καὶ τῶν ἄλλων ἁπάντων· ὁπότ'
ἀναγκασθεῖμεν ἀποληφθέντες που, οἷα δὴ ἐπὶ στρατείας,
220 ἀσιτεῖν, οὐδὲν ἦσαν οἱ ἄλλοι πρὸς τὸ καρτερεῖν· ἔν τ' αὖ
ταῖς εὐωχίαις μόνος ἀπολαύειν οἷός τ' ἦν τά τ' ἄλλα καὶ
πίνειν οὐκ ἐθέλων, ὁπότε ἀναγκασθείη, πάντας ἐκράτει, καὶ
ὃ πάντων θαυμαστότατον, Σωκράτη μεθύοντα οὐδεὶς πώποτε
5 ἑώρακεν ἀνθρώπων.   τούτου μὲν οὖν μοι δοκεῖ καὶ αὐτίκα ὁ
ἔλεγχος ἔσεσθαι.   πρὸς δὲ αὖ τὰς τοῦ χειμῶνος καρτερήσεις
(δεινοὶ γὰρ αὐτόθι χειμῶνες) θαυμάσια ἠργάζετο τά τε
b ἄλλα, καί ποτε ὄντος πάγου οἵου δεινοτάτου, καὶ πάντων ἢ
οὐκ ἐξιόντων ἔνδοθεν, ἢ εἴ τις ἐξίοι, ἠμφιεσμένων τε
θαυμαστὰ δὴ ὅσα καὶ ὑποδεδεμένων καὶ ἐνειλιγμένων τοὺς
πόδας εἰς πίλους καὶ ἀρνακίδας, οὗτος δ' ἐν τούτοις ἐξῄει
5 ἔχων ἱμάτιον μὲν τοιοῦτον οἷόνπερ καὶ πρότερον εἰώθει
φορεῖν, ἀνυπόδητος δὲ διὰ τοῦ κρυστάλλου ῥᾷον ἐπορεύετο
ἢ οἱ ἄλλοι ὑποδεδεμένοι, οἱ δὲ στρατιῶται ὑπέβλεπον
c αὐτὸν ὡς καταφρονοῦντα σφῶν.   καὶ ταῦτα μὲν δὴ ταῦτα·
οἷον δ' αὖ τόδ' ἔρεξε καὶ ἔτλη καρτερὸς ἀνὴρ
ἐκεῖ ποτε ἐπὶ στρατιᾶς, ἄξιον ἀκοῦσαι.   συννοήσας γὰρ
αὐτόθι ἕωθέν τι εἱστήκει σκοπῶν, καὶ ἐπειδὴ οὐ προυχώρει

d 7 καρτερίαν m: [ ]κρατειαν a   e 9 ἀποληφθέντες z: ἀπολειφ⁻
θέντες m [a]   a 4 θαυμασιωτατον a   b 1 ἦ om. m   b 4 δ'
om. a   c 3 στρατείας m

αὑτῷ, οὐκ ἀνίει ἀλλὰ εἱστήκει ζητῶν. καὶ ἤδη ἦν μεσημ- 5
βρία, καὶ ἄνθρωποι ἠσθάνοντο, καὶ θαυμάζοντες ἄλλος ἄλλῳ
ἔλεγεν ὅτι Σωκράτης ἐξ ἑωθινοῦ φροντίζων τι ἕστηκε.
τελευτῶντες δέ τινες τῶν 'Ιώνων, ἐπειδὴ ἑσπέρα ἦν, δειπνή-
σαντες (καὶ γὰρ θέρος τότε γ' ἦν) χαμεύνια ἐξενεγκάμενοι d
ἅμα μὲν ἐν τῷ ψύχει καθηῦδον, ἅμα δ' ἐφύλαττον αὐτὸν εἰ
καὶ τὴν νύκτα ἑστήξοι. ὁ δὲ εἱστήκει μέχρι ἕως ἐγένετο
καὶ ἥλιος ἀνέσχεν· ἔπειτα ᾤχετ' ἀπιὼν προσευξάμενος τῷ
ἡλίῳ. εἰ δὲ βούλεσθε ἐν ταῖς μάχαις (τοῦτο γὰρ δὴ 5
δίκαιόν γε αὐτῷ ἀποδοῦναι)· ὅτε γὰρ ἡ μάχη ἦν ἐξ ἧς ἐμοὶ
καὶ τἀριστεῖα ἔδοσαν οἱ στρατηγοί, οὐδεὶς ἄλλος ἐμὲ ἔσωσεν
ἀνθρώπων ἢ οὗτος, τετρωμένον οὐκ ἐθέλων ἀπολιπεῖν, ἀλλὰ e
συνδιέσωσε καὶ τὰ ὅπλα καὶ αὐτὸν ἐμέ. καὶ ἐγὼ μέν, ὦ Σώκρατες, καὶ τότε ἐκέλευον σοὶ διδόναι τἀριστεῖα τοὺς στρατη-
γούς, καὶ τοῦτό γε μοι οὔτε μέμψῃ οὔτε ἐρεῖς ὅτι ψεύδομαι
ἀλλὰ γὰρ τῶν στρατηγῶν πρὸς τὸ ἐμὸν ἀξίωμα ἀποβλεπόντων 5
καὶ βουλομένων ἐμοὶ διδόναι τἀριστεῖα, αὐτὸς προθυμότερος
ἐγένου τῶν στρατηγῶν ἐμὲ λαβεῖν ἢ σαυτόν. ἔτι τοίνυν,
ὦ ἄνδρες, ἄξιον ἦν θεάσασθαι Σωκράτη, ὅτε ἀπὸ Δηλίου
φυγῇ ἀνεχώρει τὸ στρατόπεδον· ἔτυχον γὰρ παραγενόμενος 221
ἵππον ἔχων, οὗτος δὲ ὅπλα. ἀνεχώρει οὖν ἐσκεδασμένων
ἤδη τῶν ἀνθρώπων οὗτός τε ἅμα καὶ Λάχης· καὶ ἐγὼ περι-
τυγχάνω, καὶ ἰδὼν εὐθὺς παρακελεύομαί τε αὐτοῖν θαρρεῖν,
καὶ ἔλεγον ὅτι οὐκ ἀπολείψω αὐτώ. ἐνταῦθα δὴ καὶ κάλ- 5
λιον ἐθεασάμην Σωκράτη ἢ ἐν Ποτειδαίᾳ (αὐτὸς γὰρ ἧττον
ἐν φόβῳ ἦ διὰ τὸ ἐφ' ἵππου εἶναι), πρῶτον μὲν ὅσον περιῆν
Λάχητος τῷ ἔμφρων εἶναι, ἔπειτα ἔμοιγ' ἐδόκει, ὦ 'Αρι- b
στόφανες, τὸ σὸν δὴ τοῦτο, καὶ ἐκεῖ διαπορεύεσθαι ὥσπερ
καὶ ἐνθάδε, βρενθυόμενος καὶ τὠφθαλμὼ παραβάλ-
λων, ἠρέμα παρασκοπῶν καὶ τοὺς φιλίους καὶ τοὺς πολεμίους,
δῆλος ὢν παντὶ καὶ πάνυ πόρρωθεν ὅτι εἴ τις ἅψεται τούτου 5
τοῦ ἀνδρός, μάλα ἐρρωμένως ἀμυνεῖται. διὸ καὶ ἀσφαλῶς
ἀπῄει καὶ οὗτος καὶ ὁ ἑταῖρος· σχεδὸν γάρ τι τῶν οὕτω

διακειμένων ἐν τῷ πολέμῳ οὐδὲ ἅπτονται, ἀλλὰ τοὺς προ-
c τροπάδην φεύγοντας διώκουσιν.

πολλὰ μὲν οὖν ἄν τις καὶ ἄλλα ἔχοι Σωκράτη ἐπαινέσαι
καὶ θαυμάσια· ἀλλὰ τῶν μὲν ἄλλων ἐπιτηδευμάτων τάχ᾽ ἄν
τις καὶ περὶ ἄλλου τοιαῦτα εἴποι, τὸ δὲ μηδενὶ ἀνθρώπων
5 ὅμοιον εἶναι, μήτε τῶν παλαιῶν μήτε τῶν νῦν ὄντων, τοῦτο
ἄξιον παντὸς θαύματος. οἷος γὰρ ᾿Αχιλλεὺς ἐγένετο, ἀπει-
κάσειεν ἄν τις καὶ Βρασίδαν καὶ ἄλλους, καὶ οἷος αὖ
Περικλῆς, καὶ Νέστορα καὶ ᾿Αντήνορα (εἰσὶ δὲ καὶ ἕτεροι)
d καὶ τοὺς ἄλλους κατὰ ταῦτ᾽ ἄν τις ἀπεικάζοι· οἷος δὲ οὑτοσὶ
γέγονε τὴν ἀτοπίαν ἄνθρωπος, καὶ αὐτὸς καὶ οἱ λόγοι αὐτοῦ,
οὐδ᾽ ἐγγὺς ἄν εὕροι τις ζητῶν, οὔτε τῶν νῦν οὔτε τῶν
παλαιῶν, εἰ μὴ ἄρα εἰ οἷς ἐγὼ λέγω ἀπεικάζοι τις αὐτόν,
5 ἀνθρώπων μὲν μηδενί, τοῖς δὲ σιληνοῖς καὶ σατύροις, αὐτὸν
καὶ τοὺς λόγους.

καὶ γὰρ οὖν καὶ τοῦτο ἐν τοῖς πρώτοις παρέλιπον, ὅτι
καὶ οἱ λόγοι αὐτοῦ ὁμοιότατοί εἰσι τοῖς σιληνοῖς τοῖς διοιγο-
e μένοις. εἰ γὰρ ἐθέλοι τις τῶν Σωκράτους ἀκούειν λόγων,
φανεῖεν ἄν πάνυ γελοῖοι τὸ πρῶτον· τοιαῦτα καὶ ὀνόματα
καὶ ῥήματα ἔξωθεν περιαμπέχονται, σατύρου δή τινα ὑβρι-
στοῦ δοράν. ὄνους γὰρ κανθηλίους λέγει καὶ χαλκέας τινὰς
5 καὶ σκυτοτόμους καὶ βυρσοδέψας, καὶ ἀεὶ διὰ τῶν αὐτῶν τὰ
αὐτὰ φαίνεται λέγειν, ὥστε ἄπειρος καὶ ἀνόητος ἄνθρωπος
222 πᾶς ἄν τῶν λόγων καταγελάσειεν. διοιγομένους δὲ ἰδὼν ἄν
τις καὶ ἐντὸς αὐτῶν γιγνόμενος πρῶτον μὲν νοῦν ἔχοντας
ἔνδον μόνους εὑρήσει τῶν λόγων, ἔπειτα θειοτάτους καὶ
πλεῖστα ἀγάλματ᾽ ἀρετῆς ἐν αὐτοῖς ἔχοντας καὶ ἐπὶ πλεῖ-
5 στον τείνοντας, μᾶλλον δὲ ἐπὶ πᾶν ὅσον προσήκει σκοπεῖν
τῷ μέλλοντι καλῷ κἀγαθῷ ἔσεσθαι.

ταῦτ᾽ ἐστίν, ὦ ἄνδρες, ἃ ἐγὼ Σωκράτη ἐπαινῶ· καὶ αὖ
ἃ μέμφομαι συμμείξας ὑμῖν εἶπον ἅ με ὕβρισεν. καὶ μέν-
b τοι οὐκ ἐμὲ μόνον ταῦτα πεποίηκεν, ἀλλὰ καὶ Χαρμίδην
τὸν Γλαύκωνος καὶ Εὐθύδημον τὸν Διοκλέους καὶ ἄλλους

πάνυ πολλούς, οὓς οὗτος ἐξαπατῶν ὡς ἐραστὴς παιδικὰ
μᾶλλον αὐτὸς καθίσταται ἀντ' ἐραστοῦ.   ἃ δὴ καὶ σοὶ
λέγω, ὦ Ἀγάθων, μὴ ἐξαπατᾶσθαι ὑπὸ τούτου, ἀλλ' ἀπὸ 5
τῶν ἡμετέρων παθημάτων γνόντα εὐλαβηθῆναι, καὶ μὴ κατὰ
τὴν παροιμίαν ὥσπερ νήπιον παθόντα γνῶναι.'
    εἰπόντος δὴ ταῦτα τοῦ Ἀλκιβιάδου γέλωτα γενέσθαι c
ἐπὶ τῇ παρρησίᾳ αὐτοῦ, ὅτι ἐδόκει ἔτι ἐρωτικῶς ἔχειν τοῦ
Σωκράτους.   τὸν οὖν Σωκράτη, 'νήφειν μοι δοκεῖς,' φάναι,
'ὦ Ἀλκιβιάδη.   οὐ γὰρ ἂν ποτε οὕτω κομψῶς κύκλῳ περιβαλλόμενος ἀφανίσαι ἐνεχείρεις οὗ ἕνεκα ταῦτα πάντα 5
εἴρηκας, καὶ ὡς ἐν παρέργῳ δὴ λέγων ἐπὶ τελευτῆς αὐτὸ
ἔθηκας, ὡς οὐ πάντα τούτου ἕνεκα εἰρηκώς, τοῦ ἐμὲ καὶ
Ἀγάθωνα διαβάλλειν, οἰόμενος δεῖν ἐμὲ μὲν σοῦ ἐρᾶν καὶ d
μηδενὸς ἄλλου, Ἀγάθωνα δὲ ὑπὸ σοῦ ἐρᾶσθαι καὶ μηδ' ὑφ'
ἑνὸς ἄλλου.   ἀλλ' οὐκ ἔλαθες, ἀλλὰ τὸ σατυρικόν σου
δρᾶμα τοῦτο καὶ σιληνικὸν κατάδηλον ἐγένετο.   ἀλλ', ὦ
φίλε Ἀγάθων, μηδὲν πλέον αὐτῷ γένηται, ἀλλὰ παρα- 5
σκευάζου ὅπως ἐμὲ καὶ σὲ μηδεὶς διαβαλεῖ.'
    τὸν οὖν Ἀγάθωνα εἰπεῖν, 'καὶ μήν, ὦ Σώκρατες, κινδυ-
νεύεις ἀληθῆ λέγειν.   τεκμαίρομαι δὲ καὶ ὡς κατεκλίνη ἐν e
μέσῳ ἐμοῦ τε καὶ σοῦ, ἵνα χωρὶς ἡμᾶς διαλάβῃ.   οὐδὲν οὖν
πλέον αὐτῷ ἔσται, ἀλλ' ἐγὼ παρὰ σὲ ἐλθὼν κατακλινήσομαι.'
    'πάνυ γε,' φάναι τὸν Σωκράτη, 'δεῦρο ὑποκάτω ἐμοῦ
κατακλίνου.'   5
    'ὦ Ζεῦ,' εἰπεῖν τὸν Ἀλκιβιάδην, 'οἷα αὖ πάσχω ὑπὸ τοῦ
ἀνθρώπου.   οἴεταί μου δεῖν πανταχῇ περιεῖναι.   ἀλλ' εἰ
μή τι ἄλλο, ὦ θαυμάσιε, ἐν μέσῳ ἡμῶν ἔα Ἀγάθωνα
κατακεῖσθαι.'
    'ἀλλ' ἀδύνατον,' φάναι τὸν Σωκράτη.   'σὺ μὲν γὰρ ἐμὲ 10
ἐπῄνεσας, δεῖ δὲ ἐμὲ αὖ τὸν ἐπὶ δεξί' ἐπαινεῖν.   ἐὰν οὖν
ὑπὸ σοὶ κατακλινῇ Ἀγάθων, οὐ δήπου ἐμὲ πάλιν ἐπαι-
νέσεται, πρὶν ὑπ' ἐμοῦ μᾶλλον ἐπαινεθῆναι; ἀλλ' ἔασον,
ὦ δαιμόνιε, καὶ μὴ φθονήσῃς τῷ μειρακίῳ ὑπ' ἐμοῦ 223
ἐπαινεθῆναι· καὶ γὰρ πάνυ ἐπιθυμῶ αὐτὸν ἐγκωμιάσαι.'

b 5 ἐξαπατᾶσθε m   e 2 διαλάβῃ z: διαβαλει a: διαβάλῃ m

'ἰοῦ ἰοῦ,' φάναι τὸν Ἀγάθωνα, ' Ἀλκιβιάδη, οὐκ ἔσθ' ὅπως
ἂν ἐνθάδε μείναιμι, ἀλλὰ παντὸς μᾶλλον μεταναστήσομαι,
5 ἵνα ὑπὸ Σωκράτους ἐπαινεθῶ.'
'ταῦτα ἐκεῖνα,' φάναι τὸν Ἀλκιβιάδην, 'τὰ εἰωθότα·
Σωκράτους παρόντος τῶν καλῶν μεταλαβεῖν ἀδύνατον ἄλλῳ.
καὶ νῦν ὡς εὐπόρως καὶ πιθανὸν λόγον ηὗρεν, ὥστε παρ'
ἑαυτῷ τουτονὶ κατακεῖσθαι.'
b τὸν μὲν οὖν Ἀγάθωνα ὡς κατακεισόμενον παρὰ τῷ
Σωκράτει ἀνίστασθαι· ἐξαίφνης δὲ κωμαστὰς ἥκειν παμπόλλους ἐπὶ τὰς θύρας, καὶ ἐπιτυχόντας ἀνεῳγμέναις ἐξιόντος
τινὸς εἰς τὸ ἄντικρυς πορεύεσθαι παρὰ σφᾶς καὶ κατακλί-
5 νεσθαι, καὶ θορύβου μεστὰ πάντα εἶναι, καὶ οὐκέτι ἐν
κόσμῳ οὐδενὶ ἀναγκάζεσθαι πίνειν πάμπολυν οἶνον. τὸν
μὲν οὖν Ἐρυξίμαχον καὶ τὸν Φαῖδρον καὶ ἄλλους τινὰς ἔφη
ὁ Ἀριστόδημος οἴχεσθαι ἀπιόντας, ἓ δὲ ὕπνον λαβεῖν,
c καὶ καταδαρθεῖν πάνυ πολύ, ἅτε μακρῶν τῶν νυκτῶν οὐσῶν,
ἐξεγρέσθαι δὲ πρὸς ἡμέραν ἤδη ἀλεκτρυόνων ᾀδόντων, ἐξε-
γρόμενος δὲ ἰδεῖν τοὺς μὲν ἄλλους καθεύδοντας καὶ οἰχομένους, Ἀγάθωνα δὲ καὶ Ἀριστοφάνη καὶ Σωκράτη ἔτι
5 μόνους ἐγρηγορέναι καὶ πίνειν ἐκ φιάλης μεγάλης ἐπὶ δεξιά.
τὸν οὖν Σωκράτη αὐτοῖς διαλέγεσθαι· καὶ τὰ μὲν ἄλλα ὁ
d Ἀριστόδημος οὐκ ἔφη μεμνῆσθαι τῶν λόγων — οὔτε γὰρ ἐξ
ἀρχῆς παραγενέσθαι ὑπονυστάζειν τε — τὸ μέντοι κεφάλαιον,
ἔφη, προσαναγκάζειν τὸν Σωκράτη ὁμολογεῖν αὐτοὺς τοῦ
αὐτοῦ ἀνδρὸς εἶναι κωμῳδίαν καὶ τραγῳδίαν ἐπίστασθαι
5 ποιεῖν, καὶ τὸν τέχνῃ τραγῳδοποιὸν ὄντα καὶ κωμῳδοποιὸν
εἶναι. ταῦτα δὴ ἀναγκαζομένους αὐτοὺς καὶ οὐ σφόδρα
ἑπομένους νυστάζειν, καὶ πρότερον μὲν καταδαρθεῖν τὸν
Ἀριστοφάνη, ἤδη δὲ ἡμέρας γιγνομένης τὸν Ἀγάθωνα. τὸν
οὖν Σωκράτη, κατακοιμίσαντ' ἐκείνους, ἀναστάντα ἀπιέναι,
10 καὶ ἓ ὥσπερ εἰώθει ἕπεσθαι, καὶ ἐλθόντα εἰς Λύκειον,
ἀπονιψάμενον, ὥσπερ ἄλλοτε τὴν ἄλλην ἡμέραν διατρίβειν,
καὶ οὕτω διατρίψαντα εἰς ἑσπέραν οἴκοι ἀναπαύεσθαι.

b 8 ἓ m: εαυτον a   d 5 alt. καὶ om. a m   d 7 πρῶτον m
d 9 κατακοιμήσαντ' m   d 10 ἓ z: αὐτὸς m: om. a m

COMMENTARY

172a1–174a2: Introductory scene

Apollodorus is asked by some friends to tell them about an occasion, many years earlier, on which Socrates and others were at a party in Agathon's house. He says that only a couple of days ago he was asked the same thing by another friend; he was able to tell the story because he had heard it from Aristodemus, who was at the party, and he has checked Aristodemus' account with Socrates.

172a1 δοκῶ μοι 'I think that I...'; the apparently reflexive use of μοι is virtually confined to δοκεῖν. ἀμελέτητος 'unprepared', 'unpractised'. **a2** πρώην 'the day before yesterday', or more generally, 'the other day'. **Φαληρόθεν:** Phalerum lies on the coast east of Piraeus and two miles south-west of the city perimeter. It was one of the 170 demes of Attica, and Apollodorus' demotic is Φαληρεύς (a4). **a3** τῶν οὖν γνωρίμων τις 'a man I know'; οὖν sometimes does no more than indicate the next point in a narrative sequence (*GP* 425f.). **a4** παίζων: the humour may lie in startling Apollodorus by shouting with feigned urgency 'Hi! The man from Phalerum! *You!*' οὗτος is not always rude, but it is forceful; cf. Ar. *Birds* 1164 οὗτος τί ποιεῖς; 'Hey, what's up with *you?*' **a5** οὐ περιμενεῖς: the primary manuscripts give the present (περιμένεις) or leave the accent off. Accents had not been invented in Plato's day; but interpretation of the verb as future fits (as the present does not) colloquial usage, e.g. (on a vase-painting) οὐ παύσει; 'Stop it!' Cf. 175a10f. **a6** καὶ ὅς = 'he' survived in some fixed expressions; cf. b7 ἦ δ' ὅς 'said he'. ἔναγχος 'a little while ago'. **a7** διαπυθέσθαι...**b3** ἦσαν 'to get the whole story' (δια- and the aorist combine to suggest completeness) 'of the time when Agathon and Socrates...were all together', then, with a change of direction, lit. 'about the speeches on eros, what they were', i.e. '... (sc. and hear all) about what they said on the subject of eros'.

b3 ἀκηκοώς...**4** Φιλίππου 'having heard (sc. about it) from Phoenix the (sc. son) of Philippus'. ἀλλὰ γάρ 'but', as usually; *GP* 102f. **b5** δικαιότατος...**6** ἀπαγγέλλειν lit. 'you are most just...to report',

[77]

i.e. 'it's most appropriate that *you* should report'. τοῦ ἑταίρου 'your friend', i.e. Socrates; cf. c5f. **b8** ὅτι, unlike English 'that', can introduce direct quotation; cf. 173a5.

c2 ἐγώ γε δή 'Yes, (*sc.* I did think that)'. **c3** πόθεν 'How could you?' **c4** πολλῶν ἐτῶν '*for* many years (*sc.* past)', expressed by the genitive when joined with a negative. οὐκ ἐπιδεδήμηκεν 'has not been in Athens'; it is evident from Ar. *Frogs* 83f. that Agathon had gone (to the court of the King of Macedon, in fact) by 405. ἀφ' οὗ...6 ἐστίν 'and it's not yet three years that I've been spending my time with Socrates' (lit. 'from which...I spend...') 'and have made it my business (*sc.* in the course) of each day to know...'.

173a1 πρὸ τοῦ...**2** ὁτουοῦν 'previously, running around at random' (lit. 'whatever way I chanced') 'and thinking I was doing something (*sc.* that mattered), you can't imagine what a state I was in' (lit. 'I was more wretched than anyone whosoever'). **a2** οἰόμενος δεῖν lit. 'thinking it to be necessary', i.e. 'choosing', 'preferring'. **a3** μὴ σκῶπτ' 'don't joke', 'don't make fun of me'. **a5** ὅτι: cf. 172b8 n. ὅτε...**6** 'Αγάθων: cf. p. 9. ἢ ᾖ: ἢ ᾖ (cf. 189c3) or ἤ (without ᾖ) or ᾖ (without ἤ) are all acceptable Greek here. ἐπινίκια: the meat of the animals sacrificed as 'thanksgiving for victory' provided a good dinner, and there was plenty to drink (176a5–8). **a7** χορευταί: in *Ach.* 1154f. Aristophanes makes a comic chorus complain of the stinginess of a choregus (not dramatist) in failing to give them a dinner; possibly Agathon's generosity went further than was commonly expected of a dramatist.

b2 ἀνυπόδητος 'barefoot', like Socrates himself (174a4). **b3** ἐραστής: cf. p. 4. ἐν τοῖς...**4** τότε lit. 'among those (*sc.* who were) most (*sc.* so) of those at that time', i.e. 'as much as anyone at that time'. **b4** οὐ μέντοι ἀλλά 'but, mind you', or 'but, of course'; *GP* 30f. **b5** ἤδη 'afterwards'; the appropriate temporal adverb or phrase for translation of ἤδη must always be chosen in the light of the context. **b6** τί οὖν...**7** μοι lit. 'Why didn't you tell me, then?', i.e. 'Well, go on, tell me.' Cf. *Meno* 92d τί δ' αὐτῷ οὐ σὺ ἔφρασας; 'but why don't *you* tell him?' (*MT* 18). **b7** πάντως 'in any case'. **b9** περὶ αὐτῶν 'about it'; with this indefinite reference, Greek often prefers the plural.

c1 ἀμελετήτως: cf. 172a1. **εἰ οὖν...2 ποιεῖν** 'Well, if I'm to tell you about it too, that's what we should do'; the tone is cheerful, not grudging (cf. 175b4, 210b2). **c3 ἄλλως...4 χωρίς...5 χαίρω** 'anyway,...quite apart from...', then lit. 'extraordinarily how I enjoy it', i.e. 'it's extraordinary how...'; the idiom is common with words meaning 'wonderful', etc. (e.g. 200b1). **ἄλλως τε...6 χρηματιστικῶν** lit. 'otherwise and yours, (sc. namely) those of the rich and engaged-in-moneymaking', i.e. 'particularly the talk of you men who are rich and concerned with business'. A genitive plural following ὁ ἡμέτερος or ὁ ὑμέτερος refers to the 'we' or 'you' implicit in the possessive adjective; cf. also 193b5 n. ἀλλ- τε καί... 'both other and...' means 'especially'; thus λόγους ἄλλους τε καὶ τοὺς ὑμετέρους would mean 'your talk especially', but the adverb ἄλλως tends to oust, in phrases of this type, forms of ἄλλος and other words with the stem ἀλλ- (cf. 176d6, 194d4), and in the present passage ἄλλους τινάς has already been used to mean 'talk about subjects other than philosophy'. **c7 ἄχθομαι ...ἐλεῶ** 'get bored and feel sorry for...' **τι ποιεῖν:** cf. 173a1.

d1 καὶ ἴσως...3 οἶδα: Apollodorus misleads his friends by saying humbly 'and I think' (or 'I dare say') 'you're right', but then turns the tables on them: 'but I don't (sc. just) *think* that *you* are miserable creatures – I *know* you are!' This is banter, not preaching, as the continuation shows. **d8 μαλακός:** μανικός is a variant. μαλακός 'soft', 'impressionable' (commonly contrasted with σκληρός 'hard', 'unfeeling') suits Apollodorus, who upset everyone at Socrates' death by unrestrained howling (*Phd.* 117d). Then the point of d8 ἐν μέν...9 ἀγριαίνεις will be 'because you're always so *fierce*!' In *Rep.* 410d ἀγριότης and σκληρότης are together contrasted with μαλακία and ἡμερότης. ει καὶ δῆλον...3 παραπαίω must be sarcastic, picking up the implication of ἀγριαίνεις: 'Yes, and it's obvious, I suppose, that I'm crazy' (he means 'and aren't I *right* to be crazy?'). If Plato wrote μανικός 'crazy' in d8, the sarcasm of e1–3 would still be intelligible, but the sequence of thought in 'I *don't know why* you're called μανικός, *for* you're always so ἄγριος' would not. The variant μανικός probably originated in an ancient conjecture based on e1–3 and motivated by the fact that μαλακός (like μαλθακός) *could* be (in the sense 'cowardly', 'effeminate') intolerably opprobrious. τοιοῦτος is 'as you are now'.

e4 οὐκ ἄξιον ἐρίζειν 'let's not quarrel'. **e5 μὴ ἄλλως ποιήσῃς** lit. 'don't do otherwise (but...)', a common formula of entreaty (e.g. Ar. *Birds* 133, in a pressing invitation). **e7 τοιοίδε τινές** 'something like this', the demonstrative looking foward; then Apollodorus changes his intention (μᾶλλον δ') and decides to begin at the beginning.

174a3–175e10: Socrates arrives at Agathon's house

Aristodemus said: he met Socrates, who was on his way to a party at Agathon's house, and Socrates persuaded him to come too. Aristodemus arrived first, because Socrates, deep in thought, fell behind. Agathon welcomed Aristodemus. Socrates arrived halfway through the meal.

The narrative begins here, introduced by ἔφη in 174a3. The rest of the work is expressed in the constructions of reported speech, e.g. 175d3 καὶ τὸν Σωκράτη καθίζεσθαι 'and Socrates sat down', mixed with periodic reminders that the whole story is told by Aristodemus and also with passages which ignore this fact. Thus in 174a9 'ἀλλὰ σύ,' ἦ δ' ὅς, 'πῶς ἔχεις...' b3 'ἕπου τοίνυν', ἔφη '"but you", said (*sc.* Socrates to Aristodemus), "how do you feel...?"' And I, said (*sc.* Aristodemus to me), said "Just as you tell me." "Come with me, then," said (*sc.* Socrates to Aristodemus) ....' We have to remember that ἔφη mostly means 'Aristodemus said to me' but sometimes (e.g. 193d6) 'So-and-so said to So-and-so' within the story which Aristodemus is telling.

Where the infinitive constructions of reported speech are used, the personal pronoun referring to the narrator is the 'semi-reflexive', accus. ἕ (e.g. 175a6 καὶ ἓ μὲν ἔφη ἀπονίζειν τὸν παῖδα 'and he said that the slave washed him'), gen. οὗ (e.g. 174d6 καὶ περιμένοντος οὗ κελεύειν προϊέναι 'and when he waited (*sc.* for Socrates, Socrates) told him to go on'), dat. οἷ (e.g. 174e2 οἱ μὲν γάρ...παῖδα... ἀπαντήσαντα ἄγειν 'for a slave met him and took him...'). The dative also has an enclitic form οἱ, as in 174a3 ἔφη γάρ οἱ Σωκράτη ἐντυχεῖν 'for he said that Socrates met him'. The plural is σφᾶς, σφῶν, σφίσι, e.g. 174d4 τοιαῦτ' ἄττα σφᾶς ἔφη διαλεχθέντας ἰέναι 'he said that after talking in that way they (i.e. he and Socrates) went on their way'. The pronoun αὐτ- refers to persons other than the narrator, e.g. 174a4f. καὶ ἐρέσθαι αὐτόν 'and (*sc.* Aristodemus) asked him (i.e. Socrates)'; when such a person is subject of the infinitive, τόν may be used, e.g. 174a6 καὶ τὸν εἰπεῖν 'and he (i.e. Socrates) said...'.

174 a3 λελουμένον τε...4 ἐποίει: Socrates commonly went unshod (cf. 220b6 and Ar. *Clouds* 103). It sounds here as if he also went unwashed, and Ar. *Birds* 1554 calls him ἄλουτος. But he washes the morning after the party (223d11 ἀπονιψάμενον); we should distinguish between washing off sweat and surface dirt (ἀπονίζεσθαι) and having a good bath (λούεσθαι) followed by oiling and preening. In Ar. *Birds* 132 and *Plutus* 615 λούεσθαι is associated with feasting and celebration; we do not say 'next Wednesday have a bath and come to my birthday party', but evidently the Greeks did. **βλαύτας** 'slippers'. **εἰς 'Αγάθωνος:** as in English, 'to Agathon's (*sc.* house)'. **a7 ὄχλον:** the word is not always derogatory, any more than 'crush' in English. **a8 ταῦτα δή** 'that's why...'; cf. ταῦτ' ἄρα 'so that's why...!' **ἐκαλλωπισάμην** 'I made myself look nice'. **a9 παρὰ καλόν:** Agathon was notably good-looking (cf. 213c3–5). The first scene of Ar. *Thesmophoriazusae* (e.g. 29–35) treats him as effeminate; perhaps he shaved his beard very close, to imitate the appearance of a youth whose beard is only just growing (an appearance attractive to the Greeks; cf. *Prt.* 309ab) and to maintain in adulthood a subordinate role *vis-à-vis* Pausanias (cf. p. 8). **πῶς ἔχεις...b1 ἰέναι** lit. 'in what condition are you with regard to being willing ἄν to go...?', i.e. 'how do you feel' (cf. 176b7) 'about possibly being willing...?'. ἄν is odd, but serves to make Socrates' question tentative and diffident. The manuscripts actually have not ἄν ἰέναι but ἀνιέναι 'go up'; that, however, is never used of simply going to someone's house.

b3 ἵνα...6 παροιμίαν 'to disprove' (διαφθείρωμεν 'spoil', 'ruin', 'undermine') 'the proverb by changing it (*sc.* to make it say) that after all' (ἄρα, i.e. contrary to what is generally said) 'good men go of their own accord' (i.e. without being invited) 'to the feasts of good men'. Homer, says Socrates (b5–c4), comes close (κινδυνεύει 'risks') to treating the proverb with contempt (ὑβρίσαι) by portraying an inferior man as coming uninvited to the feast of a better man. Evidently the proverb which Plato had in mind said that good men come uninvited to the feasts of inferior men, and that is what we find in Eupolis fr. 289, where the archaic word δειλῶν is used ('cowardly' in Plato's Attic, but much less specific in archaic poetry, sometimes simply 'poor'). Such a proverb is insulting if uttered by a guest and obsequious on the lips of a host; an alternative version, with ἀγαθοί and ἀγαθῶν, is useful on a greater variety of occasions, and that is the form of the proverb cited from Hesiod (fr. 264) and implied by Bacchylides fr. 22.4–6. If Plato had that in mind, and intended the sequence of letters αγαθων (he wrote before breathings, accents, apostrophes, etc., had been invented) to be interpreted as 'Αγάθων' (accusative or dative; slightly shaky grammar, but possible), μεταβαλόντες makes sense (it would have been clearer if he had added ὀλίγον), but διαφθείρωμεν does not; in Grg. 495a and Prt. 360a to διαφθείρειν a promise or agreement is to break it and nullify it. (The proverb in Hesiod is a complete hexameter; but since very many proverbs had the metrical form ◡◡ – ◡◡ – ◡ ◡ – – Plato has inverted the ingredients of the verse so as to start off in that rhythm.)

c1 μαλθακὸν αἰχμητήν: Homer nowhere portrays Menelaus as a 'soft warrior'; he portrays Apollo as trying to bring Hector back into the battle by the taunt that he has been worsted by a 'soft warrior', Menelaus (*Il.* 17.587f.). A Greek citing poetry seldom takes notice of the context in which the words were uttered, by whom, to whom, or (most important of all) for what purpose. **c2 θυσίαν...3 θοίνην** 'when Agamemnon was performing a sacrifice and entertaining...' (in *Il.* 2.408). θοίνη is 'feast'. **c3 χείρω...4 ἀμείνονος** 'a man who was not so good to the feast of the better man'. **c5 κινδυνεύσω:** the notion of 'risk' is prominent here (cf. b5), but the word shades into 'be likely to...'. **c6 ὡς σὺ λέγεις:** with reference to b3–5. **c7 φαῦλος** 'mediocre', 'undistinguished', contrastable with any favourable evaluative term; sometimes 'useless', 'bad'. **σοφοῦ:** down to the late fifth century B.C. σοφία usually denoted artistic or technical skill (applied to a poet, σοφός is 'good'); the denotation 'intelligence', 'wisdom' (*sc.* in understanding how to live and behave) did not oust the earlier denotation, but was added to it (*GPM* 119–23). **ὅρα οὖν** 'so you'd better consider...'.

d2 σύν τε...ὁδοῦ: in *Il.* 10.222–6 Diomede asks Nestor that someone should go with him into the enemy camp, since 'when two go

together, one has an idea before the other' (καί τε πρὸ ὁ τοῦ ἐνόησεν),
i.e. one of the two has an idea which the other might not have had. If
πρὸ ὁ τοῦ is what Plato wrote, it does not fit βουλευσόμεθα at all well,
and might be taken by a reader with what precedes: 'going together,
one in front of the other'. He probably wrote πρὸ ὁδοῦ, which in
Il. 4.382 means 'further on the way', deliberately altering Homer;
he quotes the line correctly in *Prt.* 348d.   **d3 ἀλλ':** as often with
orders and exclamations, 'come on, now, ...!'   **d5 ἑαυτῷ...νοῦν**
'turning his thoughts inward.'   **d6 ὑπολειπόμενον** 'falling behind'.

e1 καί τι...2 παθεῖν: 'suffer' is often much too strong for πάσχειν;
γελοῖόν τι ἔπαθον is sometimes 'a funny thing happened to me',
sometimes 'I was put into a ridiculous position'.   **παῖδα** 'slave', as
often.   **e3 τῶν ἔνδοθεν** *sc.* παίδων.   **e4 καταλαμβάνειν** 'and he
found them' (cf. e1).   **δ' οὖν** 'anyway', i.e. in spite of his lateness.
e5 εἰς καλόν...6 ἰδεῖν lit. 'you have come into a good (*sc.* occasion)
...', i.e. 'Ah! Just the man we wanted!' Agathon's courtesy to an
uninvited guest is exemplary; we cannot easily tell whether we are
meant to think that he really looked for Aristodemus the day before.
εἰς αὖθις ἀναβαλοῦ 'put it off to some other occasion'.   **e8 Σωκράτη:**
173b2–4 explains why Agathon should have expected Socrates to be
with Aristodemus.   **e10 καὶ αὐτός** 'that *I* had come *with* Socrates',
lit. 'that I myself also...'.   **e12 καλῶς...σύ** lit. 'doing well you (*sc.*
have come)', i.e. 'I'm very glad you have!'

175a6 ἀπονίζειν 'wash' – his feet, that is, and probably also his hands,
before getting on a couch.   **a7 οὗτος:** not 'this Socrates (*sc.* whom
you told me to fetch)' but with a gesture, 'Socrates is here – he's
retreated and is standing in the porch next door', using the demonstrative pronoun, as normally, where we would use an adverb.
a10 ἄτοπόν γ' 'extraordinary', 'odd'; the word acquired an in-
creasingly derogatory flavour. Cf. W. G. Arnott, *Phoenix* 18 (1964)
119–22.

b1 ἔθος...2 ἔχει lit. 'for he has this (*sc.* as) a certain habit', i.e. 'it's
one of his ways'. 220c3–d4 relates a spectacular example.   **ὅποι ἂν
τύχῃ** '*any*where'; cf. 173a1.   **b6 πάντως...c1 ἐπαινῶμεν:** πάντως
with an imperative is 'at all costs' or 'come what may' (cf. 173b7),

but ἐπειδάν... 'when*ever*...' and νῦν οὖν 'so *now*...' (indicating that a consequence is being drawn from what precedes) show that παρατίθετε is in fact indicative: 'in any case, you serve up whatever you like whenever there's no one supervising you – and I've never supervised you. So now, ...'. Agathon is simultaneously putting his slaves on their mettle, boasting that they are so skilled as to need no supervision, and perhaps also exploiting a conventional joke that whatever one orders, one gets what the cook sends in and the slaves serve up (cf. Ar. *Clouds* 5–7 for a grumble about the difficulty of disciplining one's slaves in wartime).

c4 ἥκειν...6 δειπνοῦντας: on οὖν cf. 172a3 n. Given Aristodemus' assurance (b2f.) 'he'll be along in a moment', ὡς εἰώθει does not mean that Socrates usually spent a *long* time in this way, but qualifies διατρίψαντα. ἀλλά contrasts with οὐ although the subjects are different: 'in fact, they were about halfway through their meal'. **c7 ἔσχατον:** cf. p. 11. **c8 τοῦ σοφοῦ:** cf. 174c7 n.

d1 προθύροις: singular (a8) and plural are used indifferently in this word. **d2 οὐ γὰρ ἂν προαπέστης** 'for (*sc.* otherwise) you wouldn't have come away before (*sc.* you'd got it)'. **d3 καθίζεσθαι:** he puts his feet up later (176a1), as invited (175c8). **d4 τοιοῦτον:** a noun of any gender may have a neuter predicate; so here '...a thing of such a kind', and cf. 176d1 χαλεπόν...ἡ μέθη ἐστίν. **d6 ὥσπερ...7 κενωτέραν:** the siphoning of liquid from one cup (κύλιξ) to another by a strip or thread of wool (ἔριον) is slow, but it works.

e1 πολλοῦ τιμῶμαι 'I value very highly'. **οἶμαι...2 πληρωθήσεσθαι:** normally 'I think I shall...' would have no με, and whatever agreed with 'I' would be in the nominative; here the contrast and juxtaposition of 'I' and 'from you' cause an abnormality. **e3 ἂν εἴη** 'must be', 'is surely'; cf. *MT* 79. **ἀμφισβητήσιμος...οὖσα** lit. 'debatable as if in a dream', i.e. 'illusory'. **e4 πολλήν...ἔχουσα** lit. 'having much growth', i.e. 'with a great future before it' (cf. e5 νέου ὄντος). **ἤ γε** 'seeing that it...'; so often when γε is added to the relative. **e6 πρώην:** cf. 172a2 n. **ἐν μάρτυσι...τρισμυρίοις:** at the Lenaea (cf. p. 9). 'Thirty thousand' is the traditional number of male citizens of Athens even in the early fourth century (e.g. Ar. *Eccle-*

siazusae 1132). Socrates says Ἑλλήνων advisedly, since foreigners went to the theatre too, though at the Lenaea these would be mostly resident aliens (cf. Ar. *Ach.* 502–5). **e7 ὑβριστής:** someone who treats others with contempt, ridicule or violence, as if they had no rights. The tone here is: 'Why, you old...!'; Agathon perceives irony in Socrates' words. Cf. 215b7. **e8 διαδικασόμεθα...9 Διονύσῳ** 'we'll argue our rival claims to σοφία, and Dionysus shall be the judge' (because we shall be full of wine, his gift to mankind). In the end, it is logic, not drunken confidence or sentimentality which helps the reader to decide the question (199c3–201c9).

176a1–178a5: Eryximachus' proposal

After the meal Pausanias said ' We all drank too much yesterday, so tonight let's talk, and drink only moderately.' All agreed. Eryximachus said ' Phaedrus pointed out to me that no one has composed an encomium on Eros. Let us therefore take turns to pronounce one.' Socrates agreed, and so did they all.

The decision is taken in a manner which reflects Athenian democratic practice. When no one has spoken up in favour of hard drinking, Eryximachus says (176e4–9) 'Well, since that's agreed (δέδοκται)..., I propose (εἰσηγοῦμαι)...'. His first proposal clears the ground ('send the αὐλητρίς away'), and is followed by his statement that he has a constructive proposal (176e9f.). They wish to hear it, so he makes a speech for it (177a2f. ἡ μέν μοι ἀρχὴ τοῦ λόγου ἐστί... d5). No one, says Socrates, will 'vote against it' (d6f.); and Socrates, exhorting Phaedrus to begin, uses the phrase τύχῃ ἀγαθῇ (e5), which sometimes heads the published text of a decree passed by the Assembly.

176a2 σπονδάς...3 νομιζόμενα: after a meal libations were poured to the gods and a song of salutation (παιών) was sung (hence lit. 'having sung the god'). With 'and the usual things as well' (lit. '... the things which are done as a custom...'; cf. νόμος in 181d7, etc.) understand 'having done' (e.g. putting wreaths on their heads); for the elliptical expression cf. Hdt. 4.106 'they wear clothing like that of the Scythians, but (*sc.* speak) a language of their own'. **a5 εἶεν** 'Well, now!', recognising (as in 213e7) the establishment of a situation and suggesting that the next step should be considered. **ῥᾷστα** 'most comfortably' (cf. b1). **a6 ἐγώ...ὑμῖν** 'Well, I can

tell you!'   **a7 χθές:** cf. 173a6f. ἀναψυχῆς 'respite'. **a8 τοὺς πολλούς**
sc. χαλεπῶς ἔχειν κτλ.

b2 μέντοι often (especially in comic and prose dialogue) reinforces a
personal or demonstrative pronoun: '*that*'s a good idea!'   **b3 τὸ
παντί. . .4 πόσεως** lit. 'the providing-for-ourselves in every way a
certain taking-it-easy of our drinking', i.e. 'to make sure anyway. . .'.
βεβαπτισμένων lit. 'sunk', 'drowned'.   **b5 'Ερυξίμαχον τὸν 'Ακου-**
μενοῦ: he is a doctor (d1); we meet him in Phaedrus' company in
Prt. 315c, where they have gone to Callias' house to listen to the great
sophists. He and Phaedrus were both denounced for mutilating the
herms in 415 (Andocides 1.15, 35). Acumenus is the name of another
friend of Phaedrus (*Phdr.* 227a), of a man denounced in 415 for
parodying the Mysteries (Andocides 1.18), and of a man mentioned
by Xenophon (*Mem.* 3.13.2) as if he were a doctor. Those three
Acumeni are probably all the same man, and a brother or cousin of
Eryximachus rather than his father.   **b6 καὶ ἔτι. . .7 'Αγάθων** lit. 'and
I still want to hear from one of you in what state Agathon is with
regard to being strong enough for drinking'; ἐρρῶσθαι (~ ῥωννύναι
'strengthen') is often 'be in good health' or, as we say, 'be fit'.
Agathon, who answers in b8, is plainly the 'one of you', and Vahlen
suggested putting a comma after πίνειν and emending to 'Αγάθωνος:
'hear from one of you. . . (*sc.* namely) from Agathon'.   **b8 οὐδ' αὐτός:**
the opposite of καὶ αὐτός: '*I*'m not feeling up to it, *either*.'

c1 ἕρμαιον 'a stroke of luck'; the unexpected finding of something
good was conventionally credited to Hermes.   **c3 ἀπειρήκατε** 'have
given up'.   **c4 ἐξαιρῶ λόγου** lit. 'I take out of account', i.e. 'I make
an exception of. . .'.   **κατ' ἀμφότερα** 'either way'; on Socrates'
immunity to the effects of wine cf. 214a3–5.   **c5 ἐξαρκέσει** 'it'll be
all right with him'; cf. 177e5.   **c7 ἴσως. . .8 ἀηδής** lit. 'perhaps I
would be less displeasing telling the truth about drunkenness, what
kind of thing it is', i.e. 'perhaps you won't mind so much if I. . .'.
Eryximachus can never resist reminding the company that he
possesses specialised knowledge.   **c8 οἶμαι** is often used (like 'I
think' in English) when the speaker does not merely 'think' but feels
certain and invites no discussion.

d1 χαλεπόν 'harmful', 'a bad thing'; on the neuter, cf. 175d4 n.

d2 ἑκὼν εἶναι: when immediately following ἑκών, ἐνθάδε or νῦν, εἶναι '(*sc.* so as) to be' means much the same as γε: 'I wouldn't wish – if I could help it, anyway –'. **πόρρω** lit. 'far', here 'deep'; cf. English 'far on', 'far gone'. **d3 συμβουλεύσαιμι** *sc.* πόρρω πιεῖν. **ἄλλως τε καὶ κραιπαλῶντα** 'especially when one has a hangover'; on ἄλλως τε cf. 173c5 n. The accusative of the participle is used, not a dative agreeing with ἄλλῳ, because the analysis is not 'I couldn't advise another, when he has a hangover, to drink deep' but 'I couldn't advise another that one should drink deep when one has a hangover.' **d5 Φαῖδρον τὸν Μυρρινούσιον:** cf. b5 n. Phaedrus' deme (cf. 172a2 n.) is Myrrhinus. An inscription shows that he is the Phaedrus named, without demotic, by Andocides 1.35 as denounced in 415 for mutilating herms. **d7 καὶ οἱ λοιποί** *sc.* πείσονται; cf. a8 n.

e2 οὕτω 'simply', 'just' (joined in 180c5 with ἁπλῶς). **e3 πρὸς ἡδονήν:** the opposition to διὰ μέθης (e1; cf. e5f.) carries the revealing implication that excessive drinking at a party could be more a social obligation than a pleasure; cf. p. 11. **e5 ἐπάναγκες** 'compulsory'. **e6 τὸ μετὰ τοῦτο εἰσηγοῦμαι** 'the next thing I propose is...'. **τὴν μέν...ἐᾶν** lit. 'allow...to rejoice', i.e. 'let go', 'not bother about...'; the idiom is based on the use of χαῖρε as a word of farewell. Slave-girls playing αὐλοί (not 'flutes', but more like recorders) are often depicted on vase-paintings at parties (cf. 212c8), and the paintings also suggest that when everyone had drunk a lot these girls might interest the guests more as sexual partners than as accompanists of the singing. **e7 ταῖς ἔνδον:** the womenfolk of a household kept to their own quarters while male guests were entertained; recollection of the presence of a woman at a symposium could be used in court (Dem. 59.48) as evidence that she was not of citizen status.

177a1 φάναι...βούλεσθαι 'they all said that they did want (*sc.* him to)'. **a3 κατὰ τὴν Εὐριπίδου...4 μῦθος:** in a citation (fr. 484) from a lost play of Euripides, *Melanippe the wise*, the heroine prefaces a didactic speech about the origin of the world with the words οὐκ ἐμὸς ὁ μῦθος ἀλλὰ τῆς μητρὸς πάρα. **a5 πρός με:** after πρός the enclitic με is not uncommon in place of the expected ἐμέ. **ἀγανακτῶν**

'complaining', 'taking it hard'. **a7 παιῶνας:** cf. 176a3 n. **a8 τηλικούτῳ** 'so old'; cf. 178a8–c2.

b1 εἰ δὲ βούλει κτλ. 'or, if you like to look at the good sophists, that they write speeches in praise of Herakles…'; since σκοπεῖν (aorist σκέψασθαι) is not used with the accusative and infinitive to mean 'consider that…', the infinitive συγγράφειν must be regarded as still depending on οὐ δεινόν 'isn't it extraordinary…' in a5. The words from καὶ τοῦτο μέν (b4) to ἐγκεκωμιασμένα (c1) are grammatically a self-contained parenthesis; when the main sentence is resumed, τὸ οὖν…ποιήσασθαι (c1f.) recapitulates the point made in the parenthesis, and Ἔρωτα δὲ κτλ. in c2 states a contrast not with 'Herakles and others' but with 'things like that' (c1 τοιούτων μέν). In c1 τό with the infinitive is most easily interpreted as an indignant exclamation, 'to think that…'; *MT* 321. **b2 τοὺς χρηστοὺς σοφιστάς:** σοφιστής originally denoted a good practitioner of any art or skill (cf. 174c7 n.), but later someone who taught skills, including oratory and political practice, and it acquired a certain connotation of dishonest or amoral purpose; hence Phaedrus' specification 'the *good* sophists'. χρηστός (to be distinguished from χρήσιμος 'useful') is the most general word of commendation in fourth-century Attic. **b3 καταλογάδην συγγράφειν:** συγγράφειν is the word normally used of all prose writing, whether literary or documentary; for poetry the appropriate word is ποιεῖν (cf. 205b8–c10). καταλογάδην 'in prose' is contrasted in Isocrates 2.7 with 'in metre'. **b4 Πρόδικος:** Prodicus of Ceos, well known in late fifth-century Athens (cf. *Prt.* 315cd), was the author of an allegory (summarised in Xen. *Mem.* 2.1.21–34) in which Virtue and Vice present Herakles with a choice between opposing paths, and he chooses the path of Virtue. **b4 ἧττον καὶ θαυμαστόν** 'not so very surprising'. **b5 ἀνδρός…6 ὠφελίαν:** Isocrates 9.12 refers to people who compose encomia on 'bumble-bees and salt (ἅλες) and the like', and there is strong reason to think he is referring to the early fourth-century sophist Polycrates. πρὸς ὠφελίαν is lit. 'with reference to usefulness'.

c1 πέρι: περί often follows the substantive which it governs, and is then accented on the ε; cf. 181c3, 208d6. **c3 τετολμηκέναι** 'to have ventured'. **ἀλλ':** contrasting with the negative in μηδένα (c2); cf.

175c4. **c5 τούτῳ:** i.e. Phaedrus. **ἔρανον:** most commonly used of a loan made for (sometimes organised) philanthropic motives; here 'contribution'. **c6 ἅμα δ':** we expect another infinitive clause dependent on ἐπιθυμῶ, but a fresh sentence begins, as commonly in a μέν/δέ coordination; *GP* 371f. **c7 κοσμῆσαι** 'adorn'.

d1 διατριβή can connote delay or idleness, but often does not; in e2 it is close to 'occupation', and here 'enough to keep us busy' seems appropriate. **d2 λόγον...3 Ἔρωτος** 'a speech (*sc.* as) praise...'; cf. *Phdr.* 260b συντιθεὶς λόγον ἔπαινον κατὰ τοῦ ὄνου 'composing a speech in praise of the donkey'. **ἐπὶ δεξιά...4 κατάκειται:** cf. p. 11. **d5 πατήρ:** so in *Phdr.* 257b Socrates calls Lysias 'father' of a speech which a provocative composition by Lysias has 'compelled' (237a) Socrates to utter. **d8 ἐρωτικά:** cf. p. 4. **Ἀγάθων καὶ Παυσανίας:** the implication that Agathon and Pausanias are erotic partners is made explicit in 193b7; cf. p. 3. In *Prt.* 315e they are together in Callias' house, Agathon a 'youth' at the time, and Socrates says 'I shouldn't be surprised if he's Pausanias' paidika.' When Agathon emigrated to Macedon (cf. 172c4 n.), Pausanias followed (Aelian, *Varia historia* 2.21).

e1 περὶ Διόνυσον καὶ Ἀφροδίτην: the characters in Aristophanic comedy greatly enjoy alcohol and sex, the provinces of Dionysus and Aphrodite respectively, but we should form a curiously deficient idea of the nature of that comedy if it were all lost and we had only this passage to go on. **e3 οὐκ ἐξ ἴσου...ἡμῖν** 'it isn't fair on us'. **e5 ἐξαρκέσει** implies 'we shan't compete'; cf. 176c5. **τύχῃ ἀγαθῇ:** a verbal obeisance to good fortune; cf. p. 85.

178a3 ἃ δὲ μάλιστα *sc.* ἐμέμνητο. **καὶ ὧν...ἀξιομνημόνευτον** 'and what it seemed to me to be worth speaking of'; the grammar is odd, implying that one could say *ἀξιομνημόνευτόν ἐστιν αὐτῶν = ἄξιόν ἐστι μνησθῆναι αὐτῶν 'it is worthwhile to speak of them'.

178a6–180b8: Phaedrus' speech

Eros is among the oldest of deities, and he has brought the greatest blessings to mankind; for the erastes is anxious to excel, and afraid to fall short, in the eyes of his eromenos. Eros inspires courage and self-sacrifice; consider the legendary examples – Alcestis, Orpheus, Achilles. The gods respect him who is inspired by Eros.

Phaedrus confines himself to certain ingredients of standard encomia: nobility of lineage and responsibility for good consequences. The continued existence of a Greek city-state was felt to depend on the willingness of its defenders to fight bravely and die, if need be, in its defence; hence the 'greatest blessing' for a community was that its members should be inspired with courage. Cf. *GPM* 161–3.

178a6 ὥσπερ λέγω: the reference (for the present tense cf. 186e4) is to 177d3f.–e5f. **a7** ἐνθένδε...ὅτι lit. 'from here from somewhere, that...', i.e. 'by making the point, more or less, that...'. The vagueness reminds us (as does the fact that Phaedrus' opening is only summarised) that exact recollection is not guaranteed. **a8** πολλαχῇ ...γένεσιν lit. 'in many other ways, and not least...'; English usually omits the forward-looking 'other'. **a9** οὐχ...δέ 'and not', common only with fixed phrases such as 'not least' or 'not only'; cf. however 180c7 n. and *GP* 186f. τὸ γάρ...**b1** τίμιον: the clause τό...θεόν is the subject, τίμιον (*sc.* ἐστί) the predicate. For ἐν τοῖς πρεσβύτατον 'among the oldest', cf. c1; ἐν τοῖς with a superlative which does not agree with τοῖς is a fixed phrase.

b2 γονῆς...**3** ποιητοῦ: after 'evidence for this is...', which we would commonly follow with a colon in English, an introductory γάρ is normal; cf. *GP* 58f. οὔτε λέγονται is untrue, for many poets (e.g. Alcaeus fr. 327) had specified the parents of Eros; but different poets gave him different parents, and Phaedrus naturally gives most weight to the poets cited in the next few lines, 'specialists' in divine genealogy. ἰδιώτου 'layman', contrasted here with 'poet', elsewhere with 'doctor', 'craftsman', 'magistrate', 'politician' or (as in d3) 'state'. **b3** Ἡσίοδος: in *Theog.* 116f., 120 (Phaedrus omits 118f.). **b6** ἕδος 'seat'. **b8** Ἡσιόδῳ...σύμφησιν: after the quotation from Hesiod the manuscripts continue: φησὶ μετὰ τὸ Χάος κτλ. The absence of any connecting particle is odd, and the simple restatement of what is already stated in the quotation is no less so. The probability is that Plato wrote here the words which in the manuscripts come after the quotation (b11) from Parmenides, and that the word φησί is a stop-gap interpolation occasioned by the misplacing. Stobaeus (*Eclogae* 1.9.12) omits the quotations from b3–11 (they have already been given, on their own, in 1.9.5 and 1.9.6), and then goes on 'Ἡσιόδῳ δὲ καὶ 'Ακουσίλεως ξύμφησιν ἐν τοῖς πρεσβυτάτοις (sic) εἶναι; from this the classical and characteristically Platonic σύμφησι is worth rescuing, in preference to the banal ὁμολογεῖ of the manuscripts. **b9 Παρμενί-δης...b10** λέγει 'Parmenides speaks of his birth, (*sc.* saying)...' or '...says, on the subject of his birth, ...'. **b11 μητίσατο:** the subject of the verb ('devised') in this isolated line (b13) is uncertain; Plutarch makes it Aphrodite, Simplicius 'the deity who steers all things' (b12.3). *HGP* ii 60 n. 3, recalling 195c1–3, suggests Ananke, 'Necessity'.

c1 πολλαχόθεν 'in many sources', 'by many authorities'. **ἐν τοῖς πρεσβύτατος:** cf. a9 n. **c3 ὅτι** 'what' (agreeing with ἀγαθόν), not 'that...'. **c4 εὐθὺς νέῳ ὄντι** lit. 'at once for one being young', i.e. 'right from boyhood'. **c5 παιδικά** *sc.* χρηστά; on the noun, cf. p. 4. **ἀνθρώποις...βίου:** ἡγεῖσθαι + dative + genitive is 'lead (a person) in (a thing)'. **c6 συγγένεια** 'kinship', *sc.* with distinguished people. **c7 τιμαί:** particularly election to public office.

d1 τὴν ἐπί...2 φιλοτιμίαν: any act or condition is αἰσχρόν which makes the agent seem inferior, for any reason, in the eyes of others, but especially if it is induced by cowardice (cf. d5f.), meanness, sloth or lack of ambition. φιλοτιμία 'love of honour' is what makes us strive for achievements which will earn the admiration of others; cf. *GPM* 230–42. **οὐ γάρ...4 ἐξεργάζεσθαι:** ἐστί 'it is possible' may be followed by a dative and infinitive ('it is possible *for* a man to...') or (as here) by an accusative and infinitive ('it is possible *that* a man should...'). It is a common Greek belief that the desire to be honoured and the fear of incurring contempt are the essential motives of good action; cf. *GPM* 232. On ἰδιώτης cf. 178b3 n. **ἄνδρα ὅστις ἐρᾷ** '...that a man who is in love...'. **d5 πάσχων:** cf. 174e2 n. **d6 δι' ἀνανδρίαν μὴ ἀμυνόμενος** 'failing, through unmanliness, to defend himself'.

e1 ταὐτόν...2 ὅτι lit. 'and we see also the eromenos this same (*sc.* thing) that...', i.e. 'and we see that the eromenos too, in just the same way, ...'. **αἰσχύνεται:** not 'is ashamed *of*...', but 'feels shame *towards*...'. **e3 εἰ οὖν...γένοιτο:** Phaedrus presents the idea of a city or army (στρατόπεδον) of erastai and their eromenoi as a purely hypothetical possibility (cf. Hdt. 5.3.1, imagining the Thracians united, and Thuc. 2.97.6, on the Scythians). What is said in Xen. *Smp.* 8.32 about such an army (with explicit mention of Thebes) is in more restrained terms; cf. p. 10. **e5 οὐκ ἔστιν... 179a1 ἀλλήλους:** *prima facie* 'they would run their own (*sc.* country) in the best possible way' (lit. 'there is not a way in which better...'); then ἤ 'than' comes as a surprise, for it makes us retranslate 'there is no better way they could run their own country *than by* abstaining...'. We can understand 'as erastai and their eromenoi naturally would', but Rückert's deletion of ἤ is tempting: 'for they would abstain...'. οἰκεῖν, often 'inhabit', also covers constitutional, administrative and social practice.

179a1 καὶ μαχόμενοί γ' ἂν μετ' ἀλλήλων 'yes, and if men like that fought beside one another...'; English 'fight with...' in the sense 'fight against...' is expressed in Greek by the dative or by πρός + accusative. **a2 ὡς ἔπος εἰπεῖν** lit. 'so as to say an utterance', i.e. 'virtually', qualifying πάντας; in Attic prose the expression most often occurs with 'all' or 'none' (cf. however 192c1, 209d6). **a3 ἤ λιπών...ἀποβαλών:** 'leaving (*sc.* one's place in the) formation', i.e. desertion in the face of the enemy, was a serious offence, and the charge that a man had 'thrown away his arms' (particularly his heavy shield, in order to run away faster) was an extreme insult. **a5 πρὸ τούτου** 'rather than that'. **a6 ἐγκαταλιπεῖν** 'and as for leaving one's paidika behind (*sc.* in difficulties)'; the relation of the infinitive to οὐδεὶς κτλ. is very loose indeed. **κινδυνεύοντι:** masculine singular because of what παιδικά means, without regard for the grammatical form of παιδικά. **a7 κακός** 'cowardly', just as ἀγαθός, applied to an adult male, is 'brave'. **ἔνθεον** 'having a god in him', i.e. 'inspired'. **a8 τῷ ἀρίστῳ φύσει** 'him who is by nature bravest'.

b1 ἀτεχνῶς '(*sc.* it is) absolutely (*sc.* true that...)'. **ὃ ἔφη...2 τοῦτο** 'what Homer said, (*sc.* namely) that the god ..., this...'. The notion that a deity 'breathes valour into' a man is recurrent in Homer; it is not always the same deity, and '*the* god' often means, in effect, '*a* god'. ἡρώων 'heroes' in the Greek sense, i.e. demigods and other larger-than-life characters of the legendary past. **b5 οὐ μόνον ὅτι:** the expression (as in Thuc. 4.85.6) conflates 'not only' with οὐχ ὅτι (cf. 208a1), which sometimes connotes 'to say nothing of...'. **αἱ γυναῖκες:** it is not uncommon for the article to be absent from the first member of a pair of nouns but present with the second; cf. Arist. *Poetics* 1449a1 'Ιλιὰς καὶ ἡ 'Οδύσσεια. **b6 "Αλκηστις:** Apollo, owing a good turn to Admetus, obtained for him the privilege of finding a substitute when he was fated to die in the prime of life. Neither of Admetus' aged parents was willing to be the substitute (cf. b8–c3), but his wife Alcestis was. In Euripides' *Alcestis* she is brought back to Admetus by Herakles, who wrestles with Death at the tomb. It seems from c6–d1 that Plato may be using an older and simpler form of the legend (see A. M. Dale's edition of the play (Oxford 1954) vii–xvii). **b7 ὑπέρ...λόγου:** there is a slight tautology in τούτου...μαρτυρίαν ...ὑπὲρ κτλ. 'evidence of this in defence of my argument'. **εἰς τοὺς "Ελληνας** 'for all the world to see'.

c1 ὑπερεβάλετο...2 ἔρωτα: a case, then, where eros generates that extreme φιλία which motivates self-sacrifice. It is clear from 180b4f. that Phaedrus thinks of Alcestis as being in love with Admetus but not of Admetus as being in love with Alcestis. **ἀποδεῖξαι αὐτούς** 'make them appear'. **ἀλλοτρίους** 'alien', the antonym of οἰκεῖος. **c5 ὥστε...6 θεοί** 'so that, although many ..., the number of those to whom the gods have given this privilege is very small indeed'. **c7 ἀνεῖναι:** amplifying τοῦτο, 'that they should send up...' (~ ἀνίημι); Hommel's conjecture ἀνιέναι, 'that...should come up...' (~ ἀνέρχομαι) is very plausible.

d2 ἀρετήν: here, as often, the 'valour' which makes one hold one's own life cheap; ἀρετή is the abstract noun corresponding to ἀγαθός, on which cf. 179a7 n. **'Ορφέα:** according to the legend in sources later than Plato (notably Virgil, *Georgics* 4.453–527), Eurydice, wife of the great legendary musician Orpheus, died of snakebite. Orpheus entered the underworld to find her, relying on the power of his music to disarm the opposition (cf. d6f.), and was allowed to bring her back on condition that he did not turn round and look at her on the upward journey. He broke this condition and lost her for ever. d3 φάσμα ('phantom')...4 δόντες suggests that Plato has a simpler version of the legend in mind. **d3 ἀτελῆ** 'without accomplishment', i.e. 'empty-handed'. **d4 αὐτήν** '(*sc.* his wife) herself'. **μαλθακίζε-σθαι ἐδόκει** 'they regarded him as faint-hearted'; cf. 174c1. **d5 κιθαρ-ῳδός:** by contrast with the warrior and farmer, the musician was sometimes regarded as unmanly; Euripides' *Antiope* contained (frr. 184–8) a famous debate on this theme. **d8 καὶ ἐποίησαν...9 γενέσθαι:** Orpheus was torn to pieces by maenads; Aeschylus (in *Bassarai*) made his slighting of Dionysus the cause of this, and we do not know if anyone before Plato linked the fate of Orpheus with his venture into the underworld.

e1 οὐχ ὥσπερ...ἐτίμησαν 'not in the way in which...they honoured...', i.e. 'it was different with Achilles; they honoured him...'. **e2 μακάρων νήσους:** the souls of some legendary heroes were regarded (e.g. by Pindar, *Olympian Odes* 2.79f., cf. Hes. *WD* 170–3) as living in 'the islands of the blessed', much the same idea as Homer's 'Elysium' (*Od.* 4.561–9). **πεπυσμένος...4 τελευτήσοι:** in *Il.* 9.410–16 Achilles explains that his divine mother Thetis has told him that he can choose between two destinies: to stay and fight at Troy, die there, and obtain immortal fame, or to go home, live to old age and be forgotten. After his companion Patroclus has been killed by Hector, he chooses (*Il.* 18.88–96) to avenge Patroclus although, as Thetis tells him, this means that he will never return home. *Ap.* 28cd uses Achilles as the supreme example of heroism. **e5 βοηθήσας** 'striking a blow for...'. **ἐραστῇ:** Homer does not portray the mutual affection of Achilles and Patroclus as a homosexual relationship, but it was so interpreted in classical times; cf. 180a4 n.

180a1 ἐπαποθανεῖν: Achilles could not die ὑπέρ Patroclus, since Patroclus was already dead; he could only add (ἐπ-) his own death as a foreseeable consequence of avenging Patroclus. **a2 ὅθεν...3 ὅτι** 'and in consequence..., because ...'. For ὑπεραγασθέντες 'in the greatest admiration', cf. b1 ἄγανται. **a4 Αἰσχύλος:** *Myrmidons* (frr. 228f.) refers explicitly to 'kisses' and 'thighs'; the latter suggests a mode of homosexual intercourse depicted in vase-painting, the dominant partner pushing his penis between the thighs of the sub-ordinate partner. Aeschylus often modified tradition drastically to suit the attitudes and interests of his own time, and may have been the first to make Achilles the erastes of Patroclus. φλυαρεῖ is 'talks nonsense'; cf. 211e. **a5 καλλίων...6 ἁπάντων:** *Il.* 2.673f. **ἀγένειος:** Achilles is a beardless youth in fifth-century vase-painting, though not always so earlier. **a7 νεώτερος πολύ:** Homer says that Achilles was the younger of the two (*Il.* 11.786f.), but he does not say '*much* younger'; Phaedrus' addition illustrates how easily (in ancient and modern times alike) the evidence of texts can be bent. **ἀλλὰ γάρ** 'anyway, ...'; cf. *GP* 103.

b2 ἀγαπᾷ: cf. 181c6 and p. 2 n. 1. **b3 θειότερον...4 ἐστι:** he who has the god Eros in him (cf. 179a7); respect and devotion to the erastes is therefore a kind of worship, and the gods naturally react favourably to that. **b7 εἰς ἀρετῆς...τελευτήσασιν:** the εὐδαίμων man is the man who has succeeded in being, having and doing what he wishes to be, have and do (cf. 205a1–3), so that εὐδαιμονία is 'happiness' (not a subjective feeling, but as in the phrase 'health and happiness'). One possesses it, and ἀρετή too – '(*sc.* reputation for) excellence' – if one is remembered and celebrated in song and story; cf. *GPM* 228f., 235f.

180c1–185c3: Pausanias' speech

There are two Erotes, not one, for Aphrodite and Eros are inseparable, and there are two Aphroditai – one 'Heavenly', the other 'Popular'. An action does not in itself deserve praise or blame, but only as it is performed with honourable or shameful intentions. Popular eros, concerned only to use the body of the love-object, as ready to use females as males and preferring a weak and unintelligent object, has got eros a bad name, and should be prohibited by law, like adultery.

In some parts of the Greek world all eros is accepted, and in other parts all is condemned. Athenian custom is ambivalent; we tolerate, even encourage, the pursuer, and yet we try to frustrate his aims, and we blame his quarry for yielding. This is because we want to distinguish the pursuer who desires only the body (a desire which fades when the body ages) from him who 'desires the soul' (a desire which is educative and the foundation of lasting love). If the intention is honourable in both partners, any homosexual act is justified.

The second speech of the series is the obvious point at which to introduce a distinction between good and bad eros. What Pausanias

contrasts with the simple desire for orgasm in contact with a handsome body is not an emotional and intellectual relationship from
which all contact is excluded, but a complete relationship in which
orgasm is both the reward of devotion to the whole person and the
generator of future devotion; that much is clear from his use of
χαρίζεσθαι and ὑπουργεῖν (e.g. 184d, and cf. p. 8). What he praises
differs from heterosexual love in its characteristically Greek insistence
on the wish to improve, and to be improved, in skills and courage
and thus in usefulness to the community (cf. *GPM* 296–9).

Pausanias' relationship with Agathon (cf. p. 3 and 177d8 n.) is
reflected in his contempt for women (181b3–c6), his criticism of those
who desire immature boys (181c7–182a6), and the importance he
attaches to permanence (181d3–7, 183d8–e6).

On his description of ambivalence in Athenian attitudes cf. p. 8.

180c2 ἄλλους τινὰς εἶναι *sc.* λόγους, probably; 'there were some
others (*sc.* who spoke)' is possible English, but would be odd Greek.
c5 τὸ ἁπλῶς... παρηγγέλθαι '(*sc.* I mean,) that the injunction has
been given'.   **c6** νῦν δέ...εἷς: this γάρ is related to d1 οὖν 'but as it
is – for he is not one... – I, then, will try'; cf. *Laches* 200e 'but as it is
(νῦν δέ) – for all of us alike (ὁμοίως γάρ) were at a loss – why, then
(τί οὖν), ...?' and *GP* 71.   **c7** μή: one would expect οὐκ, '*since* he is
not one', but μὴ ὄντος is equivalent to εἴπερ μὴ ἔστι 'if (*sc.* as we are
satisfied is the case)...'. On μή...δέ cf. *GP* 186f.

d1 ὁποῖον 'which kind (*sc.* of Eros)'.   **d2** ἐπανορθώσασθαι 'set
right'.   φράσαι '(*sc.* that is, I will try) to explain'.   **d4** οὐκ ἔστιν...
'Αφροδίτη: it is not true that one cannot desire and enjoy sexual
intercourse without being in love, but Pausanias is exploiting the
notion that Eros is an agent inseparable from Aphrodite and always
at her service.   **d5** ἀνάγκη *sc.* ἐστί: 'it necessarily follows that...'
(which, strictly speaking, it does not).   **d6** ἡ μέν...9 καλοῦμεν:
according to Hes. *Theog.* 190ff., Aphrodite was born from the genitals
of Uranus (Sky), which were lopped off by his son Cronus and fell
into the sea. In *Il.* 5.370–430, on the other hand, Aphrodite is the
child of Zeus and Dione. Pausanias treats the alternative genealogies
as evidence for the existence of two distinct Aphroditai. Both οὐράνιος
and πάνδημος are known as epithets of Aphrodite and of other

deities, at Athens and elsewhere. Eur. *Hippolytus* 59f. 'Artemis
οὐρανία daughter of Zeus' and fr. 781.15–17 'Aphrodite οὐρανία
daughter of Zeus' show that οὐράνιος was not normally felt to mean
'of Uranus'. πάνδημος probably means 'worshipped by all the people
of the land' (*sc.* and not simply by particular families or in particular
localities); later, it meant 'vulgar', 'ordinary'.

e3 ἐπαινεῖν...θεούς: a verbal gesture to avert nemesis; he does not
in fact find anything to commend in Eros Pandemos.   **e4 εἴληχε:**
each deity who has a 'province' (e.g. Ares: war; Aphrodite: sex) is
treated as having 'obtained it by lot'.

181a1 οἷον 'as, for example, ...'.   **a2 αὐτό** 'in' (or 'by') 'itself'.
a3 τοιοῦτον ἀπέβη 'that' (i.e. conforming to ὡς ἂν πραχθῇ) 'is how
it turns out'. The aorist indicative is commonly preferred to the
present in stating a general truth; cf. *MT* 53f. (where, however, it is
hard to make sense of the statement that the aorist is 'more vivid').
a4 μὴ ὀρθῶς δέ: cf. 180c7 n.; but here the conditional force of μή is
clear.   **a5 τὸ ἐρᾶν καὶ ὁ Ἔρως:** the two are treated as one, so that the
following words are masculine.   **a6 ὁ καλῶς...ἐρᾶν** 'the (*sc.* Eros)
who induces being in love in a good way'.   **a7 ὡς ἀληθῶς** 'truly', 'in
the true sense'.

b1 ὅτι ἂν τύχῃ: cf. 173a1 n. on ὅπη τύχοιμι.   **καὶ οὗτος...ἐρῶσιν**
'and this is the eros of *ordinary* people'; cf. 174c7 n.   **b3 οὐχ ἧττον...
παίδων:** Pausanias will not allow 'heavenly' Eros ever to be heterosexual; c4–6 is his explanation.   **ὧν καὶ ἐρῶσι** 'of those with whom
they *are* in love'; for καί cf. 177a1 καὶ βούλεσθαι.   **b4 ὡς ἄν...
ἀνοητοτάτων** 'the least intelligent possible'.   **b5 διαπράξασθαι**
'achieve their object', i.e. orgasm in contact.   **b7 τοῦτο** picks up ὅτι
ἂν τύχωσι.   **b8 τοὐναντίον** 'the opposite', a common euphemism for
'bad'.   **ἀπό:** not 'born of...', for Pausanias (unlike later authors)
does not treat Eros (the subject of ἔστι here) as son of Aphrodite,
but rather 'proceeding from...', 'sent by...'.

c2 καὶ θήλεος καὶ ἄρρενος: Dione and Zeus.   **c4 πρεσβυτέρας:** the
mutilation of Uranus occurred long before Zeus (son of Cronus) was
born.   **ὕβρεως ἀμοίρου** 'having no portion (μοῖρα) of lawless

violence'. On ὕβρις cf. 174b6, 175e7 nn.; it was regarded as characteristic of the young (*GPM* 103).   **c5 ἔπιπνοι** 'inspired'; cf. 179a7,
b1 nn.   **c6 τὸ φύσει...ἔχον**: that males are usually bigger and
stronger than females is observable; that they are more intelligent,
more stable emotionally and better able to resist impulses is a belief
which served as a rationalisation of the Greeks' treatment of women –
a treatment which, in so far as women accepted men's estimation of
them and accepted the role they were given, tended to make the
belief come true. Cf. *GPM* 95–102.   **ἀγαπῶντες:** cf. 180b2.   **c7
εἰλικρινῶς** 'genuinely', 'purely'.

d1 παίδων: so far (b3, c4, cf. c7), παῖς has meant 'younger male';
now it is given a more restricted sense, 'boy' well below the age
(d2f.) at which the beard begins to grow, and henceforth Pausanias
will use παῖς in this sense (e.g. e1f.) but 'eromenos' or 'paidika' in
speaking of the younger partner in a homosexual relationship.
d2 ἐπειδάν...ἴσχειν: in the Greek view, when children grow up,
they get more sense; they do not lose 'innocence' (*GPM* 102, 104).
πλησιάζει τῷ γενειάσκειν 'is near to the growing of a beard'; in
Prt. 309ab Socrates approves of *Il.* 24.348, where a youth is called
χαριέστατος at the age when his beard is first appearing.   **d5 κοινῇ:**
not as a rule under the same roof, but perhaps Pausanias and Agathon
did.   **ἀλλ' οὐκ...7 ἀποτρέχοντες:** ἀλλ' οὐκ...οἰχήσεσθαι is coordinated with ἐρᾶν, and both depend on d3 παρεσκευασμένοι...
εἰσιν: 'and not deceive (*sc.* the paidika) – whom they got at a time
when he had no understanding, as (*sc.* he would not have, being)
young – and contemptuously' (lit. 'having laughed at him') 'abandon
him, running off after someone else'.   **d7 νόμον:** the word can mean
'law', 'custom', 'usage', etc.; here clearly 'law', as e4–7 shows.

e1 παίδων: cf. d1 n.   **εἰς ἄδηλον** 'on (*sc.* something of which the
outcome is) uncertain'.   **ἀνηλίσκετο:** in a purpose-clause dependent
on a main clause which asserts what might or would or ought to have
happened, the past tenses of the indicative are used; cf. *MT* 120f.
e2 οἱ...3 σώματος lit. 'whither of badness and goodness it ends concerning soul and body'.   **e5 προσαναγκάζειν τὸ τοιοῦτον** 'impose
a compulsion of that kind on...'.   **e6 ἐλευθέρων γυναικῶν:** women
or girls who are not slaves and whose father, husband or nearest male
relative is their κύριος and has the right to give them in marriage.

182a1 οἱ...2 πεποιηκότες 'those who have brought the (*sc.* familiar) reproach into being'. **τολμᾶν** 'go so far as to...'; cf. 177c3 n. **a4 τήν...ἀδικίαν** lit. 'non-observance of καιρός, and injury'; ἀκαιρία is doing things at the wrong time, to the wrong extent, and in the wrong way. **δήπου**: a persuasive 'surely'. **a5 νομίμως:** Pausanias has in mind the νόμος of e3f. and the νόμος he later commends (184d4) as implicit in Athenian practice (185e5f.). **a8 ὥρισται** 'has been defined'; ὅρος is 'boundary', then 'definition'.

b1 καὶ ἐν Λακεδαίμονι: it has been suggested that these words should be deleted or transposed to follow 'in Elis and Boeotia', since the inarticulateness predicated of the two latter in b2 is a notorious characteristic of Sparta. But the Spartan attitude to homosexuality was indeed ποικίλος 'complicated', 'intricate', as described by Xen. *Lacedaemoniorum Respublica* 1.12ff.; Xenophon there contrasts Sparta with Boeotia and Elis. **ἐν Ἤλιδι...2 Βοιωτοῖς:** there is a common modern belief that homosexuality was especially Dorian, but neither the Eleans nor the Boeotians were Dorians. **b4 ἵνα οἶμαι...6 λέγειν** 'so as not to have the trouble, I imagine, of trying...'. Inability to persuade by words could as well have had the opposite consequence; but many an argument of Pausanias *non sequitur*. **τῆς δέ...πολλαχοῦ** 'in many parts of Ionia and in (*sc.* many) other places'. Since the Ionians were often regarded as effete (the opposite of the crude and fierce Boeotians), the passage reminds us that the Greeks did not associate the pursuit of paidika with effeminacy, though the compliant paidika himself could be reproached as effeminate. **b7 ὅσοι ...οἰκοῦσιν:** all the Ionian states were in the Athenian Empire at the 'dramatic date' of *Smp.*; but at the time of writing, the Ionians of the Asiatic mainland, thanks to the peace treaty of 387/6, were under Persian rule. On the correlation of ὅσοι with τῆς...πολλαχοῦ cf. Democritus B30 ἐνταῦθα, ὃν νῦν ἠέρα καλέομεν. **b8 τυραννίδας:** Pausanias has in mind the story of the Athenian tyrannicides (c5–7; ἐνθάδε is 'at Athens', as in a8), and draws the conclusion that absolute rulers necessarily fear and discourage homosexual relationships.

c2 φρονήματα...ἀρχομένων lit. 'that big ideas' (cf. 190b6) 'of their subjects should come about in (*sc.* their domain)', i.e. 'that their subjects should entertain proud ambitions'. **c3 ὅ:** object of ἐμποιεῖν, and referring primarily to φρονήματα...ἐγγίγνεσθαι, to which οὐδὲ φιλίας κτλ. is supplementary. **c4 φιλεῖ** 'is accustomed to...'. **τά τε ἄλλα πάντα** i.e. philosophy and physical training (c1); the form of the expression (cf. 173c5 n.) suggests 'and Eros (sc. most of all)'. **c5 ὁ γάρ...7 ἀρχήν:** as told by Thuc. 6.54–9, the story is that Aristogeiton was in love with Harmodius; so was Hipparchus, the brother of the tyrant Hippias. Aristogeiton and Harmodius conspired to kill both brothers, but succeeded only in killing Hipparchus. Thucydides emphasises that this did not end the tyranny, but popular tradition (used here by Pausanias) said that it did. The φιλία of Harmodius is here the affectionate response generated in the eromenos by the erastes; cf. p. 4. The feminine forms of βέβαιος, as of some other adjectives in -ιος, are commonly replaced by the masculine. **ἐτέθη** 'it has been laid down (sc. that it is)...'; cf. b2f. τιθέναι is the usual word for making a law or creating a custom; in d1 and d3 the middle τίθεσθαι is used rather than the active because the communities concerned have not consciously performed a legislative act but have accepted a custom.

d2 πλεονεξίᾳ 'aggrandisement'. **ἀνανδρίᾳ:** cf. 178d6. **d3 ψυχῆς ἀργίαν** 'mental laziness', with reference to b2–6. **d5 ἐνθυμηθέντι ...183a2 ὀνείδη:** the skeleton of the sentence is (lit.) 'for to anyone who reflects that (d5 ὅτι) being in love openly is said..., and again that (d7f. καὶ ὅτι αὖ) the encouragement...is extraordinary...and (d9 καί) it is regarded as creditable...and (e1 καί) our custom has given ...'; then e3–183a2 ἃ εἴ τις...ὀνείδη is a comment on θαυμαστά in e2, whereupon the sentence breaks off as Pausanias enlarges (a2 εἰ γάρ...) on what he has just said, never reaching the main clause which ἐνθυμηθέντι has led us to expect. **d7 αἰσχίους ἄλλων** 'less handsome than others'; 'X is worse than Y' is normal Greek for 'X is not as good as Y'. **d8 παρακέλευσις** 'encouragement'. **d9 καὶ ἑλόντι...εἶναι** 'and it is regarded as being to his credit if he has got the better of (sc. the paidika)'.

e1 ἐξουσίαν 'freedom', 'opportunity'. **e2 θαυμαστά** 'extraordinary', with a rather more derogatory flavour than in d8.

183a1 [φιλοσοφίας]: it is hard to see how 'philosophy' comes into it, since the reproaches would be uttered by people in general, not just by philosophers. Unless the word is being used in a very unusual sense ('understanding of how one ought to live'?) and an unusual construction (since ὀνείδη *of*...are normally reproaches *against*...), it must be corrupt or interpolated or the surviving portion of a longer expression which clarified the sense. **a2 εἰ γάρ...b2 αὐτῶν:** the εἰ-clause extends to a7 οὐδείς, and ἐμποδίζοιτο ἄν is the verb of the main clause; a4 ἱκετείας...a7 οὐδείς enlarges on a4 οἷάπερ οἱ ἐρασταί (*sc.* ποιοῦσι), and b1 τῶν μέν...b2 ὑπὲρ αὐτῶν enlarges on a8 ὑπὸ φίλων καὶ ὑπὸ ἐχθρῶν. **a3 ἀρχὴν ἄρξαι** 'hold (*sc.* elected) office'. **δύναμιν** 'influence' (*sc.* λαβεῖν); cf. 184a8. **a4 ἱκετείας...5 ποιούμενοι** 'employing' (lit. 'making') 'supplication and entreaties in their requests'. **a6 κοιμήσεις ἐπὶ θύραις** lit. 'lyings-down-to-sleep at doors' (*sc.* ποιούμενοι or κοιμώμενοι; for the ellipse cf. 176a2), i.e. in the doorway of the paidika. The lover spending the night, wet and frozen, in the doorway of a heartless mistress is a common motif in later poetry.

b1 τῶν μέν...τῶν δέ 'his enemies...and his friends...'. **κολακείας καὶ ἀνελευθερίας** 'gross flatteries and behaviour unworthy of a free man'. **b2 νουθετούντων** 'admonishing'. **b3 χάρις ἔπεστι:** they respond favourably, as to 'charm' or 'attractiveness' in his behaviour. **b4 ὡς...5 διαπραττομένου** 'since he is regarded as trying to achieve some wholly admirable end' – a switch into the genitive absolute, though a dative in agreement with b2 τῷ δ᾽ ἐρῶντι would have been grammatical. **b5 ὃ δέ...7 ὅρκων:** we seem to have a conflation of (1) 'and, what is most extraordinary, even when he swears (*sc.* an oath), according to what most people say, ...' with (2) 'and, what is most extraordinary, most people say that even when he swears ...', or with (3) 'and the most extraordinary thing is that, according to what most people say, even when he swears ...'. Plato seems to have written 'and, what is most extraordinary, according to what most people say, that even when he swears ...'; the conflation is probably his own, not a copyist's error. Cf. d4. The notion that the gods are indulgent to perjury by lovers goes back to Hesiod (fr. 124). **b7 εἶναι:** for the sense 'be valid', cf. εἶναι 'be true' in Thuc. 6.16.5 (of a claim) and Soph. *Electra* 584 (of an excuse), or 'be fulfilled' in Aeschines 3.100 (of hopes).

c2 ταύτη...d3 νομίζεσθαι: at last Pausanias comes back to the point he made in 182d5. The sentence beginning at c4 ἐπειδάν consists of a multiple subordinate clause down to d2 λέγοντας, and its main clause then begins with εἰς δὲ ταῦτα, in which δέ is not a connective but the repeated δέ which we find in, e.g., 196b3 or Andocides 3.1 'that (ὅτι μέν) it is better to make peace . . ., I think you all know; but that (ὅτι δέ) the politicians. . .oppose. . ., this (τοῦτο δέ) you do not all perceive'. **c4 φίλους:** cf. 182c6 and p. 4. **παιδαγωγούς:** slaves whose business it was to take their masters' sons to and from school and gymnasium. προστεταγμένα is 'imposed (*sc.* as a duty)'. **c7 ἡλικιῶται** ('*sc.* boys) of his own age'.

d3 αἴσχιστον. . .νομίζεσθαι 'that behaviour of this kind is regarded here as most disgraceful'. **τὸ δέ. . .ἔχει** 'but, I think, the situation is: . . .'; cf. 198d7. **d4 ὅπερ. . .5 αἰσχρόν** 'a point which was made (*sc.* by me) at the start, (*sc.* in saying that) . . .'. **d6 αἰσχρῶς μὲν οὖν** *sc.* πράττειν (and not πραττόμενον), as is clear from the infinitive χαρίζεσθαι. **d7 πονηρῷ. . .8 καλῶς:** πονηρός is the normal antonym of χρηστός; the adverb χρηστῶς is rarely used.

e1 καὶ γάρ. . .2 πράγματος 'for also he is not a lasting (*sc.* erastes), in so far as what he desires is not lasting either'. **e3 ἅμα. . .λήγοντι** 'as the flower. . .fades' (lit. '. . .ceases'). **οἴχεται ἀποπτάμενος:** *Il.* 2.71 (-χετ' ἀπο-). **e4 καταισχύνας** almost 'devaluing', i.e. showing to be of little worth. **e6 συντακείς** 'fused', 'intimately joined' (∼ συντήκειν). **τούτους** good and bad erastai.

184a1 τοῖς μέν. . .3 φεύγειν 'and that (*sc.* eromenoi) should comply with the good erastai but keep clear of the bad ones. So for that reason (*sc.* our custom) encourages the erastai to pursue and the eromenoi to flee'. **ἀγωνοθετῶν** 'organising a competition', 'putting on a contest'. **a4 βασανίζων** 'putting to the test (*sc.* to see. . .)'. **a6 ταχύ:** with ἁλίσκεσθαι. **a7 τὰ πολλά** 'most things'. **a8 πολιτικῶν δυνά-μεων** 'acquisition of influence in the community' – 'political' in the broadest sense, not the narrow sense, for we are concerned here with adolescents. **αἰσχρόν** *sc.* νενόμισται.

b1 ἐάν τε. . .πτήξῃ 'if he knuckles under' (lit. 'cowers') 'when ill-treated (*sc.* by threats, blackmail, slander, etc.)'. **ἄν τ'. . .2 μὴ καταφρονήσῃ** 'and if, offered favours. . ., he does not reject them with contempt'. **b4 χωρίς:** cf. 173c4.   **b6 ἔστι...7 νόμος:** this does not fit syntactically with οὕτω δὴ κτλ., and its sense is repeated in c4 νενόμισται γὰρ δὴ ἡμῖν; but to delete it would leave b7 ἦν (*sc.* νόμος) unintelligible and ὥσπερ κτλ. without any connective to link it to b5 μία δή...6 παιδικά.   **b7 ἐθέλοντα** accusative singular as referring to the unspecified subject of the infinitive δουλεύειν (cf. 176d3f. n.), and virtually adverbial, 'voluntarily'.

c3 περὶ τὴν ἀρετήν lit. 'involving goodness'; here 'in furtherance of self-improvement'.   **c4 θεραπεύειν** 'treat as his superior', 'cultivate', 'comply with the wishes of...'.   **c5 κατὰ σοφίαν...6 ἀρετῆς:** Pausanias has in mind both apprentices, e.g. of a musician or sculptor, and disciples of a philosopher (such as Apollodorus in relation to Socrates; cf. 172c5f.).

d2 συμβῆναι 'come about that...'.   **d3 εἰς τὸ αὐτὸ ἔλθωσιν** 'meet', 'come together'.   **d4 νόμον ἔχων ἑκάτερος** 'each having a principle'. **ὁ μέν...7 ὑπουργῶν:** with ὁ μέν... we must understand 'thinking' or 'believing', and so too with ὁ δέ..., giving the content of the νόμος involved in each case. In d7 older manuscripts have ὑπουργῶν, later manuscripts ὑπουργεῖν; if we adopt the participle, we must understand the infinitive.   **φρόνησιν** 'intelligence'.

e1 συμβάλλεσθαι 'contribute'; cf. 185c3.   **εἰς παίδευσιν...2 κτᾶσθαι:** if this is what Plato wrote, we must understand φρόνησιν καὶ ἀρετήν as object of κτᾶσθαι; but if εἰς were deleted (as by Schütz) παίδευσιν...σοφίαν would be the object, and the sentence would be easier to follow.   **e3 συμπίπτει** 'comes about'.   **e4 ἐπὶ τούτῳ** 'on this condition', 'on these terms'.   **e5 ἐξαπατηθῆναι:** to be deceived is normally αἰσχρόν, since it shows carelessness or stupidity, but not all would agree with Pausanias in e5f.; Xen. *Anab.* 7.6.21 declares that to be deceived by a friend is more creditable than deceiving a friend. **e6 αἰσχύνην...μή** lit. 'it brings shame both for one who is deceived and (*sc.* for one who is) not'. φέρει has no specifiable subject.

185a1 ὡς πλουσίῳ 'in the belief that he is rich'.   **a3 οὐδὲν ἧττον αἰσχρόν** 'just as discreditable (*sc.* as it would have been if his belief had been true)'.   **τό γε αὐτοῦ** 'his own character', 'the part he is playing'.   **a6 διὰ τὴν φιλίαν ἐραστοῦ** 'through the affection (*sc.*

expected) of an erastes' (cf. 179c1 n.) ; normally, e.g., '*the* head of *a* lion' is 'head of lion' in Greek, and τήν here means more than simply 'the'.

b1 καλή: for the eromenos, that is.   **b2 τὸ καθ᾿ αὑτόν** 'his own part (*sc.* in the relationship)'.   **b3 πᾶν ἂν παντί**: here, as in b4 πᾶν πάντως, Pausanias' fervency in advocating homosexual eros shows through. **b6 ἰδιώταις**: cf. 178b3 n.   **b7 πολλήν...c1 ἐρώμενον** lit. 'compelling the erastes to take much care himself of himself with regard to goodness, and (*sc.* compelling) the eromenos too'. αὐτός (in the relevant case) is often coupled with the reflexive αὑτ-; indeed, in some dialects the two fuse into a single word.

c2 ὡς ἐκ τοῦ παραχρῆμα 'as best I can on the spur of the moment'.

185c4–e5: Aristophanes' hiccups

It was now Aristophanes' turn, but he had hiccups. Eryximachus told him how to stop the attack, and said that he himself would speak next.

Much humour in Old Comedy is founded on bodily processes, and it is appropriate that Aristophanes, rather than anyone else, should have hiccups; but Plato lets him off lightly, for hiccups are among the less offensive consequences of overeating. Plato may also wish to suggest (1) that Aristophanes artfully gains time for composing his speech, and (2) that Eryximachus is over-anxious to enlighten the company.

185c4 ἴσα λέγειν 'to speak in equal units', involving in this case (Παυσανίου ∼ παυσαμένου) assonance as well as symmetry; the phenomenon is obtrusive in Gorgias (cf. p. 123), and its influence on the epideictic oratory of the late fifth and early fourth centuries is obvious.   **c5 οἱ σοφοί** *sc.* λέγειν 'those skilled in speaking'.   **c6 πλησμονῆς** 'over-eating', 'satiety'.

d1 ἐν τῇ κάτω *sc.* κλίνῃ; cf. p. 11.   **d2 δίκαιος εἶ**: cf. 172b5 n.   **d5 μέρει** 'turn'.   **d6 ἐὰν μέν...7 λύγξ**: in sentences of the form 'if μέν...; but if not, ...' the first 'if' can be translated 'perhaps' or 'possibly'. ἀπνευστί...χρόνον 'holding your breath for a long time'.

e1 ἀνακογχυλίασον 'gargle'.   **ἰσχυρά** 'severe', in medical language (again in e3); Thuc. 2.49f. overworks the word in describing the plague. **e2 τοιοῦτον οἵῳ** 'of such a kind that... by it... '. **κινήσαις** lit. 'move', i.e. 'irritate'. **πτάρε** 'sneeze'. **e4 οὐκ ἂν φθάνοις λέγων** lit. 'you could not be beforehand speaking', i.e. 'start speaking as soon as you can'. **e5 ταῦτα** 'what you said'.

185e6–188e5: Eryximachus' speech

The two Erotes are manifest throughout nature, and not only in human reactions to human beauty. We must gratify (χαρίζεσθαι) what is healthy in the body (good eros) and refuse what is unhealthy (bad eros); that is the doctor's business. It is also his business to implant healthy eros, making opposites (e.g. dry and wet) desire each other and so be reconciled. So in tuning an instrument a musician must reconcile high and low and must gratify and fortify the good eros in his audience. When opposing principles in the climate are reconciled, all is well; when the bad eros gets the upper hand, disasters follow. And in dealings between men and gods it is the business of the seer and the religious expert to cherish and gratify the good eros in men.

Eryximachus, who feels (186a7–b1, cf. b4f.) that the study of medicine qualifies him to go beyond what Pausanias has said (186a1f.), runs together (1) the contrast between good desires or tendencies and bad desires or tendencies, and (2) the contrast between the good consequences of reconciling opposites and the bad consequences of failure to reconcile them. In (1) he stretches the denotation of the word 'eros' wide enough to diminish its utility very greatly, and in (2) he stretches it even further by treating an adjustment between two extremes as creating an eros of the extremes for each other. It is tempting to believe that Plato composed this speech (reminiscent at times of Teilhard de Chardin, and justly assessed by Hamilton, 15) in order to ridicule the tendency of scientific theorists to formulate excessively general laws governing the phenomena of the universe. Medical writers sometimes criticise such generalisation (e.g. Hipp. *De vetere medicina* 13–16, *De victu* 2.39), but they are none the less addicted to it (e.g. *De victu* 1.3–10; cf. *De flatibus* 1–5). Inasmuch as Eryximachus breaks away from the treatment of eros as an aspect of human sexuality, his speech might be regarded as looking ahead to Diotima's treatment of eros as a groping after absolute good; but its dualism, which attributes a positively bad eros to the order of nature, is alien to Diotima's metaphysics.

185e6 ἀναγκαῖον...186a1 δεῖν: the tautology is caused by the need to recapitulate (in δεῖν) after the ἐπειδή-clause has intervened between ἀναγκαῖον εἶναι and the infinitive group which is the subject of εἶναι.

186a1 τέλος ἐπιθεῖναι 'round off', adding what Pausanias omitted (οὐχ ἱκανῶς ἀπετέλεσε). **a2 τὸ μέν...3 διελέσθαι** lit. 'he seems to me well to have made the distinction that Eros is twofold'. **a4 καλούς:** conforming with Pausanias, Eryximachus seems to ignore heterosexuality, but οἱ καλοί can mean 'handsome males and beautiful females' (as it does in Xen. *Cyropaedia* 5.1.14). **a7 μοι:** cf. 172a1 n.

b1 ὡς μέγας...τείνει '(*sc.* seeing) how great and wonderful (*sc.* the god is) and (*sc.* how) the god extends over everything'. **b3 πρεσβεύωμεν** 'give pride of place to...'; cf. 188c4. **b6 ἕτερόν τε...7 ἐρᾷ** 'are (*sc.* each) different and unlike (*sc.* one another)'; then (lit.) 'and the unlike desires unlike things'. **ἐπὶ τῷ ὑγιεινῷ** 'in' (cf. a3) 'the healthy body'. **b8 ὥσπερ...9 ἔλεγεν** 'as Pausanias said, (*sc.* namely) that...'; cf. 179e1 and 183d4.

c1 ἀκολάστοις (~ κολάζειν 'punish', hence lit. 'unchastised' or 'incorrigible') 'immoral', the antonym of σώφρων (cf. 188a5 n.). **c2 τοῖς μέν...ὑγιεινοῖς** 'the good and healthy (*sc.* elements)'. **c3 καὶ δεῖ** 'and one should (*sc.* do so)'. **c4 αἰσχρόν** *sc.* χαρίζεσθαι. **c5 τεχνικός** 'a true practitioner' (lit. 'having to do with a scientific, technical or artistic skill'). **ὡς...6 εἰπεῖν** lit. 'so as to speak in sum total', i.e. 'essentially'. **τῶν...ἐρωτικῶν...7 κένωσιν** 'the operations of eros in respect of filling and emptying'; cf. Hipp. *De flatibus* 1 'emptying cures fullness, filling (*sc.* cures) emptiness, and rest (*sc.* cures) exertion', on the principle that every condition is rectified by its opposite. **καὶ ὁ διαγιγνώσκων...d1 οὗτος:** as one can say ὅστις ἂν διαγιγνώσκῃ, οὗτός ἐστι κτλ., so after a long substantival expression the thread may be picked up by a demonstrative.

d2 ὁ μεταβάλλειν ποιῶν 'he who brings about a change (*sc.* in their balance)'. **d3 κτᾶσθαι:** the patient is the understood subject. **d4 καὶ ἐνόντα ἐξελεῖν** 'and how to remove (*sc.* the opposite eros) when it is there'. **ἂν εἴη:** after ἐστιν in d1, a very clear case of variation for purely aesthetic reasons. **d5 δημιουργός:** the word is applied to all, irrespective of wealth or birth, whose technical skills serve the community's needs. **τὰ ἔχθιστα...6 φίλα** sc. ἀλλήλοις, in both cases.

e2 ὁ ἡμέτερος...3 τέχνην: in historical times certain families (in Stagirus and the Dodecanese) which practised medicine in successive generations claimed descent from Podalirius or Machaon, who in *Il.* 2.731f. are healers and sons of Asclepius. The profession of medicine was not restricted to these families, but there was an increasing tendency for all doctors to call themselves, and to be called by others, Ἀσκληπιάδαι, as if adopted into the family by virtue of their science. Asclepius in Homer is a healer (*Il.* 4.449) who learned from the wise centaur Chiron (*Il.* 4.219). Hesiod fr. 51 makes him a son of Apollo, and he was worshipped in many places as god; evidently by Plato's time he was regarded as the founder of medicine. Legend was the province of poets; hence οἶδε οἱ ποιηταί, where the demonstrative includes Agathon and Aristophanes. **e4 τοῦ θεοῦ** sc. Eros.

187a1 κυβερνᾶται lit. 'is steered', 'is piloted', hence 'is governed'. **γυμναστικὴ καὶ γεωργία:** both entail bodily exertion; the former trains the human body, while the latter is concerned with the health of crops and beasts. **μουσική:** sometimes 'music' in the strict sense, sometimes 'music and poetry', sometimes, more broadly, 'culture'. **a2 τῷ...νοῦν** 'who gives it even a moment's thought'. **a3 ὅτι... τούτοις** 'that it is in the same situation as what I have been describing'. **a4 ἐπεί...λέγει:** Eryximachus explains why he said 'perhaps' (a3, cf. a8). Heraclitus of Ephesus, a philosopher active at the beginning of the fifth century, expressed himself concisely and enigmatically; hence here 'in the actual wording' (as opposed to his meaning (βούλεται λέγειν)) 'he does not say it well'. **τὸ ἕν...6 λύρας:** what Heraclitus meant and what Plato thought he meant might be different; and what Plato wished to portray Eryximachus as thinking Heraclitus meant might be different again. Here, the subject is 'the One'; in *Sophist* 242e the subject of διαφερόμενον ἀεὶ συμφέρεται is 'that which is', τὸ ὄν, described there as being 'many and one, held together (συνέχεται) by enmity and friendship'. Ancient authors cite Heraclitus B51 (212 KR) in different forms: 'they do not understand how being at variance (διαφερόμενον) it agrees (ξυμφέρεται or ὁμολογεῖ) with itself; the fitting-together (ἁρμονία) is stretched back (παλίντονος; or παλίντροπος 'turning back') as of bow and lyre'. It is true that the unity of a complex is often constituted by the balance of opposing forces in it. One string of a lyre produces a given note by virtue of being put under a given tension; the tuning of the whole lyre to a given mode is accomplished by putting all the strings under certain tensions; and a bow only functions as a bow because its two ends are forced towards each other when, left to themselves, they would be further apart (see G. S. Kirk, *Heraclitus: the cosmic fragments* (Cambridge 1954) 203ff.). **πολλή...8 εἶναι** 'it is much irrationality to say...', i.e. 'it is quite absurd to say...'; cf. ἀνάγκη (180d5) 'it follows necessarily that...'. It is uncertain whether ἁρμονία (the understood subject of b2 γέγονεν) is here (1) the tuning of one string, treated as the forcing of 'agreement' (cf. c2–4) on the higher (ὀξύς) register which the string would produce if tightened and the lower (βαρύς) which it would produce if slackened, or (2) the tuning of a whole lyre to a given mode, in which the note of each string is neither higher nor lower than what is required by the relationship between the strings which constitutes the mode. The words immediately following point to (1).

b4 συμφωνία: it is doubtful whether in Plato's time this ever meant the simultaneous sounding of two different notes; in all examples, it can be interpreted as the relationship between those notes which belong to one and the same mode. Cf. *Rep.* 617b 'from all (*sc.* these notes), which are eight in number, μίαν ἁρμονίαν συμφωνεῖν'. συμφων-εῖν, -ία, -ος are commonly used of 'harmony' in the figurative sense. **b6 διαφερόμενον...7 ἁρμόσαι:** i.e. it is not possible, on the other hand (αὖ), to 'fit together' the components of anything except by making them cease to be at variance. **b7 ὥσπερ γε...c2 γέγονε:** there is the same room for doubt as in a8–b2. One unit of movement may follow the preceding unit either quickly or slowly; and a sequence of units may constitute a recognisable rhythm by virtue of their interrelation.

c3 ἐκεῖ 'in what I said before'. **c5 ἐρωτικῶν:** it is easy to think of varied impulses and appetites in the body (186c6f.), but far-fetched to speak of 'high' and 'low' or 'fast' and 'slow' as manifesting eros on the part of strings or drums, let alone on the part of notes or beats, which do not exist until an instrument produces the sound of which they are an aspect. **c6 συστάσει** 'construction'; cf. 188a1. **c7 οὐδέ …8 ἐστίν:** it comes as a surprise, after reading c3–5 with 186c5–e3 in mind, to hear now that there is no bad eros in mode and rhythm. **c8 καταχρῆσθαι:** occasionally 'use up' or 'misuse', but clearly not so here or in 205b6. The twofold eros is to be sought, according to the present argument, in those who listen to the music.

d1 ποιοῦντα 'composing'; cf. 197c4, and on the grammar cf. 176d4 n. **d2 μέλεσί τε καὶ μέτροις:** a song necessarily has '(*sc.* rhythmical) measures' as well as a musical mode, but μέλη 'songs' must here be 'tunes' considered as sequences of notes without regard for their rhythm. **d3 παιδεία:** in *Rep.* 376e παιδεία 'education', 'culture', is said to be γυμναστική for the body and μουσική for the soul; this reflects normal Athenian practice in secondary education, since boys were taught to memorise poetry and sing it to the accompaniment of the lyre. **d4 δημιουργοῦ:** cf. 186d5 n. **ὁ αὐτός** *sc.* as in 186b7–c5. **τοῖς μέν…5 καὶ ὡς ἄν…6 χαρίζεσθαι** 'gratify those people who are orderly and (*sc.* implant good eros (cf. 186d3f.)) in such a way that those who are not yet so are enabled to become so'. **d6 τούτων:** masculine, referring to those who are, or have been caused to become, orderly. **d7 ὁ οὐράνιος…e1 ὁ πάνδημος:** in Hes. *Theog.* 75–9 the list of the Muses contains a Urania and a Polymnia; the allocation of particular functions to particular Muses is a later development (Plutarch, *Quaestiones convivales* 9.14 illustrates the state of the game in Roman times). Eryximachus utilises these two names as being nearest to the οὐρανία and πάνδημος Aphroditai distinguished by Pausanias (180d6–e3). It seems from d4–6 that eros 'of' a given kind of music or poetry is the desire for it which exists in the hearer; in e1–3 we are told of the 'application' of this eros *to* the hearer, which (in the light of c7f.) must be the arousal and gratification of good or bad eros in the hearer by means of what is applied.

e1 ὁ δέ…πάνδημος 'but the other one is of Polymnia, (*sc.* I mean) the popular one'. **εὐλαβούμενον** 'taking care', 'being cautious'. **e2 προσφέρῃ** *sc.* τις. The composer 'applies' (cf. Thuc. 2.51.2 'do good by applying (προσφέροντας) a cure'), the hearer 'enjoys' (c3), and the composer 'implants' (e3), as the doctor 'deals with' (e5 χρῆσθαι) the patient's desires and the patient 'enjoys' (e6 καρπώσασθαι 'gather' as a crop) the resultant pleasure.   **e3 ἀκολασίαν:** cf. 186c1 n. **e4 ὀψοποιικήν** 'cookery'; ὄψον is used of virtually any prepared food other than bread.   **e8 παρείκει** lit. 'permits'; impersonally (as often; cf. φέρει in 184e6) 'is practicable'.   **φυλακτέον** 'one must look out for...', 'one must be careful about...'.   **ἔνεστον γάρ:** except, apparently, in tunings and rhythms (187c5–8).

188a1 ἡ τῶν...σύστασις 'the composition of the seasons of the year' (cf. 187c6).   **a2 πρὸς ἄλληλα...3 ἔλεγον:** Eryximachus treats the elements of nature as 'hostile to one another', like the elements in the body, and as needing to be harmonised (νυνδή refers to 186d7). **a4 κρᾶσιν...σώφρονα:** the notion of the right 'mixture', i.e. balance and adjustment, of opposites, was fundamental to Greek medical theory (e.g. Hipp. *De vetere medicina* 14, 16). κρᾶσις is used also of a temperate climate (e.g. Hipp. *De aeribus aquis locis* 12; cf. Pl. *Phd.* 111b). As σώφρων human action entails abstaining from reckless expression of one's own wishes and emotions, a mid-point between climatic extremes is here called 'sensible', 'reasonable'.   **a5 εὐετηρίαν:** a state of affairs which we would describe, in respect of herds and crops, as 'a good year'.   **a6 οὐδὲν ἠδίκησεν** 'does no damage' (cf. *GPM* 181f.); on the aorist cf. 181a3 n.   **a7 ὕβρεως:** cf. 181c4 n.   **ἐγκρατέστερος** 'in control', 'having the upper hand'; the sense 'self-controlled' is a later development.

b1 οἳ τε...5 ἐρωτικῶν 'for from such events plagues and other abnormal diseases are wont to arise and affect both beasts and plants; for frost and hail and blight...'. The importance attached by Greek medical theory to climatic difference and climatic change is evident from Hipp. *De aeribus*, especially chapter 2. γίγνεται is strikingly un-grammatical – all its subjects are feminine plural – and unless it is corrupt we have to suppose that the intervening neuter plural ἄλληλα led Plato into a solecism; cf. English sentences of the very common type 'the difficulty created by these conditions are intractable'. **b6 ἀστρονομία:** for a Greek 'astronomy' included meteorology; con-spicuous stars, such as Sirius, were regarded as 'bringing' (cf. Aesch. *Agamemnon* 5), even as causing, the seasonal changes to which the health of living beings is linked. φοραί are 'courses', 'movements'.

θυσίαι...7 ἐπιστατεῖ: by sacrifices a man conciliates gods and tries to secure their cooperation, or at least non-intervention, in the furtherance of his ambitions. In μαντική, which comprises clairvoyance, inspired utterance and the interpretation of omens on principles which can be learned, men glimpse past and future and the intentions of the gods. Seers (μάντεις) and interpreters (ἐξηγηταί) of sacred law often prescribe sacrifices, observances and taboos as means of winning divine favour or averting divine displeasure. Here they have the opportunity to encourage in their fellow-men the desire for morally good actions and to discourage the desire for bad.

c2 περί...ἴασιν: watching for the indications of good or bad eros (187e8), preserving the good eros (187d7) and curing (ἴασις is the abstract noun of ἰᾶσθαι 'heal') the bad (cf. 186d2f.). **c3 φιλεῖ:** cf. 182c4 n. **ἐάν...4 χαρίζηται:** in isolation one would take these words to refer simply to the following of moral rules; in this context the reference must be to the moral advice offered by those who interpret the will of the gods. **πρεσβεύῃ:** cf. 186b3 n. **c5 καὶ περί...6 θεούς:** one's behaviour towards one's parents is treated by the Greeks as 'pious' or 'impious' no less than one's behaviour towards gods. **c6 ἅ:** object of τοὺς ἐρῶντας, 'those who have these desires'; cf. 181b2. For προστέτακται cf. 183c6 n.

d1 φιλίας...δημιουργός 'creator of good relations between...'; cf. b7–c2. **d2 τείνει πρὸς κτλ.:** intransitive (lit. 'stretch towards...') 'concern', 'be relevant to...'; cf. 186b1 ('extend over'). **d5 συλλήβδην:** reinforcing πᾶς (as often), 'as a whole', 'in general', contrasted with the specific ὁ δὲ κτλ. **d6 ἀποτελούμενος** 'realised', 'satisfied' (cf. *Rep.* 581e 'such desires ἀποτελοῦνται'), not (as LSJ) 'worshipped'. **d7 οὗτος:** cf. 186c7 n. **d8 δυναμένους** *sc.* παρασκευάζει ἡμᾶς.

e1 οὐ μέντοι ἑκών γε: we can well believe that. **e2 σὸν ἔργον** 'it's up to you now', 'it's your business', a common colloquialism.

189a1–c1: Aristophanes prepares to speak

Aristophanes recovered from his hiccups, and Eryximachus warned him that he must be serious.

189a1 ἐκδεξάμενον 'taking over', 'taking up (*sc.* his cue)'.   **a2** πταρ-
μόν: 185e2.   **a4** ψόφων καὶ γαργαλισμῶν lit. 'noises and ticklings'.
οἷον 'the kind of thing which...'.   **a7** ὅρα τί ποιεῖς 'now then!'

b1 σεαυτοῦ: the point of using the reflexive rather than the possessive
adjective σοῦ is that Aristophanes is himself acting in a way preju-
dicial to his own speech. ἐάν 'in case', 'to see if...'.   **b2** ἐξόν σοι
'when it's open to you (*sc.* by *not* behaving as you are)...'.   **b4** ἄρρητα
'unsaid'; commonly elsewhere 'unspeakable', 'shocking' or 'secret',
'not to be divulged'.   **b6** οὖ τι μή...εἴπω: the insertion of τι (cf.
Rep. 331b οὖ τι παντὶ ἀνδρί, ἀλλὰ κτλ.) saves the hearer from taking
οὐ μή...εἴπω in the sense 'I shall not say...'.   **b7** ἐπιχώριον lit.
'belonging to the country', hence 'native to...', 'characteristic
of...'.   καταγέλαστα 'contemptible', a quite strongly derogatory
word.   **b8** βαλών...ἐκφεύξεσθαι lit. 'having cast...you think you
will escape', i.e. 'you think that you've had your fling and you'll get
away with it'.   **b9** οὕτως...λόγον 'in the knowledge that you'll be
called to account'; διδόναι λόγον is used by Plato (e.g. *Rep.* 534b) of
expounding the steps of a rational hypothesis, but the Athenians were
most familiar with the expression in connection with the financial
account which every magistrate had to render at the end of his year
of office.

c1 ἴσως...ἀφήσω σε: on Eryximachus' authoritarian handling of the
situation here and in a8–b2, cf. p. 11.

189c2–d6: Aristophanes' speech

*Human beings were once two-bodied and four-limbed and could be any one of
three sexes – male–male, female–male, or female–female. They were arrogant
and threatened the gods. Zeus therefore split each of them in half. Ever since,
each of us has sought his or her 'other half'; that is why, when we are in love,
we want a more complete and lasting union than sexual intercourse by itself can
achieve. If we are not careful, we shall be split in half yet again; but if we are
mindful of our moral and religious duties, we may regain our original nature.
In the meantime, Eros brings us as near to that as we can come.*

'Once upon a time...' is a motif used by intellectuals in the fifth
century (e.g. *Prt.* 320c), and its reflexes appear in tragedy (Aesch.
Prometheus 436ff., Moschion fr. 6); moreover, speculation on the origin

of the human species had a long history, and Empedocles (B57–62 (336–8 KR)) postulated an epoch of 'double' beings. But taken as a whole, Aristophanes' speech exhibits the characteristics of a folktale or fairy-tale; the notion (a world-wide feature of aetiological tales) that 'once upon a time' humans were different; the biological naivety of treating people who exist now as if they were the immediate product of their ancestors' bisection; the moral drawn from the story (193ab); and the wish at the end (193cd) for the future happiness of story-teller and audience. Cf. the Hesiodic story (*Theog.* 570ff., *WD* 54ff.) of the first woman, the Aesopic story (Callimachus fr. 192.15f. Pf.) of the days when beasts and birds and fishes could talk, and Socrates' idea (*Phd.* 60c) that a story of how Pleasure and Pain had their heads fastened together would be typically Aesopic (see further *J.H.S.* 86 (1966) 41ff.). Aristophanes' story does not resemble the plots of his extant comedies, except in being amusing and fanciful, nor, so far as our evidence goes, had anyone composed a comedy on a comparable theme; the *Ant-men* of Pherecrates was a burlesque version of a myth in which ants were turned into men, and the *Anthropogony* of Antiphanes, whatever its theme, is unlikely to have been earlier than *Smp.*

Plato's reason for giving Aristophanes a speech of this kind may well be that he regarded comedy, fairy-tales and fables as reflecting the same popular attitudes and values; he was aware of the extent to which comic poets used fairy-tale motifs and techniques (e.g. in *Birds*). Aristophanes, unlike all the other speakers in *Smp.*, recognises that when you fall in love you see in another individual a special and peculiar 'complement' to yourself; for you, union with that individual is an end, most certainly not a means, not a step towards some 'higher' and more abstract plane, and very often you continue to love and desire that person even when much more powerful sensory or intellectual stimuli impinge upon you from alternative sources. Having composed for Aristophanes the only speech in *Smp.* which strikes a modern reader as founded on observable realities, Plato later makes Diotima reject and condemn its central theme (205de, cf. 212c).

Aristophanes' notion that in sexual eros we are groping in ignorance after something beyond temporary union (192c4–d3) might itself be regarded as an uninformed but not totally misdirected groping after the metaphysical world perceived and expounded by Diotima (210a–

212a); and his statement that the permanence we seek is a return to our 'original nature' (192c5, d4) might be seen as a faint apprehension of the doctrine, developed in *Phdr.* 247c–249c, *Meno* 81a–87b, *Phd.* 72e–77c, that the individual is enabled to progress towards systematic knowledge of the good and the beautiful by 'recollection' of the ideas which his soul once perceived directly. However, recollection and the existence of the soul before union with the body are nowhere mentioned by Diotima, and we cannot be sure what view Plato took of the recollection theory when he wrote *Smp.*

189c5 αἰσθανόμενοί γε 'if they *did* realise it'. **c6 κατασκευάσαι** sc. ἐμοὶ δοκοῦσιν. **c7 οὐχ ὥσπερ...αὐτόν:** for the construction cf. 179e1 n. **c8 φιλανθρωπότατος:** applied to a deity (as in a flattering address to Hermes, Ar. *Peace* 392) who is notably benevolent to mankind, but more commonly (especially in the orators) applied to people: 'kind', 'decent', 'nice'. Plato is precluded by his metaphysics from treating φιλανθρωπία as a virtue.

d1 ἐπίκουρος 'helper'. **d2 τούτων...3 εἴη** lit. 'of those(sc. defects) which having been cured there would be happiness...' (on εὐδαιμονία cf. 180b7 n.). **d4 τῶν ἄλλων** 'others', as commonly in Greek, without the specific reference of English 'the others'. **d5 τὰ παθήματα αὐτῆς** 'what has happened to it', 'what has been done to it'. **d6 αὐτή** = ἡ αὐτή. **d7 ἀλλοία** 'of another kind'. **γένη** 'sexes', as is clear from what follows.

e2 ἀνδρόγυνον...4 θῆλεος lit. 'for at that time (sc. there was) one (sc. of the three which) was androgynous in form and shared name (sc. made up) from both, male and female'. **ἀλλ' ἤ** 'except'. **ἐν ὀνείδει:** as, e.g., in Eupolis fr. 3 (*Suppl. com.*), denoting an effeminate or cowardly man. **e6 στρογγύλον...ἔχον** 'round, with back and sides forming a circle'. **e7 τὰ ἴσα** 'the same number as...'.

190a2 ἐναντίοις κειμένοις 'facing opposite directions'. Further details become clear from the description of the transformation in 190e2–191a5, b5–c1. These original humans had two backs, but no visible chest or belly, and their genitals (αἰδοῖα) faced outwards, where the buttocks are now. **a4 εἰκάσειεν** 'infer', 'imagine'. **ὀρθόν** 'upright'. **a5 ὁποτέρωσε** 'in whichever direction (sc. of the two directions faced)'. **ὁπότε...θεῖν** 'whenever they launched themselves into a quick run'; ὁρμᾶν (cf. 185e7) with an infinitive is 'start' (energetically or eagerly) 'to...'. **a6 ὥσπερ...7 κύκλῳ** lit. 'as those who tumble' (i.e. perform acrobatics) 'and bringing their legs round upright tumble in a circle'; the reference is clearly to somersaults. **a8 ἀπερειδόμενοι** 'pushing off from the ground'.

b1 τὸ μέν...3 μετέχει 'the male (sc. sex) was originally (τὴν ἀρχήν) an offspring of the sun...'. The sun is a male deity, 'mother' earth a female deity; the notion that the moon is bisexual (despite the gender of the noun σελήνη and the frequent identification of the moon with other goddesses) occurs also in Philochorus (fr. 184) c. 300 B.C., and later in an Orphic hymn. **b4 καὶ αὐτά...αὐτῶν** 'both they themselves and their course'; cf. a4 ἐπορεύετο. **b5 ἰσχύν...ῥώμην:** the former is more strictly material, the latter denotes the moral ascendancy afforded by well-being; cf. Thuc. 7.18.2 'the Spartans had acquired a certain ῥώμη because they thought...'. **b6 φρονήματα:** cf. 182c2. **b7 ὃ λέγει...λέγεται:** Otus and Ephialtes, 'tallest men on earth', who had once imprisoned Ares for a year (*Il.* 5.385ff.), planned to overthrow the gods by piling Mt Ossa on Olympus and Pelion on Ossa (*Od.* 11.307–20), but Zeus destroyed them. Plato does not say καὶ περὶ ἐκείνων, and it seems that he is interpreting the Homeric passage as a covert or confused allusion to the double humans. Allegorical interpretation of Homer was familiar to him (*Cratylus* 407b), and in *Phdr.* 229d–e Socrates playfully offers a rationalistic interpretation of a myth.

c1 ἐπιθησομένων: on the construction cf. 183b4 n. **c2 ἐβουλεύοντο ...ποιῆσαι** 'deliberated about what to do with them'; ποιεῖν + accusative, with an adverb or phrase, is 'treat', 'do with...' or 'do to...'. **ἠπόρουν** 'they were at a loss'. **c3 οὔτε...εἶχον:** the direct deliberative question 'Am I to kill them?' or 'How can I kill them?' would be expressed in the subjunctive (e.g. 214b5, e2); then in 'I didn't know' (or 'I didn't see') 'how I could kill them' the subjunctive can be replaced by an optative (*MT* 99–101, 265f.). **c4 γίγαντας:** Zeus and the gods fought a great war against the Titans and another against the Giants; both wars are portrayed in the visual arts, and in both the thunderbolt (κεραυνός) is naturally Zeus's decisive weapon. **αἱ τιμαί...5 ἠφανίζετο** 'for the honours and sacrifices they received from men were going to disappear (sc. if they destroyed mankind'); for the imperfect cf. Antiphon 3.β.4 'if the javelin...had wounded him, no argument ὑπελείπετο to us' (i.e. '...would have remained to us'). Just as a human feels his life in society to be insupportable if his fellows do not display their regard for him, gods are treated as needing the festivals and sacrifices with which they are honoured; cf. *GPM* 226–36. **c6 ἀσελγαίνειν: ἀσελγής** is used of people whose behaviour is morally shocking. **μόγις** 'at last', 'after much difficulty'. **c7 μηχανήν...d1 γενόμενοι** 'a bright idea about how' (not 'in order that') 'men could both (sc. still) exist...'; *MT* 126.

d3 βαδιοῦνται 'they will walk'; the present is βαδίζω. **d6 ἀσκω-λιάζοντες**: ancient lexicographers relate the word to ἀσκός 'wine-skin' and explain it as denoting a game in which men jumped on to greased wineskins and tried to keep their balance. Since we require a reference to hopping on one foot, it seems that that further difficulty was part of the game. **d7 ὄα** 'sorb-apples', the fruit of *Sorbus domestica*.

e1 ταριχεύειν 'preserve' (sc. by drying). **ἢ ὥσπερ...2 θριξίν:** halving a (sc. hard-boiled and shelled) egg with a hair is possible; Plutarch, *Moralia* 770b mentions 'dividing an egg with a hair' as a proverbial expression used jokingly of the ease with which lovers, apparently so firmly united, can fall out over a triviality. The point of the comparison here is the ease with which Zeus halved individuals who had taken their own physical integrity for granted. Any reference to the fragility of love-affairs would be very much out of tune with the rest of Aristophanes' story. **e4 τομήν...τμῆσιν** 'the cut' (i.e. the place where the division has been made)...'his own division' (i.e. the fact that it has been made); but no rigid universal distinction between abstracts in -ή and abstracts in -σις can be derived from this instance. **e5 τἄλλα** sc. wounds created by the division. **e7 σύσπαστα βαλλάντια** purses which are 'pulled together' in the sense 'closed by a draw-string'. **e8 ἀπέδει** 'fastened it off'. **e9 ὀμφαλόν** 'navel'. **καὶ τὰς μέν...191a3 ῥυτίδας** 'and he smoothed out the other numerous wrinkles and put the chest together' (διαρθροῦν is to construct as an articulated or organic whole) 'with a tool of the kind which shoe-makers (sc. have) when they smooth the wrinkles of leather on the last'. Since the change in the method of human procreation was not effected until later (191b5–c8), Aristophanes passes over in silence the differentiation between male and female breasts. The simple verb λεαίνοντες picks up the compound ἐξελέαινε (a1), as 190d5 τεμῶ and d7 ἔτεμνε pick up the compound διατεμῶ (d1).

191a4 τὰς περί...ὀμφαλόν 'those in the area of the belly, that is (*sc.* in the area of) the navel'; on this use of καί, not discussed in *GP*, see W. J. Verdenius, *Mnemosyne* 4.9 (1956) 249. **a5 φύσις** '(*sc.* original) form'.

b1 καὶ τῆς ἄλλης ἀργίας 'and inactivity too'. **b2 τὸ δέ** 'and the other half'. **b3 εἴτε...5 ἀνδρός** 'whether the whole of which it encountered a half had been a woman – and we now call that half a "woman" – or a man'. Yet the half of an original androgyne must also have sought its other half, and we use 'man' and 'woman' of any human being, i.e. of any 'surviving half', without regard to its original complement. It seems that Aristophanes means to explain the co-existence of homosexuality and heterosexuality but in explaining the first does not trouble to mention the second. **b5 ἐλεήσας** 'taking pity'. **b7 τέως ...εἶχον** 'for until then they had these too on the outside', i.e. facing away from the direction in which the face now (190d2–4) points. **καὶ ἐγέννων...c1 γῆν:** it seems that the male half of a double human (and both halves of a double male) planted seed in the ground; who suckled the infant, we are not told. Both γεννᾶν and τίκτειν are used both of begetting and of bearing (cf. p. 147).

c1 τέττιγες 'cicadas', which in fact mate in the usual way; the female lays her eggs in trees, the young fall to the ground, and they live underground until emerging for their final metamorphosis into adults. Some species of grasshopper lay eggs directly into the ground, and the female has a very large, hard ovipositor. Plato may have confused cicadas and grasshoppers, and may have thought that the grasshopper's ovipositor is a penis. **c2 μετέθηκε...πρόσθεν** 'so he brought it round to their front'. **c6 πλησμονή** 'satisfaction'; cf. 185e6. **γοῦν** 'at any rate'. **c7 διαπαύοιντο** 'take a rest' from their otherwise unending quest. **c8 ἔστι...d1 ἀνθρώποις** 'so eros of one another is inborn in humanity from as long ago as that'.

d2 ἐπιχειρῶν: ἐστί...ἐπιχειρῶν 'he is one who tries' would be an uncommon (though not unparalleled) use of the participle; 'he is inborn' (adjective) ...'and a reconstructor' (agent-noun) ...'καὶ ἐπιχειρῶν' is somewhat easier; cf. 175c4, and Dem. 21.114 'he is impious and vile καὶ πᾶν ἂν ὑποστὰς εἰπεῖν', i.e. '...and a man who'd be prepared to say anything'. **d4 σύμβολον** 'tally'. If an object is cut in half and given half each to *A* in one part of the world and *B* in another, *A* and *B* can prove their identity to one another for any personal, commercial or political purpose. Arist. *De generatione animalium* 772b10 summarises Empedocles' genetic theory as 'male and female each contain, as it were, a σύμβολον'. **ψῆτται** 'flatfish'. **d6 τμῆμα** 'cut' in the sense 'cut-off piece'; contrast τομή and τμῆσις in 190e4. **d8 μοιχῶν...e1 μοιχεύτριαι** 'adulterers...adulteresses'; adultery rather than marriage, since for a man marriage is a matter of compliance with convention (192b2) and a woman is given in marriage by the male head of her family, whereas adultery requires positive sexual initiative.

e1 ἐκ τούτου...γίγνονται: these words (which recur in e5) are cumbrous and may be interpolated; if we remove them, we should put a comma after γυναῖκες. **e3 οὐ πάνυ** 'not all that', 'not so very', with the implication (unlike, e.g., 180c2) 'not at all'. **e5 ἑταιρί-στριαι** 'lesbians' in modern idiom (because of the way Sappho, a native of Lesbos, expresses her emotions about girls), though in antiquity 'Lesbian' connoted sexual inventiveness in general. This is the only surviving passage from classical Attic literature which acknowledges the existence of female homosexuality. **e6 τέως:** here (contrast 191b7) = ἕως. **e7 τεμάχια** 'slices'.

192a1 καὶ εἰσιν...7 τοιοῦτοι: since it is a taunt in Old Comedy (e.g. Ar. *Knights* 875–80, Plato Comicus fr. 186) that eminent politicians in their youth submitted shamelessly (or for money) to homosexual importunities, and this taunt, characteristic of the cynical attitudes of comedy (cf. *GH* 147f.), must have been familiar to Plato, he means Aristophanes to be speaking tongue-in-cheek. **a5 ἀρ-ρενωπίας** 'masculinity'. **ἀσπαζόμενοι** 'welcoming', 'embracing', 'being glad to see'. **a6 μόνοι...ἄνδρες:** cf. Xen. *Hell.* 7.1.24 'and they thought Lycomedes the only *man*'. For ἀποβαίνουσιν cf. 181a3.

b2 φύσει...νόμου: the contrast between 'nature' and νόμος (not simply 'law' but all the pressures created by existence in an organised society) is one of the most important issues in the intellectual life of the Greeks; cf. *HGP* iii ch. 4. **b3 καταζῆν** 'live all the time', to judge from the few contexts in which the word occurs (nowhere else in Plato). **b4 παιδεραστής τε καὶ φιλεραστής:** the former term applies to the pursuer, the latter to his younger quarry; cf. 191e7f. and p. 4. **b7 ἐκπλήττονται** 'are overcome'; the word is used of strong reactions, including fear, amazement and admiration.

c1 οἰκειότητι: a relationship in which one treats another with the affection appropriate to dealing with one's own kin. **ὡς ἔπος εἰπεῖν:** cf. 179a2 n. **c4 ὅτι...γίγνεσθαι:** the question 'what exactly is it that one *wants*?' becomes very important in Diotima's exposition (204d–206a); cf. d3–5. **c5 ἀφροδισίων:** cf. p. 2; the word covers also homosexual intercourse (*GH* 63). **c6 οὕτως** qualifies μεγάλης.

d1 μαντεύεται...2 καὶ αἰνίττεται 'divines... and (*sc.* in speaking of it) disguises'; an αἴνιγμα may be an incomplete or allusive reference, not necessarily a constructed 'riddle'. **ἐν τῷ αὐτῷ** 'together'; cf. e1. **d3 Ἥφαιστος:** the metal-working god (cf. 197b2). **d8 θέλω...e1 αὐτό** 'I am willing to fuse' (cf. 183e6) 'and smelt you together'; φυσᾶν is 'blow', e.g. with a bellows in working metal.

e2 ὄντα: adapted to the singular predicate rather than to the subject of ζῆν. **e6 οὐδ' ἂν εἷς** = οὐδεὶς ἄν. **e7 ἀτεχνῶς:** cf. 173d5 n. **ἄρα:** 'after all', 'all along', 'as he now realises'; cf. 174b4, 192c6. **e10 αὕτη** 'as described', i.e. double. **τοῦ ὅλου...193a1 διώξει:** 'the desire and pursuit of the whole' has become an English cliché of much wider application than in this context.

193a2 διωκίσθημεν...3 Λακεδαιμονίων: in 385 (cf. p. 10), according to Xen. *Hell.* 5.2.5–7, the Spartans destroyed the city-wall of Mantinea in Arcadia, and the population was dispersed (διῳκίσθη) at Spartan insistence into four separate settlements. Mantinea was not the only Arcadian state, but her pro-Athenian orientation in the Peloponnesian War and the service of Mantinean mercenaries in Athenian forces (e.g. Thuc. 6.29.3) no doubt created a tendency in Athens to call Mantineans 'Arcadians' *par excellence*. **a3 φόβος...5 περίιμεν** lit. 'so there is a fear... how we shall not be split in two', i.e.

'...a fear that we may be...'; cf. Dem. 9.75 δέδοιχ' ὅπως μή... ἀνάγκη γενήσεται 'I am afraid a necessity may arise...'. **a5 ὥσπερ ...7 λίσπαι** 'like those who are moulded on stelae in outline' (i.e. 'in relief') 'sawn in half down the nose, becoming like half-dice' (which were used as tallies; cf. 191d5 n.). **a8 πάντ'...εὐσεβεῖν** 'every man must exhort (*sc.* others) to be pious in all things'. παρακελεύεσθαι takes a dative, so that 'every man' must be its subject here.

b1 τὰ μέν...τῶν δέ 'that fate...what we want'. **ὡς...2 στρατη-γός** 'according as Eros (*sc.* and no other) is...'; for Eros as 'general' cf. 197d3, e2. **b4 διαλλαγέντες** 'reconciled'. **b5 τοῖς ἡμετέροις αὐτῶν:** cf. 173c6 n. **b6 ὑπολάβῃ** 'retort that...', 'interrupt (*sc.* saying) that...' and 'suppose that...' are all possible. **κωμῳδῶν:** Eryximachus has told Aristophanes to be serious (189a7–c1) and is therefore likely not so much to ridicule Aristophanes' speech as to object if Aristophanes ridicules Agathon. κωμῳδεῖν, usually 'mock', 'ridicule', needs to be translated here 'treat...as funny'; in 193d7–e2 it is seen as a consequence of such treatment that the company may not get back to serious speaking at all. **b7 Παυσανίαν...c2 ἄρρενες:** cf. p. 3 and 192c2–4. In ἴσως κτλ. 'for it may well be that *they* really are...' Aristophanes is assuring us that what he has said is not just a reckless comic slander.

c2 δὲ οὖν (a combination usually transmitted in texts as δ' οὖν) indicates resumption after a digression, but can also (as here; cf. 174e2–4, 180e3) give weight to the second member of an antithesis, dismissing the first member as unimportant. Cf. *GP* 461. **καθ' ἁπάντων** 'about all'; κατά+genitive can mean 'against', but it is sometimes impossible to draw a distinction (with 'say' and 'speak') between κατά and περί. **c3 ἡμῶν τὸ γένος** 'the human race'. **c4 ἐκτελέσαιμεν** 'fulfil'. **c8 κατὰ νοῦν αὐτῷ πεφυκότων** 'congenial to the individual himself'.

d2 ὀνίνησιν 'benefits'. **d3 ἐλπίδας...5 ποιῆσαι:** followed as it is by 'that, if *we* show piety towards the gods, he will establish us...and... make us fortunate...', ἐλπίδας παρέχεται is treated grammatically like verbs meaning 'promise' or 'declare'; as sometimes with ἐλπίζειν, the context makes it possible to use the aorist infinitive without risk of misunderstanding. **d3 ἡμῶν ...4 εὐσέβειαν** 'that, if *we* show piety..., ...'; 'we' is emphatic, while παρεχομένων, an element shared with the previous clause (καί...παρέχεται), occupies the unemphatic position immediately after the leading element of the clause.

193d6–194e3: Socrates' misgivings before Agathon's speech

Socrates expressed misgivings about his own ability to give a satisfactory speech after Agathon. He attempted to engage Agathon in a philosophical argument, but was prevented from doing so by Phaedrus.

Aristodemus himself lay next to Eryximachus (175a4f.) and should therefore have been the next to speak; but 'each of the two' (193e1) ignores his existence.

If Agathon answered the question put to him by Socrates in 194c9f., the company might never get back to the subject of Eros; Phaedrus' intervention (194d1–9) comes not a moment too soon.

193d8 κωμῳδήσῃς: cf. b6 n.

e3 καὶ γάρ...4 ἐρρήθη 'I *enjoyed* listening to your speech'; cf. 194d4. **εἰ μή...5 ἐρωτικά** lit. 'if I did not join in knowing...being formidable...', i.e. 'if I did not acknowledge...their expertise...'; συνειδέναι + dative sometimes denotes complicity, sometimes (when the pronoun is reflexive, e.g. 216b3) conscience or self-awareness, but here it denotes simply knowing something about another person which that person also knows.

194a1 ἠγώνισαι 'competed'; cf. p. 130. **a2 οὗ...εἰμι** 'in my place'. **a4 ἐν παντὶ εἴης** 'you'd be in desperate straits', 'you wouldn't know *what* to do'. **a5 φαρμάττειν** 'cast a spell on...'; it is clear from *Phd.* 95b ('Don't speak so confidently, in case some evil influence perverts the argument on which we are embarking') that excessive praise or over-confident prediction was felt to incur the jealousy of supernatural forces. **a6 τὸ θέατρον:** normally theatrical, but here 'my audience', appropriate on the lips of a dramatic poet. **προσδοκίαν** 'expectation'. **a8 ἐπιλήσμων** 'forgetful'; cf. Socrates in *Prt.* 334c: 'I'm a forgetful sort of person, and if anyone speaks at length I forget what it is he's talking about'.

b1 μεγαλοφροσύνην 'self-confidence'. **b2** ἀναβαίνοντος... ὑποκρι-τῶν 'going up on to the platform with the actors'; not 'taking a bow', but at the προαγών (note b3 μέλλοντος κτλ.), when publicity was given to the poets, producers and actors a few days before a dramatic festival. **b4** λόγους: what a play is 'about' can be called its λόγος (Ar. *Peace* 50, *Wasps* 54), but the word can be applied to any connected utterance, and a dramatic poet can certainly be said to 'display λόγοι of his own' in putting on a play. ἐκπλαγέντος: ∼ ἐκπλήττειν; cf. 192b7.

b6 οὐ δήπου...7 ἡγῇ 'surely you don't think me so obsessed with theatre' (lit. '...so full of...'); if Socrates did think so, he was not far wrong (cf. a6, 197de). **b7** νοῦν ἔχοντι 'to anyone who has any sense'. **b8** ἔμφρονες...ἀφρόνων: here 'intelligent...stupid'; some-times 'sane...insane'.

c2 ἄγροικον δοξάζων 'entertaining an impolite opinion'; ἄγροικος 'rustic' usually connotes boorishness, a fact which reflects the cultural dominance of the city in a population still heavily dependent on the land. **c3** φροντίζοις 'care about...', 'worry about...'. **c4** ἀλλὰ μή...ὦμεν 'but maybe we're not that (*sc.* σοφοί)'. μή + subjunctive is 'perhaps...', and it is negatived with οὐ; *MT* 92. **c5** ἐκεῖ 'in the theatre'.

d2 οὐδέν...3 γίγνεσθαι 'after that it won't matter to him' (διαφέρειν is 'make a difference' as well as 'be different') 'that *any* of our present purposes' (lit. 'of the things here') 'should be realised in *any* way'. ὅτῳ διαλέγηται: cf. 190c3 n. **d4** ἄλλως τε: cf. 173c5 n. **d6** ἀποδέ-ξασθαι 'exact'; ἀποδιδόναι (as in d7) denotes giving what the recipient has a right (moral or legal) to expect, and ἀποδέχεσθαι is (here, but not always) the complementary relation. **d7** ἀποδούς... 8 διαλεγέσθω lit. 'so let each of the two, having rendered to the god, thus then converse'. The point of οὕτως between participle and verb is 'only after..., then ...', 'not ... until one has ...'.

194e4–197e8: Agathon's speech

Eros is the youngest of the gods, for he has nothing to do with old age; the strife among the gods related by the poets took place before the reign of Eros began. He is tender, supple and beautiful. He is supreme in justice, being incompatible with violence; in self-control, being superior to all pleasures and desires; in courage, for he worsts Ares, bravest of the gods; and in ability, for the desire for beauty inspires all arts and skills.

Agathon attributes to Eros himself one quality, beauty, which belongs to the objects of sexual desire; two virtues, creativity and peacemaking, which depend on equating Eros with all positive volition or even (as in Eryximachus' speech) with absence of aggressiveness; and two more, self-discipline and courage, which depend on exploitation of words (196c5–d5). At the end (197e6–8) Agathon describes his speech as partly παιδιά ('sport', 'relaxation', 'entertainment') and partly σπουδὴ μετρία ('seriousness in the proper measure', 'a degree of seriousness') – 'to the best of my ability', he adds. Similarly Gorgias of Leontini concludes (B11.21) his 'defence of Helen' by calling it a παίγνιον ('trifle', 'game') – a composition, that is, which is meant to be admired for its elegance, piquancy and skill, but is not a contribution to science or philosophy, let alone to practical politics. We must recall this if we feel annoyance at Agathon's verbal sophistries or his apparent inability to draw distinctions which, if drawn, would profoundly affect his generalisations. The speech is appropriate to a man whose business in life is the manipulation of language. In so far as it subsumes under eros all kinds of desire for τὰ καλά (197b8) and seems to attribute to this desire all good in the life of gods and men, it may be regarded as expressing, although in ways which make it immediately vulnerable to systematic criticism, some degree of 'right opinion' (cf. 202a9 n.) on the role of Eros as Diotima sees it.

The speech exhibits the characteristic features of encomia (cf. pp. 11f.): first, the birth of Eros; next, his external appearance; then, his virtues. The last section (197d1–e5) consists of a chain of laudatory phrases organised in pairs or series, with a high degree of symmetry, rhyme and assonance. Its nearest analogue is Gorgias B6, a substantial citation from a funeral speech. Gorgias had a considerable influence on the stylistic development of Greek prose in the late fifth and early fourth centuries, and his influence on Agathon is explicitly recognised by Socrates in 198c1–5. It appears not only in the chain of phrases in Agathon's peroration, but also in the frequency with which the speech refers to its own features (194e4f., 197c3), legislates for the genre (195a1–5), ticks off points in order (197a7f., b4, c6f., 196a1f., b4f., d4–6, 197c1–3), and systematically adduces τεκμήρια for each assertion (195a9–b1, d6, 196a4f., e3f.); cf. Gorgias B6 lines 11f., B11 *passim*.

In the peroration (197d1–e5) nearly all the thirty-one members (or 'cola') into which the passage can be articulated by attention to the phrasing indicated by the sense are recognisable, once normal rules of Attic prosody, elision, crasis, etc., have been applied, as metrical units familiar in Greek lyric poetry. Thus d3 ἐν ἑορταῖς, ἐν χοροῖς, ἐν θυσίαις is one type of ionic trimeter (∪∪ – – – ∪ – – ∪ ∪ –), and the immediately following γιγνόμενος ἡγεμών (– ∪ ∪∪ – ∪ –) is a cretic dimeter; then (d4) comes a trochaic tetrameter, πρᾳότητα…ἐξορίζων (– ∪ – ∪ – ∪ – – ∪∪ ∪ – ∪ – ∪ – –), and after that, in φιλόδωρος εὐμενείας (∪ ∪ – ∪ – ∪ – –) the type of ionic dimeter called 'anacreontic'. The more singular 'iambo-dochmiac' ∪ – – – – – ∪ – ∪∪ ∪ – (d2 μετ' ἀλλήλων…συνιέναι) is partially repeated in e1 κυβερνήτης ἐπιβάτης (∪ – – – ∪∪ ∪ –); and ⊻ – ∪ – ∪ – – – ∪ – – in e1 παραστάτης…2 ἄριστος repeated in e4 πάντων θεῶν τε κἀνθρώπων (κἀν- = καὶ ἀν-) νόημα, is an expansion of d1 οἰκειότητος δὲ πληροῖ (– – ∪ – – ∪ – –). The total number of colon-types occurring in Greek lyric poetry is so large that some of them are bound to occur in any prose passage which is constituted by a chain of phrases, but if we attempt to set out Gorgias B6 as a lyric poem we see the difference at once; Plato has taken considerable trouble to give Agathon's peroration a poetic character in addition to caricaturing its 'Gorgianic' structure.

Phaedrus thought it high praise to call Eros oldest of the gods (178a9–c2, cf. 177a8). Agathon, however, calls him 'youngest of the gods and always young' (195c1), and in rejecting Phaedrus' view he uses language ('more ἀρχαῖος than Cronus and Iapetus') which we know from comedy to have been the language in which the young and 'modern' mocked the old and 'old-fashioned' in the latter part of the fifth century B.C. (cf. 195b7 n.). The 'generation gap' at that time was not as spectacular as in our own day, since the changes in the material conditions of life were comparatively slow and small, but there was undoubtedly a gap in taste and moral attitudes; Aristophanes' *Clouds*, in which Socrates is portrayed as self-consciously up to date, exploits it, and Agathon's high valuation of youth is another aspect of it.

194e4 ἐγώ...**5** εἰπεῖν: cf. Gorgias B6 lines 11f., εἰπεῖν δυναίμην ἃ βούλομαι, βουλοίμην δ' ἃ δεῖ.   **e6 εὐδαιμονίζειν** 'felicitate'.

195a2 οἶος...3 ᾗ lit. 'for what kind of things the person about whom the speech is, (*sc.* being himself) of what kind, is actually responsible', i.e. 'the nature of the subject of the speech and the nature of that for which he is responsible'.   **a6 εἰ θέμις...εἰπεῖν:** on θέμις cf. 188d2; ἀνεμέσητον is 'not incurring angry resentment (νέμεσις)'. Agathon's 'verbal obeisance' resembles that of Pausanias in 180e3.

b1 φεύγων φυγῇ: this curious expression recurs in *Epinomis* 974b ('elude') and *Epistles* 8.354c ('shun'); formally it resembles 'see with (*sc.* one's own) eyes' (e.g. Hipp. *De arte* 2), 'speak with the voice', i.e. '...out loud' (Lys. 6.51), etc.   **b2 ταχὺ ὄν δῆλον ὅτι** 'which is fast, obviously'; the phrase δῆλον ὅτι can be used (like οἶδ' ὅτι) simply as an adverb.   **b3 οὐδ' ἐντὸς πολλοῦ πλησιάζειν** lit. 'approach not even within much', i.e. 'not come within a mile of...', since one does not usually fall in love with old people. Cf. 181d2.   **b4 καί ἐστιν** *sc.* νέος.   **b5 πελάζει** 'draws near to...', a predominantly poetic word.   **b7 Κρόνου καὶ Ἰαπετοῦ:** Cronus, father of Zeus, was imprisoned by him (hence c4 δεσμοί); Cronus had castrated his own father, Uranus (hence c4 ἐκτομαί, and cf. 180d6–8 n.). Iapetus was one of the 'Titans', of the same generation as Cronus. In Attic usage to call someone 'Cronus' or 'Iapetus' (e.g. Ar. *Clouds* 929, 998) was to sneer at him as being hopelessly old-fashioned.

c1 τὰ δέ...3 γεγονέναι: such (lit.) 'doings involving gods' are recounted by Hesiod in *Theog.* 147–210, 453–506. What Parmenides said about them, we do not know; he did, however, speak of κρατερή...ἀνάγκη as 'holding (*sc.* Being) in the bonds (δεσμοῖσι) of a limit which confines it all round' (B8.30f. (350 KR)), and he seems (cf. A37) to have spoken elsewhere of ἀνάγκη in terms appropriate to a ruling deity, as Agathon does in 197b7 (cf. the 'decrees of ἀνάγκη' in Gorgias B11.6).   **c6 ἐξ οὗ...βασιλεύει:** Agathon is indulging (like Pausanias in 180d4–e3) in 'creative mythology', inventing a past which will be acceptable to the present.   **c7 πρὸς δέ...ἁπαλός** 'and, in addition to being young, sensitive' (or '...tender', '...delicate'). ποιητοῦ...d1 ἐνδεής 'he lacks a poet'.

d2 Ὅμηρος...**5** βαίνει: Agamemnon in *Il.* 19.91–4 describes the speed and range of Ate, 'daughter of Zeus', the deity who inspires in men foolish and disastrous decisions: '...for she does not approach over the ground' (οὔδεος is genitive of οὖδας) 'but walks along the heads of men', i.e. leaping lightly from man to man.

e2 κρανίων 'skulls'.   **e4** ἤθεσι 'characters', 'temperaments'.   **e5** ἵδρυται 'is seated', 'has taken up his abode'; the word is sometimes used of setting up statues and founding sanctuaries.   ἑξῆς 'in succession', i.e. 'just as they come'.   **e7** καὶ ποσὶν καὶ πάντη 'not only with his feet' (like Ate), 'but all over'.   **e8** μαλακωτάτοις: 'character' and 'soul' are treated here not as belonging to a category quite distinct from material bodies but as the most tenuous and rarefied elements in the body; this accords with the Homeric notion that the soul, parted from the body at death, is a kind of gaseous replica of the living body.

196a2 ὑγρός 'moist', i.e. 'supple', 'pliable'.   πάντη περιπτύσσεσθαι lit. 'wrap himself round all ways', i.e. 'enfold completely'.   **a3** διὰ πάσης ψυχῆς *sc.* of those whom he does enter; we have been told in 195e5–7 that Eros does not enter every soul.   **a4** συμμέτρου 'well-shaped' rather than 'shapely', if justice is to be done to the notion that Eros makes a perfect fit with the soul which he enters.   **a5** εὐσχημοσύνη...**6** ἀσχημοσύνη 'gracefulness...awkwardness'; at this point, in inferring that Eros is graceful from the fact that gracefulness is an attribute of the objects of eros, Agathon leaves himself vulnerable to the attack which Socrates will shortly launch upon his argument. **ὅ:** cf. 175d4 n.   **a7** χρόας 'complexion', but of the whole body, not simply of the face; the word sometimes requires translation as 'skin', 'surface', sometimes as 'colour'.   **a8** ἡ κατ' ἄνθη δίαιτα 'living among flowers'. Since the colour and texture of human skin is much more like flower-petals in youth than in later years, and the smell of flowers (cf. b2 εὐώδης) is sexually stimulating, the idea that flowers are the preferred abode of Eros is long-standing in Greek literature (Alcman fr. 58), and in vase-painting he is sometimes shown holding a flower or associated with floral patterns.   ἀνανθεῖ...**b1** ἀπηνθηκότι: like 'bloom' in English, ἄνθος is used figuratively of beauty and captivating freshness; ἀπανθεῖν is 'fade', 'lose one's looks'.

b2 ἐνταῦθα δέ: for this non-connective δέ cf. 183c2–d3 n.   **b5** ἀρετῆς:

the articulation of ἀρετή is very clear here: δικαιοσύνη (b6–c3), σωφροσύνη (c3–8), ἀνδρεία (c8–d4), σοφία (d5–197b9). Piety (εὐσέβεια) is missing, since Eros is himself a god. Cf. p. 11 and 184c6 μέρος ἀρετῆς. **b6 οὔτ' ἀδικεῖ...7 ἄνθρωπον:** a somewhat reckless statement, considering the importance of eros as a motive of violence and fraud in myth, history and everyday life. **b7 οὔτε γάρ...c2 ὑπηρετεῖ:** a person can be forced to behave outwardly as if in love, but no one can be forced actually to be in love. πᾶς γὰρ κτλ. says further that whoever falls in love is glad to do so – which is contrary to the common Greek sentiment (e.g. Sappho fr. 172, Theognis 1353–6) that Eros is a ruthless deity from whose compulsion a person in love might gladly escape. οὔτε ποιῶν ποιεῖ = οὔτε βίᾳ ποιεῖ εἴ τι ποιεῖ.

c2 οἱ πόλεως βασιλῆς νόμοι: the image is attributed by Arist. *Rhetoric* 1406a17–23 to the fourth-century rhetorician Alcidamas. **c4 εἶναι...8 σωφρονοῖ:** the σώφρων person 'overcomes' (κρατεῖ), 'gets the better of' pleasure and desire, by resisting them, and in that sense is 'superior' (κρείττων) to pleasure; cf. Thuc. 2.60.5, where Pericles proclaims himself χρημάτων κρείσσων 'incorruptible'. The pleasure of satisfying sexual desire is, for most of us, preferable (κρείττων) to all other pleasures, and thus κρατεῖ ἡδονῶν; cf. Critias B2.7 'the Etruscan gold cup κρατεῖ', i.e. is better than any other gold cups. By equating the experience of desire with the fulfilment of desire, Agathon makes it easier for himself to exploit the ambiguity. **c6 εἰ δὲ ἥττους, κρατοῖντ' ἄν** 'and if (sc. as is conceded) they are inferior, they must be worsted...'; cf. 197b1.

d1 οὐδ' "Αρης ἀνθίσταται: from Soph. fr. 235 'Necessity' (not Eros) 'even Ares cannot withstand'. **d2 Ἀφροδίτης** sc. ἔρως. Ares fell in love with Aphrodite, who was married to Hephaestus; Hephaestus made a device with chains which imprisoned the two lovers in bed, and indignantly called the gods to witness their crime (*Od.* 8.266–366; the plan misfired, for the gods laughed and envied Ares, chains and all). **d4 ἀνδρειότατος:** if victory is the only criterion of courage, yes, but that implies that the scorpion is braver than the warrior whom it stings. Greek usage normally took into account the scale of the pain or loss risked or endured, and Eros suffers no harm but wounded pride if his victim resists temptation.

e2 ποιῆσαι *sc.* ποιητήν. **κἄν...3 πρίν:** from Eur. fr. 663 (*Stheneboea*) 'it seems that Eros teaches a poet even if there is no music in him before'; in what context this was said, is not known. κἄν κτλ. is quoted also in Ar. *Wasps* 1074. **e4 ποιητής...ἀγαθός...5 πᾶσαν ποίησιν:** coupling a noun in the accusative with an adjective, to give the sense 'in...', 'in respect of...', is normal (e.g. *Laws* 899b ἀγαθαὶ πᾶσαν ἀρετήν); coupling it with a substantival expression (as here ποιητὴς ἀγαθός) is rare, but cf. Hom. *Od.* 16.242 χεῖράς τ' αἰχμητήν. **ἃ γάρ ...6 διδάξειεν:** one cannot 'give' what one does not 'have', but if it were true that a pupil can never surpass his teacher the history of the arts would be one of continuous decline.

197a1 τήν γε...ποίησιν 'creation' now in the sense of 'procreation'; on the special and general senses of ποιεῖν and words derived from it cf. 205b8–c10. For the purpose of the present passage eros is identified with sexual desire (cf. 207a7–b2), but in a moment Agathon will identify it with all desire for creation, invention and improvement. **τίς...μὴ οὐχί...σοφίαν** lit. 'will contradict...not...to be...', i.e. 'will deny that...is...'; when 'deny' is negatived or virtually negatived – as in a rhetorical question, 'who will...?' = 'surely no one will...' – μὴ οὐ introduces the infinitive clause dependent on it. Cf. 210b2. **a4 ὅτι...6 σκοτεινός** 'that whomsoever the god teaches turns out' (cf. 181a3) 'notable and conspicuous, but whomsoever he does not touch (*sc.* remains) obscure'. Agathon now argues that each art or technique was discovered because the discoverer was motivated by desire for something better than what already existed. This is personified: 'desire and Eros led the way' – so that, e.g., Apollo was a pupil of Eros. **a6 τοξικήν...μαντικήν:** Apollo founded the first oracle (*Homeric Hymn to Apollo* 214) and can inspire a human with the 'gift' of prophecy (Solon fr. 13.53f.); from the *Iliad* onwards, he is the archer-god; and he is sometimes (e.g. Ar. *Birds* 584) regarded as a healer (though Solon *loc. cit.* 57f. makes Paeon the giver of the art of medicine, and the relation between Apollo and Paeon in the history of Greek religion is complicated).

b2 μουσικῆς: we say 'pupil of (a person)' and 'learner of (a subject)', but μαθητής (like 'student of...') can be followed by a genitive of either kind. **Ἥφαιστος χαλκείας:** cf. 192d3 n. **Ἀθηνᾶ ἱστουργίας:** weaving (ἱστός = 'loom') is one of the special concerns of Athena in

Hes. *WD* 63; Solon *loc. cit.* 49f. speaks of 'the works of Athena and Hephaestus' as means by which one 'gains a living with his hands', but he was thinking of the visual arts rather than the (feminine) art of weaving.   **b3 κυβερνᾶν:** it may be that we should understand ἔμαθε; but for a simple infinitive in the sense of τοῦ + infinitive cf. Ar. *Ach.* 196f. 'they smell of ambrosia (ἀμβροσίας)...καὶ μὴ 'πιτηρεῖν σιτί' ἡμερῶν τριῶν', i.e. '...and of not keeping a lookout for (*sc.* a notice requiring one to bring) rations for three days'.   **b4 κατεσκευ-άσθη...πράγματα** lit. 'the doings of the gods were constructed', i.e. 'the activities of the gods were formed'; πράγματα here cannot have the same reference as in 195c2, since κατασκευάζειν is used οἱ building and furnishing, not of 'composing' a quarrel.   Ἔρωτος ἐγγενομένου 'when Eros had been born among them'; cf. b7f.   **b5 δῆλον ὅτι:** cf. 195b2 n.   **κάλλους:** cf. 196d2 n.   **οὐκ ἔπι** 'there is no...for...'. ἔπι = ἔπεστι.   **b6 ἐν ἀρχῇ:** 195b6–c6.   **b8 ἐρᾶν τῶν καλῶν:** in many contexts this would be taken to mean 'be in love with beautiful persons', but in the light of 197a3–b7 the absence of distinction be-tween genders in the genitive plural is important, and the translation '...with the beautiful' or '...with beauty' is required. In 201a5–c5 the ambiguity is resolved in favour of the neuter; cf. 204d3–9.

c1 πρῶτος: we might have expected πρῶτον 'in the first place', given the following μετὰ τοῦτο, and πρὸ τῶν in Stobaeus' citation of the passage may be a corruption of πρῶτον; but given the frequency with which πρῶτος is joined with αὐτός (e.g. Thuc. 6.88.8) we may (hesitantly) translate 'himself supreme as most beautiful and best'. **c3 ἔμμετρον** 'in verse' (cf. 187d2 n.).   **c5 εἰρήνην...6 κήδει** 'peace among men, on the open sea windless calm, allaying of winds and sleep when troubled'; κῆδος is 'grief', 'mourning'. Perhaps the verses are meant to be understood as Agathon's own; but he may be quoting from a source not known to us.

d1 ἀλλοτριότητος...πληροῖ 'empties us of estrangement and fills us with affection' (cf. 192c1 n.). On the style of this passage cf. pp. 124. **d2 τιθείς** 'causing'; this use of the word is highly poetic.   **d3 ἑορταῖς** 'festivals'.   **d4 πραότητα...ἐξορίζων** 'bestowing good temper and banishing harshness'; *GPM* 201–5.   **φιλόδωρος...5 δυσμενείας** 'prompt to give friendliness, never giving hostility'. ἵλεως 'gracious', a word commonly, though not exclusively (cf. 206d4), applied to a deity's attitude to men. **ἀγανός:** Usener's emendation of the manuscripts' ἀγαθός; 'kindly', 'gentle' (in Ar. *Birds* 1321 ἀγανόφρων is an epithet of ʻΗσυχία). Stobaeus' citation of this passage has ἵλεως ἀγαθοῖς, which in itself is an unobjectionable phrase but constitutes an ill-assorted trio with the next four words. **θεατός...6 θεοῖς** 'gazed upon (*sc.* with admiration) by men of accomplishment, admired by the gods'; θεατός is used here in the sense of the poetic θηητός (Ionic θηεῖσθαι = Attic θεᾶσθαι), and for ἀγαστός cf. 180b1 ἄγανται. **ζηλωτός...εὐμοίροις** 'coveted by those who have no share in him, a desirable possession to those whose share is large'; cf. 181c4. **τρυφῆς...7 χλιδῆς:** all three words denote comfort and luxury, which under any names are usually decried by Greek moralists. **χαρίτων** 'graces', 'beauties', 'elegances'; cf. 183b3. **ἱμέρου** 'desire'; Himeros and Pothos ('longing') appear in vase-painting as Eros-like figures. **πατήρ:** the association between abstract forces was very readily expressed by the Greeks in genealogical terms, but here 177d5, where Phaedrus is called πατὴρ τοῦ λόγου, may be more apposite. **ἐπιμελής...8 κακῶν** 'looking after good, careless of bad'; whether we are meant to take the genitives as masculine or as neuter is not clear.

e1 ἐπιβάτης: a technical term for a hoplite on a trireme; the function of ἐπιβάται was to protect the crews against attack when the triremes were beached. The figure of speech here is generated by the predominantly nautical sense of κυβερνήτης 'pilot'; 'defender' is the nearest we can get. **παραστάτης** 'comrade-in-arms', strictly, the hoplite posted beside one. **e2 κόσμος:** perhaps 'ornament', but it means also 'order', 'system', 'constitution' (in Crete there were magistrates called κόσμοι), and 'government' should be considered as a translation here. **e3 ἐφυμνοῦντα** 'singing to...', 'singing in honour of...'. **e4 θέλγων** 'charming'. **e7 ἀνακείσθω:** ἀνατιθέναι is to 'dedicate' a statue or votive offering. **παιδιᾶς:** cf. p. 123.

198a1–199c2: Socrates' further misgivings

I cannot compete with Agathon's speech. I agreed to take my turn because I thought we all meant to tell aspects of the truth about Eros; as it is, all the speakers have praised Eros attractively and impressively, but without regard for the truth. If you are willing, I will tell the truth as I see it and in my own way.

It is not easy to tell one's friends that none of them has shown any sign of caring whether what he said was true or false; but there are different ways of uttering hard words, and it is up to us to see and hear Socrates in our mind's eye and ear. We must remember that ψευδής (198e2) covers 'fictitious' as well as 'lying', and that most of the speakers have been talking mythology and theology; cf. 180d6 n. Moreover, Agathon could hardly be offended by the irony with which Socrates' fulsome praise of his technical skill is charged; he knew that he and Socrates valued different things.

198a2 ἀναθορυβῆσαι 'made a stir (*sc.* of applause)'; cf. *Prt.* 334c 'all those present ἀνεθορύβησαν ὡς εὖ λέγοι'. **a4** ὦ παῖ Ἀκουμενοῦ: it is hard to define the circumstances in which a Greek was addressed as 'son of...' (e.g. *Charmides* 158b, 169b); here the reason may be that Plato wished to avoid the repetition 'looking at Eryximachus, he said, "Do you think, Eryximachus, ...?"'. **a5** ἀδεές... δέος 'a fear not to be feared', i.e. an unjustified fear. **a6** νυνδή: 194a1–4. **a8** τὸ μὲν ἕτερον 'one of the two things'.

b1 ὦ μακάριε: this mode of address often carries the implication 'surely you must see...?', as in 214c8 and 219a2 (cf. *Prt.* 309c). **b3** παντοδαπόν 'rich and varied'; cf. 193e7. **b4** οὐχ ὁμοίως μέν: the repeated μέν is very rare (*GP* 386) and may be wrong. **b5** ὀνομάτων καὶ ῥημάτων 'words and expressions'; the more specialised sense 'substantives and verbs' is first developed in *Sophist* 261e–262c. **b7** ὀλίγου... **c1** εἶχον 'I nearly ran away and was gone, if I'd had somewhere (*sc.* to go)'.

c1 Γοργίου: cf. p. 123. **c2** τὸ τοῦ Ὁμήρου... **5** ποιήσειεν: in *Od.* 11. 633–5 Odysseus departs from the edge of the underworld 'lest Persephone send up (πέμψειεν) from the underworld a Gorgon's head (Γοργείην κεφαλήν), (*sc.* the head) of a dreadful monster (δεινοῖο πελώρου)'. The story that the sight of the head of the Gorgon Medusa turned people to stone is found in Pindar, *Pythian Odes* 10.44–8, Pherecydes fr. 11.

d1 ἔφην... **2** ἐρωτικά: 177d5–8. **ὡς ἔδει** '(*sc.* I mean, not knowing) how one ought...'. **d3** ἀβελτερίας 'simple-mindedness'. **d5** ὑπάρχειν 'should be the basis'. **ἐξ αὐτῶν... 6** τιθέναι 'and that we should choose simply out of that (*sc.* the truth) the best things and present them in the most attractive way'. **d8 ἦν:** coupled with ἄρα (d7, and again in e2) ἦν is used of what has turned out to be the case (*MT* 13); cf. English 'and... was... all the time!' (where we do not imply 'and is so no more').

e1 ἀνατιθέναι 'ascribe', 'attribute' (contrast 197e7). **πράγματι** 'subject'. **e2 οὐδέν... πρᾶγμα** 'no matter'; on ἦν cf. d8 n. **e4 δόξει** 'give the appearance of...'. **ἐγκωμιάσεται:** many verbs which have an active form in the present have both an active and a middle form, without any distinction of meaning, in the future.

199a3 σεμνῶς 'impressively'. **a4 οὐ δ' εἰδώς:** cf. (though *GP* 582 ~ 187 doubts the analogy) *Politicus* 284d τούτου... ὄντος ('if this is valid') ..., μὴ δὲ ὄντος ποτέρου ('but if neither is valid')... In that passage, 'but' is preferable to 'and' as a translation of δέ; here, 'and' is needed and 'but' is impossible. **a5 ἡ γλῶσσα...6 οὔ:** Socrates adapts Eur. *Hippolytus* 612, where Hippolytus, tempted in the anger of the moment to break his oath, says ἡ γλῶσσ' ὀμώμοχ' ἡ δὲ φρὴν ἀνώμοτος 'my tongue has sworn, but my heart is unsworn'. **χαιρέτω δή** 'well, let it go!' (cf. 176e7 n.), 'it can't be helped'. Given a7 οὐ γὰρ ἂν δυναίμην, Plato may have had Eur. *Medea* 1044f. οὐκ ἂν δυναίμην· χαιρέτω βουλεύματα τὰ πρόσθεν at the back of his mind. **a7 οὐ μέντοι ἀλλά...b2 ὄφλω** 'but, all the same, the *truth* I *am* willing to tell, if you're agreeable, in my own way – not in competition with *your* speeches, so that I don't make a fool of myself' (lit. '...incur laughter').

b3 εἴ τι...4 ἀκούειν 'if you want a speech of that kind, (*sc.* that is, if you want) to hear the truth...'; δεῖσθαι can be followed by a genitive or by an infinitive. **ὀνόμασι...ῥημάτων** 'words and orderings of expressions' (cf. 198b5 n.); there is a variant ὀνομάσει (*sic*), and if adopted as ὀνομάσει (dative of ὀνόμασις) it would make the feminine τις of b5 easier, as referring to both ὀνομάσει and θέσει, but the noun is otherwise unexampled. **ἄν:** if the δ presented by some manuscripts is right, the sequence of letters is to be interpreted as δἄν = δὴ ἄν, as in ἐπειδάν = ἐπειδὴ ἄν; but that would be surprising, given that in ὅταν δή (e.g. 211b5) the relative elements, ἄν and δή, appear in a different order. **b9 ἀνομολογησάμενος** 'getting his agreement (*sc.* to some points)'; cf. 200e7. **οὕτως:** cf. 194d7 n.

c1 ἀλλ' ἐρώτα: cf. 174d3 n.

199c3–201c9: Socrates interrogates Agathon

Eros is desire for something. But one desires only what one does not yet have, i.e. what one lacks. Therefore, if Eros desires what is beautiful, i.e. desires beauty, he does not have beauty, i.e. he is not beautiful. What is good is beautiful. Therefore Eros does not have what is good.

The technique of this dialogue is characteristic of the Platonic Socrates: self-deprecating (199b8 σμίκρ' ἄττα) and self-effacing (201c6–8); disarmingly complimentary (199c3–9); insistent on the need to agree at each step (200e6–7; cf. 199b9) and on the recollection of essential steps (200a1–2); courteous but firm in the rejection of hesitant answers (200a6–b2); patient in making each general question clear by taking particular cases (199d5–e6, 200c6–d6); swift and bold in forcing fallacious inferences and assumptions on the collaborator in the dialogue (201a8–b4, c2–4, v. nn.), motivated by the need to prepare the ground for doctrinal exposition (199b8–c1) and assisted both by the fallacies which the collaborator has himself committed and by the intellectual paralysis which strikes down the collaborator at any moment of Plato's choosing (200d6–7, 201b3–7, c2–6). A dialogue in which one speaker agrees at every step with the other, never offering serious resistance or making serious criticisms, differs in form from the type of continuous, authoritative exposition which Socrates decries in *Prt.* 328d–329b, 335a–336d, and differs (at least on a cursory reading) in the impression which it conveys, but does not differ in substance.

199c3 καθηγήσασθαι 'start off'. **c4 αὐτόν . . . 5 αὐτοῦ** 'himself. . . his achievements'; so in 194e5–195a5 the δόσεις of Eros, the ἀγαθά of which he is αἴτιος, were distinguished from the god himself. **c7 μεγαλοπρεπῶς** 'magnificently', 'impressively'.

d1 πότερον . . . 2 οὐδενός; 'is he of such a kind as to stand in an "of"-relationship. . . or not?' (lit. '. . . as to be eros of something/someone or of nothing/no one?'); Greek is at an advantage, for argument of this kind, in not distinguishing between persons and things in the genitive

of the pronoun). **d3 γελοῖον. . .4 πατρός:** 'of whom is *X*?' would be
a normal way of asking about *X*'s parentage, and Socrates reasonably
explains (d2 ἐρωτῶ. . .3 ἐστιν) that in asking 'is Eros ἔρως τινός?' he
is *not* saying, 'is Eros τινος?' in the sense 'has Eros a father or
mother?' He will go on to explain that eros is 'eros *of*. . .' in the sense
that it always has an *object*. (This is, of course, open to question; the
experience of desiring or fearing, without forming any idea of what it
is that one desires or fears, is not unknown, especially in dreams.) If
anyone, through inattention to the exact form of Socrates' question,
replied, 'Eros is (*sc.* son) of *X*' (e.g. of Poros, as in 203a9–e5, where
Socrates himself asks about the parentage of Eros), he would un-
wittingly be saying, 'the father of Eros is the object of eros'. By this
answer he would indeed make himself 'ridiculous'; Socrates puts the
matter a little differently by saying that *if* 'Eros is of Poros' were a
possible answer to his question, the question itself would have been a
ridiculous question. **d4 εἰ αὐτό. . .5 ἠρώτων** 'if I were asking about
"father" by itself' (cf. e3), rather than a back-reference, 'if I were
asking about that very word "father"'. **d9 ὡσαύτως:** i.e. ὑέος γε. . .
ἡ μήτηρ μήτηρ.

e3 αὐτὸ τοῦθ' ὅπερ ἐστίν lit. 'that which (*sc.* a brother) is, by itself',
i.e. *qua* brother. **e8 πάνυ μὲν οὖν:** μὲν οὖν in a response suggests that
the previous speaker is mistaken (e.g. 201c8), but often mistaken in
not expressing himself strongly enough (e.g. 202b9). Hence πάνυ μὲν
οὖν is a formula of emphatic assent, very common in Platonic
dialogue. **e8 ἐστιν** *sc.* τινος.

200a1 τοῦτο. . .2 ὅτου: Agathon's emphatic reply suggests that he
knows what the object of eros is; Socrates is therefore saying 'don't
tell me yet! Remember it, but keep it to yourself.' **a3 αὐτοῦ** is,
strictly speaking, pleonastic with ἐκείνου: cf. *Rep.* 398a, 'a man
(ἄνδρα). . .able. . .to imitate everything. . ., if he came to our
city. . ., we would salute him (αὐτόν). . .'. **a5 ἔχων. . .6 ἢ οὐκ
ἔχων:** on the equation of ἐπιθυμεῖν with ἐρᾶν (completed in a9) cf. p.
2; and the assumption that eros is desire to 'have' or 'possess' something is important for the direction which Socrates' argument takes.
a8 σκόπει. . .9 οὕτως lit. 'consider. . .whether instead of that "probability" there is a necessity (*sc.* that it should be) so, (*sc.* namely)
that. . .'.

b1 θαυμαστῶς ... 2 ὡς: cf. 173c5 n. **b4 βούλοιτ' ἄν:** for synonymy of βούλεσθαι and ἐπιθυμεῖν (though the former cannot have a substantive as object) cf. *Lysis* 207de 'Would they not wish (βούλοιντ' ἄν) you to be as happy as possible? ... If then ... they desire (ἐπιθυμοῦσι) that you should be happy ...'. **b6 ἐκ τῶν ὡμολογημένων** 'according to what we have agreed on' (a5–b3). **b7 οὐ γάρ ... ὤν** 'after all, the man who *is* (sc. tall or strong) can't be *lacking* those (sc. attributes), can he?' **b9 εἰ γάρ** 'suppose he wanted ...'. Then at ἴσως (b10) the sentence is broken off, and a long explanatory parenthesis begins. The main thread is resumed at ἀλλ' ὅταν (c5–6), where, however, the contrast indicated by ἀλλά is a contrast with the content of the parenthesis. **b10 ἴσως ... c2 ἐπιθυμεῖν** 'for one might perhaps think, (sc. on the subject of) those (sc. qualities) and everything of that kind, that those who are such and possess those (sc. qualities) also *desire* those things (τούτων) which they *have*'.

c2 ἐξαπατηθῶμεν 'be misled'. **τούτου ἕνεκα** picks up the purpose stated in ἵνα. **c3 τούτοις** is masculine. **c4 ἀνάγκη:** cf. 200a9. **c5 τούτου:** i.e. ἔχειν ἃ ἔχουσι. **c6 ὅταν ... 8 αὐτῷ** 'whenever anyone says ... we can/could say to him ...'; the optative with ἄν often replaces a present or future indicative.

d1 εἰς τὸν ἔπειτα χρόνον looks forward to the point taken up in 205ab and developed thereafter. **d6 ἄλλο τι ὁμολογοῖ ἄν:** this looks like 'would he agree to something else?' in the sense 'surely he *would* agree to what has just been said and *not* to anything else!' (cf. d3f. 'consider if you are saying something other than this', implying 'you are not saying anything other than this'). But since we often find a question of this type introduced by ἄλλο τι ἤ 'something other than ...?' = 'surely ...!', it seems that ἄλλο τι is derived from ἄλλο τι ἤ (cf. τί δ' ἄλλο γ' ἤ ...; in Comedy). Cf. e8. **d8 τοῦτό γ'** looks forward to τό ... παρόντα; ἐκείνου is picked up by ὅ (d9).

e2 οὗτος is he who ἐρᾷ in the manner described in d8–10. A real interlocutor might say, 'I am wise/rich/strong in many ways or to a great extent, but I wish to be wise (etc.) in more ways or to a greater extent.' **ἄλλος πᾶς:** as admitted in a9–b3. **e8 ἄλλο τι:** cf. d6 n. **e9 αὐτῷ:** after e2–5, one might take this most naturally to mean τῷ ἐρῶντι: but it can also refer to Eros, and since in 201b4 the conclusion is drawn that Eros is ἐνδεής, the ambiguity is important. The omission of a subject with ἐρᾶν in 201b2 also paves the way for 201b4.

201a2 ἐπὶ δὴ τούτοις 'this being so'. **a4 τοῖς θεοῖς...5 καλῶν:** 197b3–9. **εἴη:** optative because the speech is reported: 'for (*sc.* you said,) there was no eros of what is ugly'. **a8 ἐπιεικῶς** 'reasonably'; the adjective is sometimes 'decent', 'kind' or 'honest' (cf. 210b8). **a9 ἄλλο τι:** cf. d6 n.

b1 οὐκοῦν...2 ἐρᾶν: if the subject of ἐρᾶν were specified as 'he who ἐρᾷ', the conclusion in b4 would not follow; there is no logical reason why the desire for a relationship with something beautiful should not itself be beautiful. If the subject were specified as eros, the falsity of the statement ὡμολόγηται (~ 200b3–d7) would be blatant; therefore Plato prudently leaves the subject unspecified. **b5 ἀνάγκη:** if it is Eros who ἐρᾷ, yes; but it is ὁ ἐρῶν who ἐρᾷ. **b6 μηδαμῇ:** what is ἐνδεὲς κάλλους is not necessarily 'possessing beauty *in no way*', but Agathon does not object. **b9 ὁμολογεῖς** 'agree (*sc.* with popular belief)'; Socrates himself does *not* believe that Eros is καλός.

c2 τἀγαθά...καλά: Socrates appears to be making τὰ ἀγαθά a sub-class of the class καλά, but in 204e1–2 he treats τὸ ἀγαθόν and τὸ καλόν as coincident classes; so too in *Grg.* 474d, and cf. *Meno* 77b. Anything which is καλόν, i.e. which looks or sounds good (or is good to contemplate), is also ἀγαθόν, i.e. it serves a desirable purpose or performs a desirable function, and vice versa. Cf. *GPM* 69–73. **c8 οὐ μὲν οὖν...9 δύνασαι** 'no, it is rather that you cannot...'. For φιλούμενε the papyrus has the banal φίλε. A vase-inscription of the late sixth century B.C. says Φιλόκωμος φιλεῖται; whether it means '...is popular' (implying '...is lovable') or '...is loved (*sc.* by me, or by someone whom I won't name)' is uncertain; Aesch. *Prometheus* 1004, where Prometheus refers to Zeus as τὸν στυγούμενον, is similarly ambiguous. φιλούμενε here might conceivably allude to Agathon's relationship with Pausanias, but the Aeschylean parallel seems against this.

201d1–203a8: Eros as intermediary

I learned about Eros from Diotima, who explained that he is neither beautiful nor ugly, neither good nor bad, neither immortal nor mortal, but an intermediary between the human and divine worlds.

We do not know whether Diotima is real or fictitious, and it does not much matter, considering the extreme improbability (cf. p. 10) that even if she really existed she entertained the Platonic theory of ideas in any form. The male name 'Diotimos' was common; we know far fewer women's names than men's, but 'Diotima' is attested from Boeotia in the early classical period. If Plato invented Diotima, he may have made her Mantinean because of the resemblance of the place-name to μάντις 'seer' and its cognates; 'Diotima' could be analysed as 'honoured by Zeus' (on the analogy of θεότιμος in Pindar and Bacchylides) or as 'honouring Zeus' (on the analogy of ξενότιμος in Aeschylus). Female religious experts were not unknown; *Meno* 81a refers to men and women who are σοφοὶ περὶ τὰ θεῖα πράγματα (cf. 'priests and priestesses', *ibid.*), and Aeschines' mother (according to Dem. 18.259f., a hilarious caricature) offered initiation into a minor mystery-cult. It may be that cults of this kind were numerous, and normally in the hands of women; cf. Diotima's use (209e5–210a4) of the language of initiation.

There may be other reasons why Plato makes a woman his 'spokes-person' in this work. It tends to allay our suspicion that cunning self-interest might be the mainspring of arguments for what is essentially a male homosexual foundation for philosophical activity. Again, Socrates' words 'she taught me τὰ ἐρωτικά' (201d5) are a slyly humorous reminder of another kind of ἐρωτικὸς λόγος, in which a smirking youth tells his friends about the accomplishments of a hetaira ('Rhodopis taught me all I know...'). In *Menexenus* 235c–236b, 249de Plato exploits, rather laboriously, the popular idea that Pericles was the pupil of Aspasia (cf. the comic poet Callias (fr. 15) and Plutarch, *Pericles* 24.2–7), and to make the supreme philosopher, like the supreme orator, the pupil of a woman may have appealed to his sense of humour. On a more serious plane, it must not be forgotten that in *Rep.* 451c–457b Plato argues, in full awareness of the extent to which he is going against prevailing Greek assumptions, that the natural potentiality of men and women is the same in respect of intellect and moral character, differing only in so far as their bodily structure differs.

In professing to have learned about eros from Diotima Socrates avoids preaching to Agathon and his fellow-guests from a superior standpoint; he professes to have been a mere layman who, until

Diotima enlightened him, held just the same opinions about eros as
Agathon himself (201e3–7).

Throughout Diotima's exposition the reader will encounter biological and psychological statements which, although accepted by
Socrates without demur, are at least open to question and in some
cases are irreconcilable with observed fact. Given Plato's assumptions
(p. 6), it is not altogether surprising that he should discard much of
our actual behaviour, thought and feeling as error, failure or per-
version and describe what (in his view) ought to be the case as if it
actually were the case.

201d3 καὶ ᾿Αθηναίοις...5 νόσου lit. 'and on one occasion she
created for the Athenians having sacrificed a postponement, ten
years, of the disease', i.e. she prescribed the sacrifices which would
postpone the plague for ten years. This is not the only story of an
occasion on which a Greek community brought in a religious expert
when some event had suggested that an unknown deity was hostile for
an undiscoverable reason; in *Laws* 642d we find the story that
Epimenides the Cretan, brought to Athens at the behest of Delphi,
prophesied that the Persian invasion would not come for another ten
years and that when it came it would fail. The story that the Athenians
had reason in 440 to fear a plague may be fiction, modelled on the
Epimenides story; but, of course, a minor epidemic in that year may
have given them cause for anxiety. **ὃν οὖν...λόγον** simply
picks up d1 τὸν δὲ λόγον...2 ὃν ποτ᾽ ἤκουσα. **d6 ἐκ τῶν ὡμολογημένων** 'on the basis of...'. **d7 αὐτὸς ἐπ᾽ ἐμαυτοῦ**: i.e. no longer in
dialogue with Agathon.

e1 αὐτόν: cf. 199c4 n. **e3 ἀνακρίνουσα** 'examining', 'interrogating'.
e5 τῶν καλῶν: i.e. τὰ καλά are the object of eros; cf. 200e8. **e6 ὡς**
'(*sc.* demonstrating) that...'. **e8 πῶς λέγεις;** shocked and indignant, as in, e.g., Ar. *Birds* 323; πῶς φής; is also used in this way in
comedy. **e10 καὶ ἤ**: cf. 172a6 n., on καὶ ὅς. **οὐκ εὐφημήσεις;** lit.
'will you not utter words of good omen?', i.e. 'What a thing to say!',
'Hush!'

202a2 ἤ καί...ἀμαθές; '(*sc.* do you think) also that if (ἄν) (*sc.* something is) not wise, it is stupid?' In a5–9 and in 203d4–204b7 σοφία

'skill' (cf. 174c7 n.), φρόνησις 'intelligence', 'wisdom', and ἐπιστήμη 'systematic knowledge', 'rational understanding', are treated as synonymous, and ἀμαθία, sometimes 'stupidity', sometimes 'ignorance', serves as the antonym of them all. **a5 τὸ ὀρθὰ δοξάζειν:** in *Meno* 97a–99a 'true opinion' (ἀληθὴς δόξα) or 'right opinion' (ὀρθὴ δόξα) is distinguished from 'knowledge' (ἐπιστήμη) as being unstable; it turns into knowledge and acquires stability only when 'bound' (or 'linked') by 'reasoning of cause' (αἰτίας λογισμῷ). The man who *knows* can 'give a (*sc.* rational) account' (λόγον διδόναι) of what he knows; cf. 189b9 n. **καὶ ἄνευ** 'even without...'. **a7 τοῦ ὄντος** 'reality', 'the truth'. **a8 τοιοῦτον...9 ἀμαθίας:** τοιοῦτον looks forward, and is defined by μεταξύ...ἀμαθίας. *Rep.* 477a–478e explains more fully the notion that 'opinion' (δόξα) is intermediate between the opposing extremes 'knowledge' (γνῶσις or ἐπιστήμη) and 'ignorance' (ἀγνωσία or ἄγνοια).

b1 ἀνάγκαζε 'say that...necessarily follows' **b3 μηδέν τι μᾶλλον** 'do not...any the more for that' (*sc.* merely because he is neither good nor beautiful). **b4 ἀλλά** *sc.* οἷου αὐτὸν εἶναι. **b9 συμπάντων μὲν οὖν** 'why, *everyone*!'; cf. 199e8 n.

c2 οὐδὲ θεόν 'not a god at all', 'not even a god in the first place'. **c6 οὐ πάντας...7 καλούς;** on the εὐδαιμονία of gods, cf. 195a5 n. So far as poetic and popular tradition went, Hephaestus was not καλός, and some divine beings, such as the Eumenides, were hideous. Diotima assumes, however, a more sophisticated belief (no doubt widespread in Plato's time) that the gods are not characterised by any unpleasant attributes. **c10 εὐδαίμονας...11 κεκτημένους:** it would have been enough to say (1) all gods are beautiful, but (2) Eros lacks beauty, therefore (3) Eros is not a god. It would have been fallacious to say (1) all gods are happy, and (2) those who possess beauty are happy, but (3) Eros does not possess beauty, therefore (4) Eros is not a god. Plato seems at first to have elaborated a perfectly valid argument by additions which arouse our suspicion and make us waste time in checking the argument. If, however, we realise that the meaning of c10f. is not 'those who possess...are a sub-class of the class "happy"' but 'is not possession of...what you mean by "happiness"?', we see that the kernel of the argument is, (1) all gods are happy, (2) 'happy' means 'possessing what is good and beautiful', but (3) Eros does not possess what is good and beautiful, therefore (4) Eros is not happy, therefore (5) Eros is not a god.

d1 ὡμολόγηκας: cf. 201e6. **d4 ὡμολόγηκα γάρ** 'yes, I've agreed (*sc.* to that)'. **d13 δαίμων:** the word is freely used in poetry as a synonym of θεός, e.g. *Il.* 1.222, where Athena flies back to Olympus 'to join the other δαίμονες'. But it is also used specifically of supernatural beings lower in rank than θεοί, e.g. (Hes. *WD* 122) the spirits of the 'golden race', who roam the earth as beneficent guardians; and in *Ap.* 27b–e Plato's Socrates treats δαίμονες as 'either gods or children of gods' (cf. Eur. *Medea* 1391, 'what god or δαίμων...?'). The distinction now made in characterising Eros is exceptionally explicit. Since 'demon' and 'demonic' are opprobrious words, 'spirit' and 'spiritual' are preferable translations here, though 'spiritual' is far from appropriate for δαιμόνιος in many other contexts.

e3 ἑρμηνεῦον καὶ διαπορθμεῦον 'interpreting and communicating' (or '...and conveying'). **e4 τῶν μέν...5 τῶν δέ** 'men's...and gods'...'. **ἐπιτάξεις** 'impositions', 'commands'. **ἀμοιβάς** 'return (*sc.* of favours or goodwill) for...'. **e6 συμπληροῖ...7 συνδεδέσθαι** 'fills up' (or 'fills in') '(*sc.* the space between) so that the whole complex' – constituted by gods, spirits and humans – 'is bound together as a continuum'. **e7 διὰ τούτου...χωρεῖ** 'operates' (lit. 'moves') 'through this (*sc.* medium, τοῦ δαιμονίου)'. **e8 τῶν τε...
203a1 γοητείαν** 'and (*sc.* the art) of those concerned with sacrifices and rites' (τελετάς: propitiatory, initiatory, or a blend of both) 'and with spells and with all μαντεία and magic'. μαντεία, oracular or inspired utterance or (as in 206b9) understanding, supernaturally conferred, of what baffles human wits, is the field to which μαντική (*sc.* τέχνη) applies; the sequence '(1) all μαντική and (2) the art of the priests concerned with...all μαντεία...' is therefore surprising at first sight. There were, however, seers and diviners who were not priests, and at the same time there were some priests much concerned with μαντεία. Geel (before the discovery of the Cairo papyrus, which has μαντείαν) suggested the emendation μαγγανείαν, a general term for the magical arts. This is open to the objection that it is somewhat tautologous with γοητείαν. It is also an opprobrious term, as is plain from the context in *Laws* 908d and 933a (cf. μαγγανεύματα in *Grg.* 484a and μαγγανεύειν in Dem. 25.80); but so as a rule are γόης and its cognates (despite 203d8).

203a2 οὐ μείγνυται 'has no (*sc.* immediate) contact with...'. διὰ τούτου: cf. 202e7 n. **a3** διάλεκτος 'converse' (·- διαλέγεσθαι). ἐγρηγορόσι 'awake' (~ ἐγείρειν). **a4** καὶ καθεύδουσι: since gods may communicate with humans through dreams, as Zeus does with Agamemnon in *Il.* 2.5ff.; Zeus there despatches Oneiros, 'Dream', to Agamemnon, and Diotima would no doubt regard Oneiros as a 'spirit' who 'conveys' the god's intention. **a6** βάναυσος 'vulgar'; the word is applied to those skills which minister to a community's most material needs, and in *Laws* 644a it is coupled with ἀνελεύθερος, 'unbefitting a free citizen'. In *Rep.* 495de Plato probably (though the interpretation is not certain) extends it to the arts of the sophist and rhetorician, and that would accord with the sentiment given here to Diotima.

203a8–204c6: The birth and nature of Eros

The gods feasted when Aphrodite was born. Resource, drunk, went out into the garden; there Poverty seduced him, and in time gave birth to Eros. Eros takes after both his parents: restlessly seeking, acquiring, losing, dying, reviving.

There is no reason to suppose that Plato found this story in any earlier writer; the construction of relationships between forces personified as deities is a common Greek way of characterising those forces (cf. 197d7 n.), and the chief purpose of the story here is to put eros before us as a force which impels us to *seek to acquire*.

203b1 μακρότερον... διηγήσασθαι 'it's quite a long story to tell'. **b2** Ἀφροδίτη: treated here by implication as the daughter of Zeus and Dione, not as the deity born from the severed genitals of Cronus; cf. 180d6–e1 n. **b3** ὁ τῆς Μήτιδος ὑὸς Πόρος: the usual antonym of πενία, 'poverty', is πλοῦτος, 'wealth'. πόρος, etymologically cognate with πείρειν 'pierce', is applied to any means (e.g. a path or a ferry) of getting across or over land or water; then of any means which enable one to cope with a difficulty, or of the provision of monetary or other resources (cf. our expression 'ways and means'). Since Diotima will go on (203d4–e5) to speak of Eros as always seeking and intermittently able (thanks to the character he inherits from his father) to acquire skill and understanding, 'Resource' is a suitable translation of Πόρος here. A cosmogony expounded by Alcman (fr.5.2.ii) personified Poros, but Alcman probably meant 'Way' or 'Track' (in the primeval void). Metis in Hes. *Theog.* 886 is the first wife of Zeus and (fr. 343) mother of Athena.   **b4** προσαιτήσουσα...οὔσης 'to beg, as one would expect on a festive occasion'; beggars come to the door when festivities are in progress, hoping to profit by the tipsy euphoria of the guests.   Πενία: Aristophanes' *Plutus* had personified Poverty in 388, a few years before Plato wrote *Smp.*   **b6** οἶνος γὰρ οὔπω ἦν: but even when Dionysus had taught mankind the uses of the vine, nectar was still the drink of the gods (*Il.* 5.341).   **b7** βεβαρημένος 'weighed down', i.e. 'overcome'; modelled, it seems, on Homer's οἴνῳ βεβαρηότες.

c1 ἐκύησε 'conceived'.   **c2** ἀκόλουθος...**3** γενεθλίοις: Hesiod's injunction (*WD* 735f.) 'do not beget offspring when you have come home from a funeral, but from a festival of the immortals', shows the existence of a belief in some kind of connection between the character or fortunes of a child and the occasion of his or her conception.   **c4** περὶ τὸ καλόν '*of* beauty', in this context; but for the variety of translation appropriate to περί + accusative cf. 206e1 'excitement about beauty', *Phlb.* 52a 'pleasure in learning', *Laws* 888d 'impiety towards gods'.   καὶ τῆς Ἀφροδίτης καλῆς οὔσης: a genitive absolute is readily coordinated with other kinds of participial clause; hence 'because he is a lover...and (*sc.* because) Aphrodite is beautiful'.   **c5** τοιαύτη looks forward to c6 πρῶτον μὲν κτλ.   **c6** πολλοῦ δεῖ 'far from...'.   **c7** οἱ πολλοί: including Agathon (195c6-196a1).

d2 ἐν ὁδοῖς 'by the roadside', not 'in (*sc.* the middle of) roads'.   **d4** τοῖς καλοῖς καὶ τοῖς ἀγαθοῖς: if καλοῖς had stood alone, there would be a strong temptation to take it as masculine, but the addition of καὶ τοῖς ἀγαθοῖς directs our attention more to the generalising neuter, as in 201c1-5; καλός and ἀγαθός are here, as there, treated as having the same reference, and so later in 204e1-2. The expression καλὸς κἀγαθός (204a5, cf. n.) is different.   **d6** φρονήσεως: cf. 202a2 n.   **d7** φιλοσοφῶν 'a seeker after (*or* lover of) knowledge'; the reason for the choice of this word becomes apparent in 204a1-b5.   **d8** σοφιστής: cf. 177b2 n.

e2 ὅταν εὐπορήσῃ: Wilamowitz suggested that Plato wrote these words not here but after ἀναβιώσκεται in e3; most of us would prefer them there (given the following τὸ δὲ ποριζόμενον κτλ.), but that is not quite a strong enough reason for emendation.

204a1 φιλοσοφεῖ: the sense requires the translation 'is a *lover* of knowledge', not 'is a lover of *knowledge*'; it is impossible to make the point in English by using the stem 'philosoph-'. **a2 οὐδ'...οὐ φιλοσοφεῖ**: οὐ reinforces the negative element in the connective οὐδέ; cf. Aeschines 3.78 οὐδέ γε ('nor, again') ὁ ἰδίᾳ πονηρὸς οὐκ ἂν γένοιτο δημοσίᾳ χρηστός, and *GP* 196f. **a4 αὐτὸ γὰρ τοῦτο** 'for in precisely this respect', specified by τὸ μὴ ὄντα...δοκεῖν....**χαλεπόν**: cf. 176d1 n. **a5 καλὸν κἀγαθόν**: a general laudatory term used predominantly, though not exclusively, of men; it differs from 'good' in taking account not merely of moral disposition (as manifested in courage and generosity) but also of attributes (e.g. wealth, good physique and skills) which enhance one's value to the community. Cf. *GPM* 41–5.

b1 οἱ μεταξὺ τούτων: cf. 202a5–9. **b2 τῶν καλλίστων...3 τὸ καλόν** 'knowledge (σοφία) is (*sc.* one) of the most beautiful things and eros is (*sc.* desire) of beauty' (cf. 203c4); this step in the exposition is made possible by the fact that καλός has a much wider denotation than 'beautiful', 'handsome' or 'pretty' (cf. p. 2). **b6 σοφοῦ**: there is no necessary connection between σοφία and wealth, nor did the Greeks think that there is, save that wealth facilitates the acquisition of skills; cf. 203b3 n. on πόρος. **b8 ὄν...c1 ἔπαθες** lit. 'who *you* thought Eros to be, you underwent nothing surprising', i.e. 'it's not at all surprising that you took the view you did of Eros'. Cf. 174e1 n.

c2 τὸ ἐρώμενον...3 τὸ ἐρῶν: this was characteristic, though not consistently so, of Agathon's speech; it has been implicitly rejected ever since 200a5. **c4 τὸ τῷ ὄντι...5 μακαριστόν**: of the two poles in an eros-relationship, τὸ ἐραστόν (the object possessing the attributes which attract eros) is the one which in reality is beautiful, etc.; not just 'the object of eros is beautiful', for the second τό would not then be appropriate. For ἁβρόν cf. 197d7; τέλεον is 'perfect', μακαριστόν 'blessed' (~ μακαρίζειν 'congratulate'). **c6 ἔχον** *sc.* ἐστίν.

204c7–206a13: Eros is desire to possess good always

He who desires what is beautiful desires that it should be his. All men desire that good should be theirs. Popular usage restricts 'eros' to sexual desire; and some say, wrongly, that we most desire that which is 'our own'. In fact all desire is desire for good; and we necessarily desire that good should be ours always.

It was agreed in 201c1–7 that ἀγαθά are καλά; whether anything can be καλόν but not ἀγαθόν was not considered. Diotima now makes Socrates agree that (1) 204d3–7: desire (eros) for καλά is desire to have them; (2) 204d8–e4: desire for ἀγαθά is desire to have them; (3) 204e5–205a4: to have ἀγαθά is to be happy (εὐδαίμων); (4) 205a5–8: we all necessarily wish to be happy; (5) *ibid.*, this universal wish to be happy is eros; (6) 205d1–206a8: all eros is a desire to have what is ἀγαθόν; (7) 206a9–13 – and to have it always.

Stage (5) is crucial; Diotima refers to 'this wish and this eros' as if it were agreed that 'eros for ἀγαθά' is not just analogous to 'eros for καλά' or a species of it, but identical with it. From now on καλός and ἀγαθός are treated as alternative designations of the same class. In 205e6 Diotima speaks no longer of τὰ ἀγαθά (which in normal Greek usage denotes enjoyable material things) but of τὸ ἀγαθόν, thus giving a metaphysical turn to her exposition and preparing the way for the part which τὸ καλόν will play in her peroration (201c2 etc.). Stage (7), which is needed for her argument about the desire for immortality (206b–208b), does not rest on reasoning at all; it is foreshadowed by 205a6f. πάντας τἀγαθὰ βούλεσθαι αὑτοῖς εἶναι ἀεί, where, although a Greek reader would be bound to say (if asked) that ἀεί goes with βούλεσθαι (as it does with ἐρῶσι in b1), the collocation εἶναι ἀεί is meant to lodge in our minds and reduce the likelihood of our objecting to 206a9–12. Naturally, as long as the alternative possibilities of having good and having bad exist, we wish to have good, but it does not follow from that that we ourselves wish to exist for ever.

There are particular senses in which we wish to 'have' or 'possess' persons with whom we are 'in love' or objects and situations which we strongly desire, but in a general sense it is absurd to say that we wish to treat as items at our disposal those whom we love. Hence κτήσει in 205a1, which accords with 200d1f. and 201b6, is the last we shall hear from Diotima about 'possession'; the phrasing εἶναι (or γενέσθαι) + dative (204d6 etc.) is more appropriate.

Throughout this section Plato uses the art of rhetoric more subtly than when he is caricaturing the verbal sophistries of others (e.g. 196c3–d4, *Euthd.* 276ab), but no more honestly. Since he is here using it in the service of doctrines to which he adhered passionately (cf. pp. 6–8), it is improbable that he wished us to regard Diotima as a dishonest sophist.

204c7 εἶεν δή: cf. 176a5 n. For the structure of the whole sentence cf. Eur. *Troades* 998f. lit. 'εἶεν· for you say that my son took you by force; who at Sparta perceived it?' (*GP* 68f.). **c8 χρείαν** 'function'; the point is, 'what is the role of Eros in human life?'

d1 τοῦτο δὴ μετὰ ταῦτ': since 'I will try...' in 180d1, 186a1 and 189d3 refers to something on which the speaker will embark at once, it seems that ταῦτα here refers to what Diotima has already said. **d2 τοιοῦτος** 'as I have said'. **d3 τῶν καλῶν, ὡς σὺ φῄς:** 201e5; cf. 203c3f. (περὶ τὸ καλόν), d4 (ἐπίβουλος...τοῖς καλοῖς). **d4 τί τῶν καλῶν...6 τί ἐρᾷ:** having asked 'why' (or 'in what respect') 'is eros (*sc.* a desire) of what is beautiful?', Diotima naturally has to put it 'more clearly' (d5). τί ἐρᾷ; invites, and receives, a reply in the form of an infinitive clause, since ἐρᾶν can be used (e.g. 206a6f.) like ἐπιθυμεῖν 'desire that...'. **d11 προχείρως** 'readily'.

e1 ὥσπερ ἄν...2 πυνθάνοιτο 'as if one, making a change, using "ἀγαθόν" instead of "καλόν", were to enquire'. **e7 εὐδαίμων:** formally, Socrates answers as if the question had been ποῖός τις ἔσται;

205a2 οὐκέτι προσδεῖ: evidently εὐδαιμονία (cf. 180b7 n.) is defined as that situation or condition in which one wishes to be, and 'I do not wish to be εὐδαίμων' is regarded as a self-contradictory proposition. **ἵνα τί** 'to what end', 'for what purpose'; *Ap.* 26d ἵνα τί ταῦτα λέγεις; is the only other example of the idiom in Plato, though Comedy provides some more. **a8 οὕτως** 'as *you* say'.

b1 εἴπερ γε 'if, that is (*sc.* as we have just agreed), ...'. **b4 ἀφελόν-τες...5 ἔρωτα** 'for, as we can now see (ἄρα), we separate a particular species of eros and call it, giving it the name of the whole, "eros"'. On γὰρ ἄρα cf. *GP* 56. **b6 τὰ δὲ ἄλλα** *sc.* ὀνομάζοντες. **καταχρώ-μεθα:** cf. 187c8 n.; here its connotation is 'use thoughtlessly'.

b7 ὥσπερ τί: the question is a 'feed'; Diotima is ready with an analogy. **b8 οἶσθ'...cι ποίησις** 'you know that "creation" is manifold; for, after all (τοι), that which is the cause (lit.) for anything whatsoever passing from not-being to being is, all of it, creation'.

c2 δημιουργοί: cf. 186d5 n. **6 τὸ περί...μέτρα** '(sc. namely) that which is concerned with music and verse'; cf. 187d2 n.

d1 τὸ μὲν κεφάλαιον lit. 'the summary', i.e. 'in general'; cf. 186c5, 196e4. **d2 ὁ μέγιστος...ἔρως: δολερός** 'treacherous', 'crafty', is not a common word in Attic prose (though it occurs in *Hippias Minor* 365c, of Odysseus), and its irrelevance to the argument here suggests that the whole phrase is a poetic quotation, in which μέγιστος is the relevant element. **d3 παντί** 'for everyone'. **d4 χρηματισμόν:** cf. 173c6. **d5 οὔτε...6 ἐρασταί** 'are not said to "be in love" and are not called "lovers"'. **d7 ἔρωτά τε...8 ἐρασταί:** ἔρωτα fits one construction (apposition to τό...ὄνομα), ἐρασταί fits another; cf. *Laws* 956c 'διαιτηταί' ὄνομα...ἔχοντες. **d10 λέγεται...λόγος:** by Aristophanes, in fact (191d–193d); that the reference is to him is clear from 212c4–6.

e2 ἐάν...3 ὄν 'unless, my friend, it is actually good'; που connotes '...as may be the case in given circumstances'. **e5 τὸ ἑαυτῶν...6 ἀσπάζονται:** cf. 192a5, and note Aristophanes' use of ἀσπάζεσθαι there and in b5. **εἰ μὴ εἴ τις** 'except if someone...'; cf. 221d2 and *Grg.* 480b εἰ μὴ εἴ τις ὑπολάβοι. **e7 ἀλλότριον:** cf. 179c2 n.

206a1 δοκοῦσιν sc. ἄλλου του ἐρᾶν. **a3 ἁπλοῦν:** cf. 183d4 n.

206b1–207a4: Reproduction in a beautiful medium

All human beings are fertile and desire to reproduce. Beauty stimulates them to do so, but ugliness inhibits them. It is through reproduction that mortals achieve a kind of immortality; that is why eros is a desire for reproduction.

Sexual eros is here treated as the paradigm, on the material level, of the individual's desire to secure immortality. Since on most occasions people have sexual intercourse for its own sake and not as a means to procreation (indeed, they usually hope, and try to ensure, that procreation will not result), the argument requires the assumption that humans, like animals (207a5–c1), are impelled by forces of which they are not aware.

In Greek generally τίκτειν, γεννᾶν, τόκος and γέννησις are used both of 'begetting' and of 'bearing' offspring (cf. 191b7–c1 n.), whereas κυεῖν 'be pregnant' and κυῆσαι 'conceive' are used only of females. In this passage Diotima treats the ejaculation of semen by the male, rather than the complete process of creating a child, as a τόκος of that with which the male is 'pregnant' ('fertile' will sometimes be found a less paradoxical translation). The mechanism of ovulation could not be known before the invention of the microscope, and many Greeks believed (cf. Arist. *De generatione animalium* 1.17.2, 19.19; contrast Aesch. *Eumenides* 658–66) that the female emitted semen, necessary for conception, at the moment of orgasm; this belief is still to be encountered in our own country.

It is noteworthy that of the vivid physical terms in which reaction to beauty and ugliness is expressed (206d3–e1) συσπειρᾶται (d6) 'contracts', ἀνείλλεται (d6) 'shrinks', 'curls up' and σπαργῶντι (d8) 'swelling' describe equally the reactions of the male and of the female genitals to sexual stimulus or revulsion, and διαχεῖται (d4) 'melts', 'relaxes' is more appropriate to the female; ὠδίς (e1), commonly the pains of childbirth, is also a general term for pain and can here denote the tension created in either sex by strong stimulation.

'Both in body and in soul' (206b8, repeated in c2f.) stakes a claim for the subsequent (208e5–212a7) development of the notion of spiritual reproduction.

206b1 ὅτε δή 'now that (*sc.* we have seen that)...'. τῶν τίνα τρόπον...3 καλοῖτο lit. 'of those pursuing it in what way, and in what activity, would the zeal and exertion' (cf. 203d5 σύντονος) 'be called eros?', i.e. 'in what way must men pursue the eternal possession of good, and in what activity, if their zeal and exertion are to be called eros?' **b5** οὐ μεντἂν σέ...ἐθαύμαζον 'I can assure you (μέντοι), (*sc.* if I *could* tell you)' (cf. 175d2 n.), 'I wouldn't be admiring...'; cf. *GP* 402. **b6** ἐφοίτων παρὰ σέ: φοιτᾶν is 'go (*sc.* regularly or frequently)', commonly used of pupils going to school; it is also used (and Plato had enough sense of humour to know what he was writing) of a sustained sexual relationship. **b7** τοῦτο *sc.* τὸ ἔργον (b3). **b9** μαντείας...λέγεις 'I need divination (*sc.* to discover) what you

mean'; ποτε is used like 'ever' in 'what ever do you mean?' For
μαντεία cf. Soph. *Oedipus Tyrannus* 393f. 'the riddle was not one that
the first comer could solve; μαντεία was needed'.

c5 ἐν δὲ τῷ καλῷ: if the medieval manuscripts are right here, against
the papyrus, in having τῷ, there is no shift from 'a beautiful (*sc.*
medium)' to 'Beauty (*sc.* in the abstract)'; for the definite article, see
179b5 n. **ἡ γάρ...ὁ τόκος ἐστίν**: Diotima needs to make the
assertion that intercourse is a kind of τόκος. The point of γάρ is:
'yes, (*sc.* I *am* talking about intercourse, as you might infer from
ἐπιθυμεῖ and καλῷ), for...'. **θεῖον**: Archilochus fr. 196A.15 uses τὸ
θεῖον χρῆμα of vaginal intercourse, as opposed to other modes of
sexual contact, but Diotima is not simply praising intercourse, as an
experience, in hyperbolic terms; the words immediately following
explain why she calls it 'godlike' or 'divine'. Cf. 208b1. **c8 τὰ δέ**:
not exactly 'they (*sc.* pregnancy and reproduction)', for everyone is
fertile (c1–2), but 'the process', i.e. the bringing to birth, in a
beautiful medium, of that which is waiting to be born. **ἀναρμόστῳ**
'unbefitting', 'incompatible'.

d1 ἀνάρμοστον δ'...τῷ θείῳ: cf. 202c6–8. **d2 Μοῖρα...2 γενέσει**:
Eileithyia was the goddess who presided over childbirth and made it
easy or hard, and one or more of the Fates (Μοῖραι) were regarded
also as present; Diotima, for this occasion, personifies the abstract noun
'beauty' as a deity, and gives her the role of Eileithyia and Moira in
the 'birth' of that with which 'all humans are pregnant both in body
and in soul'. **d4 ἵλεων**: cf. 197d5 n. **εὐφραινόμενον** 'gladdened'.
d5 σκυθρωπόν 'frowning'. **d8 πτοίησις** 'excitement'.

e2 οὐ τοῦ καλοῦ: cf. 204d3 n. **e6 εἶεν**: cf. 204c7. **e7 πάνυ μὲν οὖν**:
cf. 199e8 n. **τί δὴ οὖν** 'now, why (*sc.* is eros eros)...'. **e8 ὡς θνητῷ**
lit. 'as for (*sc.* something) mortal', i.e. 'as far as can be the case for
something mortal'. **ἀθανασίας...207a1 ὡμολογημένων**: 'immortality with good' is equated here with 'the eternal possession of
good'; the 'agreement' was in 206a9–13.

207a5–208b6: Immortality by replacement

We see in animals the strength of the impulse to reproduce, rear and protect offspring; this proves that mortal nature strives after immortality. During a creature's life every element in the body perishes and is replaced; the same is true of the soul, wherein thoughts, emotions and knowledge are constantly renewed.

Now Diotima treats the eros consciously experienced by humans as one manifestation of a greater force which operates in all 'mortal nature' (207d1), whether consciously apprehended or not. Her argument from animals and birds is not impressive, for some species behave as she describes, but many do not; philosophers and moralists generalising about the animal world have seldom shown respect for evidence. Her assimilation of psychological processes to physiological growth and death is striking; she treats change of character or of opinion as a continuous replacement of dead and dying thoughts and feelings by new ones, and the possession of knowledge similarly as requiring constant renewal. The analogy might seem vitiated by the discontinuity of the occasions on which we experience a given emotion or recall our knowledge of a given subject, contrasted with the absolutely unbroken continuity of the body, but in fact our total cognitive, intellectual and emotional state at any given point falls within a continuum coexistent with that of the body. Mortality may seem exalted by the reproductive process which gives it 'a share in immortality' (208b3), but 'the divine' (208a8–9) is spared the ceaseless flux and instability of the mortal.

Nowhere in *Smp.* does Plato say, as he says in *Phd.*, *Meno* and *Phdr.*, that the soul is immortal, and this passage has been taken as proof that when he wrote it he did not believe in the immortality of the soul. It is proof, if 'and everything else' (208b3–4) includes the soul and if 'immortal' (b4) refers to gods (cf. 208a8–b1) and ideas, not souls. However, the substitution of the imprecise 'and everything else' for the expected 'and soul' after 'both body . . . ' (contrast 206b8, c2f. and above all 207e1f.) directs our attention to the succession of states of a soul fused with a body; then 'immortal' in b4 can include the soul which existed before the body and will exist after the body's death. If Plato did not think it would enter his readers' heads that he disbelieved in the immortality of the soul, it is understandable that he did not take more trouble to guard against misinterpretation. We must also remember that whereas in *Phd.* Socrates, consoling his friends, asserts the continuity of the individual ('*I* shall exist when *my body* is dead', 115c–e), Plato may generally have preferred the formulation '*something which is in me* will still exist when *I* am dead'.

207a9 νοσοῦντα 'stricken'; νόσος and its cognates are commonly used of other unwelcome conditions as well as disease.

b3 καὶ ἕτοιμα...4 ὑπεραποθνήσκειν: the observation that even 'the most feeble' act in this way goes beyond the point made by Phaedrus in 179b4–5. τούτων is said as if τῶν γενομένων had been written in b2. **καὶ αὐτά...5 ἐκεῖνα** 'themselves... their young...'. **παρατεινόμενα** 'worn down', 'laid out'. **b6 τοὺς μέν...c1 διατίθεσθαι:** Democritus B278 makes the same point, but does not offer the same explanation.

c5 ὅπερ νυνδὴ εἶπον: 206b5–6. **c8 ἐκείνου** refers back to 206e5 and 207a3–4. **c9 πολλάκις** is intelligible in the light of 207a5–6 (ignored in 207c5). **ἐνταῦθα** 'in the animal world', considered more recently than the point to which ἐκείνου in c8 refers.

d1 τὸν αὐτόν...λόγον: adverbial expressions containing τρόπος 'way' may use simply the accusative (e.g. 206b1) or may be introduced by κατά (e.g. *Phlb.* 20a καθ' ἕτερόν τινα τρόπον); those containing λόγος 'principle' have κατά (e.g. *Rep.* 366b κατὰ τίνα... λόγον), but Plato here models a λόγος-phrase on the τρόπος-phrases without κατά, presumably because κατὰ τὸ δυνατόν is to come later in the clause. **d4 ἐπεί...καλεῖται** 'since in (*sc.* the course of the time for) which each single creature is said to "live"...'. **d5 οἷον:** here the sentence breaks off and a fresh start is made with οἷον 'for example'. **ὁ αὐτὸς λέγεται** 'a man is spoken of as the same man'. **d6 οὐδέποτε...7 ἀλλά:** the emphasis lies on the participial clauses, 'never having..., but always...'. **d7 τὰ δὲ ἀπολλύς** 'and losing other elements'. **d8 καὶ κατά...e1 σῶμα** 'in hair, flesh, bones, ...'.

e1 μὴ ὅτι: a commoner alternative to οὐχ ὅτι (cf. 179b5 n.), and μή is probably to be explained as imperatival, 'don't (*sc.* say) that...'. Cf. 208a1.

208a2 οὐδέ 'even'; the negative in it reinforces the negative in οὐδέποτε. **a4 μελετᾶν** 'practise'. **ὡς...ἐπιστήμης** 'exists because knowledge goes out (*sc.* of us)'. **λήθη** 'forgetting'. **a6 μνήμην:** the papyrus has μνημη, by which the dative may be intended, 'by re-collection'; the accusative of the medieval text must be the object of ἐμποιοῦσα, 'implanting new recollection'.

b4 ἀθάνατον δὲ ἄλλη '(*sc.* something) immortal (*sc.* participates in immortality) in a different way'. Creuzer, with 207d2 in mind, suggested the emendation ἀδύνατον δὲ ἄλλη 'it is impossible (*sc.* for anything mortal to participate in immortality) in any other way' (cf. 184e4), but there is no adequate reason to reject the transmitted text. The notion that the human race φύσει τινὶ μετείληφεν ἀθανασίας is developed in *Laws* 721b–d, where the desire to be remembered by one's descendants is treated as a motive for marriage (cf. 208c–e below, and Arist. *De anima* 415a26–b7). **b5 ἀποβλάστημα** 'offspring'. **b6 ὁ ἔρως:** the naming of this universal force comes in appropriately at the end of this stage of the argument; for 'this zeal *and* eros' = this zeal, which *is* eros', cf. 206d5, e5.

208b7–209e4: Immortal offspring

People seek the immortality of posthumous fame; otherwise, they would not sacrifice their lives for others. Those fertile in body beget human children in their effort to achieve a kind of immortality; those fertile in soul procreate philosophical knowledge, poems and laws.

Although 'all human beings are fertile both in body and in soul' (206c1–3), a distinction is now drawn between those who are (*sc.* more) fertile in body and those who are even more fertile in soul. We return in 209a8–c7 to 'procreation in beauty' (the doctrine of 206c4–e6), and it is obvious that Plato thinks of the man who is 'fertile in soul' as attracted by a younger male who is beautiful both in body and in soul (209b7 τὸ συναμφότερον); beauty of soul without beauty of body is not considered there (cf. however 210b8). The older male tries to 'educate' the younger (209c1f.) and they jointly 'bring up' their philosophical 'offspring' (c4–7). (There is a superficial re-semblance here to *Tht.* 149e–151e, where Socrates speaks of himself as 'midwife' to Theaetetus and to other young men who are philo-sophically 'pregnant', but there is a profound difference too; a midwife's role is not a progenitor's, and in *Tht.* 150cd Socrates denies his own 'fertility'.) Diotima does not explain the beautiful medium 'in' which Homer 'generated' poems or Solon laws, but it can only be the virtuous character of the societies for which Homer sang and Solon legislated.

In this section love of an individual for the individual's sake is decisively rejected, and Platonic eros parts company with love. It does not wholly part company with common Greek sentiment; cf. Hyperides 6.42 'as for those who have died (sc. in battle) childless, the praises accorded them by the Greek world will be their immortal children'. Perhaps the notion that Alcestis would not have died for Admetus had she not been sure of posthumous fame, or that 'everyone' (209c6–d4) would rather compose a memorable poem than procreate real children, would not have seemed so grotesque to a Greek as it does to most of us.

208c1 οἱ τέλεοι σοφισταί 'the real sophists', almost 'professional sophists'; cf. 177b4, 204c5 nn. εὖ ἴσθι, a common enough phrase, is uttered by sophists in answer to a question in *Euthd.* 274a and *Hippias Major* 287c, and Plato (in a better position to know than we are) evidently regards it as characteristic of them. **c2 καὶ τῶν ἀνθρώπων:** the contrast is with the animal world implicit in πᾶν (b5). **c3 φιλο-τιμίαν:** cf. 178d2 n. **τῆς ἀλογίας** sc. τῆς σῆς. **c4 δεινῶς διάκεινται:** cf. 207a8. **c5 καὶ κλέος...6 καταθέσθαι:** the source of this hexameter is not known; on the sentiment cf. 208b4 n.

d2 Ἄλκηστιν: cf. 179b5–d2. **d3 Ἀχιλλέα:** cf. 179e1–180a7. **d4 τὸν ὑμέτερον Κόδρον:** Codrus, a mythical king of Attica (in saying 'your', Diotima speaks as a non-Athenian), made sure that he was killed by Dorian invaders, knowing that an oracle had told them that they would take Athens only if they avoided killing its king. **d5 μὴ οἰομένους** 'unless they thought'. **d8 ὅσῳ...ει μᾶλλον** lit. 'by whatever amount they are better, by so much more', i.e. 'and the better they are, the more they do that'.

e1 τοῦ γὰρ ἀθανάτου ἐρῶσιν: a reassertion of 207a3f., 208b5f. **e4 εὐδαιμονίαν:** cf. 205d2.

209a1 εἰσί...οἳ κτλ. 'there are those who...'. The sentence takes a new turn, and we never come to a verb of which οἱ δὲ κατὰ τὴν ψυχήν can be subject. **a2 ἅ...3 τεκεῖν:** the clause as a whole is the object of αἱ κυοῦσιν; 'grow within them what it is fitting...'. **a4 ὦν...5 εἶναι** 'of which (sc. φρόνησις etc.)...are procreators, and (sc. so are) all those craftsmen who...'; lit. 'of the craftsmen as many as...'. **a5 πολύ...8 δικαιοσύνη** lit. 'by far the most important and beautiful (sc. intelligence) of intelligence (sc. is) regulation in respect of what has to do with cities and settlements...'. The context, together with d4–e4, suggests that 'self-discipline and righteousness' here are not simply orderly behaviour on the part of the citizens, but the virtues displayed by good statesmen, legislators and political philosophers, virtues diffused through the community once embodied and promoted by good law and theory. **τούτων...b2 ζητεῖ δή**: ἤθεος 'unmarried' is Parmentier's emendation of θεῖος, and it makes good sense if we take it with positive connotations, 'belonging to the very young adult male age-group' and 'looking for a philosophical partner as a youth looks for a girl'. So: 'whenever one of these..., (sc. then,) when he is an "eligible bachelor" and ..., he desires...So he seeks...'. The papyrus text, with θεῖος and ἐπιθυμῇ, means 'when one of these (sc. the fertile in soul) is, early in life, pregnant in soul, being divine, and, his maturity having come, desires now to procreate and generate, (sc. then) he seeks...'. θεῖος is 'godlike', 'superhuman', or 'belonging to the gods', 'manifesting the divine power'; since all humans are 'fertile in body and soul' (206c1–3), it would be curious if Plato characterised the fertile in soul as θεῖος, implying that the fertile in body are not (cf. 206c6, where sexual procreation is θεῖον in so far as it achieves a kind of immortality). To take θεῖος as = ἔνθεος 'inspired' (cf. 179a7) does not help; in any case, when Socrates in *Meno* 99cd argues that politicians who achieve success without understanding should be called θεῖος because they must be 'possessed and inspired by the god', he is consciously manipulating language, not following existing usage. The medieval text (with θεῖος ὤν and ἐπιθυμεῖ) means: 'when one of these is, early in life, pregnant in soul, (sc. then), when he is divine and his maturity has come, he desires...So he seeks...'. δή is no problem here, because connective δή 'then', 'so', is common (cf. 191d5 ζητεῖ δή, 219e3 ἠπόρουν δή; *GP* 236–40), but θεῖος is still a problem, for it would have to imply 'when the power of Eros (sc. previously latent) is manifested in him'.

b3 οἶμαι: this is not diffident; cf. 176c8 n., and c2 below.   **τὸ καλόν ...4 γεννήσει**: cf. 206c4f., d3–e5.   **b6 εὐφυεῖ** 'naturally gifted'.

b8 περὶ οἷον κτλ.: perhaps '(*sc.* the question) with what the good man should be concerned' (on περί...εἶναι cf. LSJ περί c.ι.3), but 'about (*sc.* the question) what the good man should be like' cannot be ruled out, although one would then expect either no περὶ or περὶ τὸ οἷον (cf. *Rep.* 327c 'one thing is left, τὸ ἦν πείσωμεν...ὡς χρή...', i.e. '...the argument that...').

c1 καὶ ἃ ἐπιτηδεύειν = καὶ περὶ ἃ χρὴ ἐπιτηδεύειν. **c3** καὶ παρὼν ...μεμνημένος 'in his presence and remembering him in absence'. **c4** ἐκείνου: the reference is the same as that of αὐτῷ in c3. **c5** τῆς τῶν παίδων 'than partnership in children'.

d2 ζηλῶν: cf. 197d6 ζηλωτός. **οἷα** = ὅτι τοιαῦτα, as often. **d4** αὐτὰ τοιαῦτα ὄντα 'because they (*sc.* the offspring) are themselves such (*sc.* immortal)'. **εἰ δὲ βούλει:** cf. 177b1 n. **Λυκοῦργος:** the half-legendary Lycurgus was regarded as creator of Spartan laws and institutions, which are therefore his 'children' here – 'saviours' of Sparta because of the military power which Sparta wielded, and of Greece by virtue of the part played by Sparta in the Persian Wars. After the Peloponnesian War, the Spartan exercise of imperial power, and the Corinthian War, Plato's Athenian readers had some reasons to deny Spartan institutions the title 'saviours of Greece'. **d6** παρ' ὑμῖν: cf. 208d4 n. **d7** Σόλων: Solon, the poet, moralist and legislator of the early sixth century, was the dominant figure in Athenian moral and social tradition, and the Athenians normally designated Attic law 'the laws of Solon'.

e2 ἀποφηνάμενοι: ἀποφαίνεσθαι is commonly 'perform' when the act performed is conspicuous or memorable. **e3** ὧν καὶ ἱερά...γέγονε lit. 'of whom many sacred things, too, have come into being'; ἱερά denotes temples and sanctuaries as well as rites and sacrifices.

209e5–212c2: Progress towards the comprehension of Beauty

(i) **209e5–210e1.** *Rightly directed, one begins with eros for the beauty of one body; then one becomes an erastes of the beauty which is manifested in all beautiful bodies; thereafter of institutions, and of sciences.*

Having parted company with love, Platonic eros now takes wing; cf. p. 2 and 205d10–206a1.

The massive sentence beginning at δεῖ γάρ in a4 is composed of six items dependent on δεῖ: (1) 210a4 ἄρχεσθαι...a6 σώματα 'begin... to turn towards...'; (2) a6 καὶ πρῶτον μέν...a8 καλούς 'to be in love...'; (3) a8 ἔπειτα δέ...b3 κάλλος 'to realise that...'; (4) b4 τοῦτο δ'...b6 ἡγησάμενον 'to become a lover...'; (5) b6 μετὰ δέ... c6 εἶναι 'to consider..., so that (b8 ὥστε)...it is enough..., in order that (c3 ἵνα) he may be compelled to contemplate...and see..., in order that (c5 ἵνα)...'; (6) c6 μετὰ δέ...e1 τοιοῦδε 'to lead..., that (c7 ἵνα) he may see...and no longer (c7 καί...d1 μηκέτι)...be..., but (d3 ἀλλ') generate..., until (d6 ἕως ἄν)...'. With (2) and (3) αὐτόν is inserted as subject of the infinitive, but not with (4) and (5). In (1)–(5) it is the young, growing person who 'must begin...' etc., as is clear from a5 νέον ὄντα and a6f. 'if his guide directs him aright'; cf. 'when he has grown in strength and stature' (d6f.) and e2f. ὃς γὰρ ἄν...παιδαγωγηθῇ. But in (6) it is the guide, the older partner, who must 'lead (sc. the younger) to the sciences, that he (sc. the younger) may see...'; ἀγαγεῖν (c7) cannot mean 'go' in classical Greek (note 211c1 ἰέναι ἢ ὑπ' ἄλλου ἄγεσθαι), and it resists emendation (one might think of ἀνάγειν 'set sail', given d3f. ἐπὶ τὸ πολὺ πέλαγος τετραμμένος, but it is specious and no more). See further 211b5–c1 nn.

209e5 κἂν σύ 'you too'; 'even you' would be carrying Socratic mock-modesty (210a2, a4) too far.

210a1 μυηθείης...ἐποπτικά: μύειν is 'initiate', ἐπόπται are those admitted to the final secrets of a mystery-cult (e.g. the Eleusinian mysteries), and τέλεος (cf. 204c5, 208c1 nn.) is applied in *Phdr.* 249c to the 'rites' (τελεταί) in which the philosopher is 'initiated' (τελού-μενος). **καὶ ταῦτα** 'that teaching' (e5); cf. *GP* 295f. **a7 ἐνταῦθα** 'with it', 'in it'; the idea of 'procreation in a beautiful medium' (last encountered in 209b1–3) is maintained throughout (c1, d5).

b1 ἀδελφόν 'akin'; cf. *Rep.* 402c 'the manifestations of self-restraint and courage...καὶ ὅσα τούτων ἀδελφά'. **b2 εἰ δεῖ...καλόν** 'if beauty (sc. manifested) in appearance is to be pursued'. **πολλὴ ἄνοια** '(sc. it is) quite ridiculous'; cf. 180d5, 187a7 nn. **μὴ οὐχ:** cf. 197a2 n. **b5 τὸ σφόδρα τοῦτο** sc. ἐρᾶν. **b6 σμικρόν** 'trivial', 'of no account'.

b8 ἐπιεικής: cf. 201a8 n.   **κἄν:** ἐάν…κἄν (= καί + ἄν, not καί + ἐάν) is surprising, but attested several times with σμικρός, e.g. Ar. *Plutus* 126 ἐὰν ἀναβλέψῃς σὺ κἂν σμικρὸν χρόνον 'if you recover your sight…'.

c1 ἐρᾶν sc. τούτου.   **καὶ τίκτειν…3 νέους:** the transmitted text means 'and generate arguments of that kind' (but of what kind?) 'and seek (sc. arguments) which will make the young better'. But the words καὶ ζητεῖν, deleted by Ast, will not do; the seeker (cf. 209b2f.) has already found his partner (b8f.), he does not 'seek' arguments, and τοιούτους obviously looks forward to οἵτινες κτλ.   **c4 καὶ τοῦτ'…5 ἐστιν:** τοῦτ' refers to the fact given by ὅτι κτλ.; lit. 'that (sc. beauty) is all akin itself to itself' means that the beauty manifested in all beautiful things is ultimately one (cf. 211b1–5).   **c7 ἀγαγεῖν:** cf. p. 155.

d1 ὥσπερ οἰκέτης: the notion that it is 'slavish' to be content with the beauty of particulars resembles the argument of *Tht.* 172c–173b, where those trained in law and politics, contending always with a multitude of pressures, are contrasted, as 'slaves' with free men, with philosophers who have time to think about abstract issues.   **d3 σμικρολόγος:** in *Tht.* 175a σμικρολογία is the 'pettiness' of those who attach importance to what is, from a philosophical standpoint, trivial and transitory. On φαῦλος cf. 174c7 n.   **d4 πέλαγος** '(open) sea'. θεωρῶν sc. 'it' as object.   **d5 μεγαλοπρεπεῖς:** cf. 199c7 n.   **d6 ἀφθόνῳ** 'ungrudging', hence 'unlimited'. ῥωσθείς: cf. 176b7 n.   **d7 τινά …ει τοιοῦδε:** not 'one science (sc. out of many)…', but 'a science which is one (sc. as distinct from the many particular sciences) and of such a kind that it is the science of a beauty which I will now describe' (cf. 173e7 n.).

(ii) 210e1–212a7. *The final reward is contemplation of unchanging, imperishable Beauty itself, beside which beauties manifested in particulars are worth little.*

Although this section describes more fully, in exalted language, the καλόν with which the previous section ends, it also recapitulates the doctrine of methodical progress ('steps', 211c3) from beautiful particulars to the contemplation of wholly incorporeal beauty (the μαθήματα of 211c6 are clearly the ἐπιστῆμαι of 210c6). The progress which begins with looking upon (210e3 θεώμενος; cf. 211d7) what is

visibly beautiful leads to a vision (210e4 κατόψεται) of eternal beauty
and on to a plane of enlightenment in which one looks upon (212a2
θεωμένου; cf. d2 θεωμένῳ) that beauty with 'the eye of the mind'. The
visible beauty of particulars is explicitly (211d3–8) and contemptuously (e1–3) denigrated. We are reminded in 210e3 παιδαγωγηθῇ
and 211b5 παιδεραστεῖν of the terms in which the topic of eros was
opened by Phaedrus and Pausanias, but Socrates is careful, by the
repeated use of ἔφη (210a3, a4, e1, 211d8, e4, 212a2) and especially
211d1f. ἔφη ἡ Μαντινικὴ ξένη, to maintain the fiction that he is a
narrator, not a preacher. He could say, as Eryximachus said (177a3f.)
in proposing the praise of Eros, οὐκ ἐμὸς ὁ μῦθος (and, for what it is
worth, Euripides' line continued ἀλλὰ τῆς μητρὸς πάρα).

210e2 μέχρι ἐνταῦθα: cf. d6 ἐνταῦθα.   **e3 παιδαγωγηθῇ:** on παιδα-
γωγοί cf. 183c4 n. Here the reference is to teaching and guidance
rather than mere custody, in accord with 209c2 παιδεύειν, 210c7
ἀγαγεῖν, 211b5 παιδεραστεῖν, 211c1 ἄγεσθαι.   **e4 ἐξαίφνης:** the
notion that a vision of overwhelming beauty is the reward of long toil
(e6) may make us think of the view from a summit after a long ascent,
but mountaineering was not a Greek sport, and a closer analogy
would be the excitement of glimpsing a wonderfully simple, comprehensive answer to a problem after a process of reasoning which was
full of difficulties and discouragements.   **e5 τοῦτο ἐκεῖνο:** the
expression has a somewhat exclamatory and dramatic character (cf.
Arist. *Poetics* 1448b17 οὗτος ἐκεῖνος 'that's him!').

211a1 ἀεί...2 φθίνον: the language used here of Beauty (αὐτὸ τὸ
καλόν, c8f., d3) is close to that of *Phd.* 78d, where each 'αὐτὸ τό...'
is eternal and invariable; cf. also *Rep.* 508d, contrasting the soul's
rational comprehension of 'truth and being' with its fluctuating
opinions when it attends to 'what becomes and perishes'.   **ἔπειτα...5
αἰσχρόν:** a negative preceding a μέν/δέ complex negatives the whole
of it, not just the μέν-part; hence 'not beautiful-in-one-respect and
ugly-in-another...nor beautiful-by-one-standard (πρὸς μὲν τό) and
ugly-by-another...'.   **φαντασθήσεται** 'will appear', with a suggestion of illusion, appropriate to the particulars (a6–b1) with which
abstract beauty is contrasted.   **a7 οὐδέ...8 τινί** *sc.* φαντασθήσεται;
but with b1 ἀλλ' κτλ. it is more appropriate to understand φανεῖται
'it will clearly be...'. ἑτέρῳ implies 'than itself'.

b1 ἀλλ' αὐτό...2 ὄν: cf. *Phd.* 78d μονοειδὲς ὂν αὐτὸ καθ' αὑτό, i.e. not associated in any way with anything but itself. **μετέχοντα:** particulars are said by Plato to 'participate' in Ideas (e.g. *Phd.* 100c, 101c), but in *Phd.* 100d he hesitates over the right word for the relationship; cf. p. 7. **b3 τοιοῦτον...5 μηδέν** 'in such a way that...', ἐκεῖνο (the Idea) being subject of the infinitives. **γιγνομένων...ἀπολλυμένων:** cf. a1. **παιδεραστεῖν:** a reminder that Diotima is not speaking of solitary mysticism, but of the 'right' use (ὀρθῶς recurs throughout: 210a2, a4, a6, e3, 211b5, b7) of the emotional relationships about which Phaedrus and Pausanias were talking.

c1 ἀρχόμενον...d1 καλόν: essentially a recapitulation of 210a4–211b4, but replacing ἐπιστῆμαι (210c6–e1) by μαθήματα (211c5–d1). **c3 ἐπαναβασμοῖς** 'ascending steps'. **c6 καί...7 τελευτῆσαι...d1 καλόν:** given ἀρχόμενον...ἐπανιέναι (c1f.), we expect an infinitive τελευτῆσαι in c7 and then in c8 either καὶ γνῶναι...τελευτῶντα or ἵνα (or ἕως ἄν) γνῷ...τελευτῶν; but the transmitted text has τελευτήσῃ and καὶ γνῷ...τελευτῶν. The minimum emendation needed to make sense would be ἵνα for καί in c6: but the run of the sentence is more convincing if τελευτήσῃ is changed to τελευτῆσαι and καὶ γνῷ (c8) to ἵνα γνῷ.

d1 ἐνταῦθα τοῦ βίου 'in this region of life'. **d2 εἴπερ που ἄλλοθι:** we say 'if any', 'if anywhere', etc., but Greek adds 'other', 'else-'. **βιωτόν** '(*sc.* it is) livable', i.e. '(a man) should live'; cf. Socrates' credo in *Ap.* 38b 'a life exempt from scrutiny is οὐ βιωτὸς ἀνθρώπῳ'. **d3 κατά** 'in the same way as...', 'on the plane of...'. **d6 ὁρῶντες** 'so long as you can see'. **d8 τί...οἰόμεθα** 'what do we think (*sc.* it would be like)', i.e. 'what are we to imagine...?' **εἴ τῳ...e4 κατιδεῖν** 'if it were possible for someone to see beauty itself, pure' (cf. 181c7), 'clean, unmixed and' (lit. 'but') 'not defiled..., but he were able...'. ἀνάπλεως is literally 'full of...', but Thuc. 2.51.4 uses the verb ἀναπιμπλάναι of infection by disease, and cf. *Phd.* 67a, where it is said that knowledge is best attained by our souls if we have as little as possible to do with the body μηδὲ ἀναπιμπλώμεθα τῆς τούτου φύσεως. On μονοειδές cf. b1 n.

212a1 ἐκεῖνο...2 θεωμένου 'contemplating that' (*sc.* τὸ καλόν) 'by that by which it is necessary (*sc.* to contemplate it)', i.e. by 'the eye of the soul', as it is called in *Rep.* 533d; cf. a3 ᾧ ὁρατόν and *Rep.* 490b 'to grasp the nature of each entity itself by that (*sc.* element) of the soul by which it is appropriate' (προσήκει) 'to grasp' (ἐφάπτεσθαι; cf. a4f. below) 'such a thing'.   **a3 μοναχοῦ** 'only', qualifying ἐνταῦθα. **a4 εἴδωλα** lit. 'images', with the connotation 'poor imitations', 'remote and partial copies'; cf. *Rep.* 586a, where the imperfect pleasures of the ignorant are called 'εἴδωλα of true pleasure'. **a5 ἀληθῆ** *sc.* offspring.   **a6 θρεψαμένῳ:** cf. 209c4.   **θεοφιλεῖ:** in a relation of mutual φιλία with the gods, who do not love a sinner but do not reject a devotee. Phaedrus asserted (180a7–b5) that the gods honour an eromenos who sacrifices himself for his erastes, and both Eryximachus (188c6–d2) and Aristophanes (193c8–d5) ended with a kind of exhortation to piety.   **καὶ εἴπερ...7 ἐκείνῳ** lit. 'and (*sc.* to become), if any other of mankind' (cf. 211d2 n.), 'immortal, he too'.

(iii) 212b1–c3. *I believe what Diotima said, and I honour Eros accordingly.*

The passage is comparable with two others which follow a description of the afterlife, *Phd.* 114d and *Grg.* 526de. The former is a little more diffident (Socrates does not 'insist' that what he has described is exactly so, but thinks that the 'risk' of believing it is well worthwhile, for it is a beneficial 'incantation' in the face of death), and the latter more urgent (Socrates is, after all, threatening Callicles with hellfire). With b2 πέπεισμαι, b6 ἀσκῶ, b2f. 'I try to persuade others too' and b6f. 'I exhort others' compare *Grg.* 526d3f. 'I am persuaded by these accounts', d6 τὴν ἀλήθειαν ἀσκῶν and e1f. 'I call upon all other men . . . '. Diotima has not offered us good grounds for believing any of her psychological, religious and metaphysical assertions, nor does she (any more than Socrates elsewhere in Plato) say 'I've *been* there!'; from 209e onwards she has adopted the tone of an initiator, confident that ineffable vision and knowledge are attainable, raising the hopes of a candidate for initiation. Socrates declares his spiritual allegiance with fervour. Later, the effect of his faith upon his life will be displayed in Alcibiades' speech; Plato was probably inclined to believe, contrary to ordinary experience, that there is a correlation between the truth of a belief and its effect upon the conduct of the believer.

212b3 τούτου...4 ἀμείνω 'a better collaborator with human nature in acquiring this possession (*sc.* becoming θεοφιλής and immortal)'.

b8 ἀνδρείαν: we have been told (210e6) that progress towards the comprehension of beauty is full of πόνοι 'privations', 'hardships', and in *Meno* 81d it is required of the man whose soul seeks to 'recollect' true knowledge that he should 'be brave and not flag in the search'.

c2 εἰ δέ...3 ὀνόμαζε 'or if (*sc.* you prefer)', then lit. 'what and in what way you rejoice naming (*sc.* it), name it that'.

212c3–215a3: Arrival of Alcibiades

Alcibiades arrives, drunk, to crown Agathon with ribbons of victory. After jocular pretence that he and Socrates are involved in a jealous and possessive erotic relationship, Alcibiades declares that he will speak in praise not of Eros but of Socrates.

212c5 ὅτι ἐμνήσθη...6 λόγου: 205d10–206a1.   **c6f. τὴν αὔλειον θύραν:** the door which gave access from the street to the court (d4 αὐλῇ) round which the house was built.   **c7 κωμαστῶν:** participants in a κῶμος, a mobile drinking-party, sometimes celebrating a success, sometimes serenading and besieging a boy or hetaira.   **c8 φωνήν:** the word can denote the sound of a musical instrument, but in d3 it is 'voice', and so probably here too.

d1 ἐπιτηδείων: not 'suitable (*sc.* for our intellectual gathering)', but 'people I know'; cf. *Phd.* 58c 'who of his ἐπιτήδειοι were with him?' **καλεῖτε** 'ask them in'; cf. 174e7.   **d6 ὑπολαβοῦσαν** 'supporting him'.

e1 κιττοῦ 'ivy', specially associated with Dionysus and thus appropriate to a drunken reveller.   **e2 ταινίας** 'bands', 'ribbons', customarily tied round the head of a victor.   **e3 πάνυ σφόδρα** qualifies μεθύοντα. Despite his drunkenness (and cf. 213e12–214a2) Alcibiades proves to be prodigiously articulate.   **e8 ἀνειπὼν οὑτωσί** is Hermann's emendation of ἐὰν εἴπω οὑτωσί, which would mean not 'if I may say so' but 'if I speak (*sc.* of him) thus'; ἀνειπεῖν denotes proclamation (including proclamation of victors) by a herald (e.g. *Rep.* 580b), and οὑτωσί will refer to the fulsome terms τοῦ σοφωτάτου καὶ καλλίστου.

213a2 αὐτόθεν 'straight away'.   **ἐπὶ ῥητοῖς** 'on agreed terms'; Alcibiades is asking them to make the choice which he offered in

212e3–5. **a4 καὶ τὸν ἰέναι:** cf. p. 81. **a5 ὑπὸ τῶν ἀνθρώπων:** 212d6f. **περιαιρούμενον** 'untying (*sc.* from his own head)'.

b1 παραχωρῆσαι 'move over'. **b2 ὡς ἐκεῖνον κατιδεῖν** 'when he (*sc.* Socrates) saw him (*sc.* Alcibiades)'; for ὡς + infinitive in this sense, dependent on a main clause expressed in the accusative and infinitive of indirect speech, cf. 174e4f. The medieval text, however, has καθίζειν, not κατιδεῖν; ὡς must then = ὥστε (as in *Rep.* 365d and a few other passages of Plato), and the sense is 'so as to seat him' (for καθίζειν cf. *Chrm.* 153c). On either reading it is curious that ἐκείνου in b1 refers to Agathon but ἐκεῖνον a few words later to Alcibiades. **b4 ὑπολύετε** 'take off...sandals'. **b5 ἐκ τρίτων** 'to make a third'; cf. *Grg.* 500a 'do you too vote with us ἐκ τρίτων?' **b9 ἦν:** cf. 198d8 n. **ἐλλοχῶν** 'lying in ambush'.

c1 ὥσπερ εἰώθεις lit. 'as you were accustomed...to appear'; English is more inclined to make 'as...accustomed' (etc.) a self-contained parenthesis and say 'appearing, as you were accustomed to, ...'. Cf. 179e1 n. **c2 καὶ τί...3 κατεκλίνης:** what is formally a question may be in substance an exclamation, 'and lying *here*, too, eh?' ὡς οὐ κτλ. then gives the answer to the question, which is at the same time the justification of the exclamation. **c4 ἐστί τε καὶ βούλεται:** considered as an object or as a functioning unit of society, a man may be good or bad through no doing of his; to add '...and he is willing to be so' is to double the praise or blame (e.g. Eur. *Helen* 998 'I am by nature pious and I am willing to be so', Andocides 1.95 'who is the worst of men and is willing to be so'). Aristophanes is 'laughable' because he is a comic poet; whether he was laughably ugly, we do not know – it is clear from *Peace* 771 that he was bald – but a contrast between γελοῖος and κάλλιστος is understandable enough. **c5 τῶν ἔνδον** 'of those in the room'. **c6 ὅρα εἴ μοι ἐπαμυνεῖς** lit. 'see if you will defend me', i.e. 'you'll defend me, won't you?'; despite 214e6 (v. n.), the future ἐπαμυνεῖς should be preferred here to the present ἐπαμύνεις; cf. d4 ὅρα...μή...ἐργάσηται. **c7 ὁ τούτου ἔρως** 'my passion for him' (cf. c8–d1); Alcibiades' emotion (Socrates jocularly treats him as an impossibly jealous boy, and Alcibiades plays up in d7–9) is φιλεραστία (d6), not ἔρως. Cf. p. 4. **οὐ φαῦλον πρᾶγμα** 'no light matter'.

d2 ἤ...3 ἐργάζεται 'or (sc. if I do), he, in his jealous resentment against me, behaves in an extraordinary way'. **d4 ἀλλά** 'but (sc. instead of his doing something like that now)'. **d8 εἰς αὖθίς σε τιμωρήσομαι** 'I'll get my own back on you another time'.

e3 αὐτόν 'him himself'. **ἐν λόγοις:** Alcibiades will have much to say (215c–216c, 221d–222a) about Socrates' λόγοι; the utterances of a dramatic poet are also λόγοι, and Agathon's production two days before (hence e4 πρώην) is so designated in 194b4. **e5 ἔπειτα:** a participial clause followed by ἔπειτα conveys 'although..., nevertheless...', usually in a tone of suprise or indignation. **e9 ὡμολόγηται:** 213a2–4. **ἄρχοντα:** cf. p. 11. **e10 φερέτω:** in comedy we often find δότω τις, φερέτω τις, etc., in orders to slaves, and the omission of τις (implying as subject 'whoever's job it is') is abnormal; but we cannot easily dispense with punctuation between φερέτω and Ἀγάθων, for even when drunk Alcibiades would not give orders to his host as if to a slave. **e11 μᾶλλον δὲ οὐδὲν δεῖ:** Alcibiades corrects himself; 'no, that's not necessary at all'. **e12 ψυκτῆρα:** the big 'cooling-vessel' in which the wine was kept before it went into the 'mixing-bowl' to be mixed with water.

214a1 ὀκτὼ κοτύλας χωροῦντα 'holding eight kotylai', i.e. nearly half a gallon. **a2 ἐκπιεῖν** 'drank off', 'drank up'. One hesitates to say that *no one* could drink half a gallon of wine quickly when already drunk and still talk coherently, but Plato seems to be giving his Alcibiades a touch of epic treatment. **a3 τὸ σόφισμά μοι οὐδέν** 'my trick's no good at all', implying 'I shan't get *him* drunk'. **a5 οὐδὲν ...μεθυσθῇ:** a combination of οὐδὲν μᾶλλον 'none the more for that' and οὐ μή + aorist subjunctive, 'he won't...'. **a6 πίνειν:** contrast ἐκπιεῖν; Socrates does not show off. **a7 πῶς...b2 πιόμεθα:** not 'how are we doing?' in the sense 'how are things going?' but 'what's this that we're doing?' Then οὕτως is 'like this' and ἀλλ' ἀτεχνῶς κτλ. 'are we simply going to...?'

b3 ὦ Ἐρυξίμαχε...4 χαῖρε: a touch of drunken magniloquence, to which Eryximachus replies primly. **b7 ἰητρός...ἄλλων:** with these words Idomeneus in *Il.* 11.514 urges Nestor to take the wounded healer Machaon out of the battle. Alcibiades is becoming tediously noisy and voluble, especially for an ἄρχων τῆς πόσεως, and Eryximachus and Socrates between them deserve the gratitude of the company for bringing him under control. **b10 ἐπὶ δεξιά:** cf. 177d3.

c3 δίκαιος: cf. 172b5 n.   **c7 μεθύοντα...8 ᾖ** 'but maybe it's' (μή... ᾖ; cf. 194c4) 'unfair' (οὐκ ἐξ ἴσου) 'to compare a drunken man' (i.e. a drunken man's speech) 'with speeches of sober men'.

d3 οὐκ ἀφέξεταί...χεῖρε: Alcibiades says of Socrates what Socrates said of him in 213d3f.   **d5 οὐκ εὐφημήσεις:** cf. 201e10 n.   **d6 μὰ τὸν Ποσειδῶ:** the oath 'by Poseidon' is frequent in comedy but otherwise unexampled in Plato; it may have had bullying overtones. **μηδέν...ταῦτα** 'don't you say a word against it!'   **d9 οὕτω** 'as you say'.

e1 δοκεῖ χρῆναι 'is it agreed that that's what I'm to do?'   **e4 οὗτος** 'hi!' in a tone of alarm (unlike 172a5, v. n.).   **ἐπὶ τὰ γελοιότερα** 'in a way that will make them laugh at me'.   **e6 ὅρα εἰ παρίης** lit. 'see if you allow me', i.e. 'do you allow me to?' Cf. Crito's words to the dying Socrates in *Phd.* 118a, ἀλλ' ὅρα εἴ τι ἄλλο λέγεις. The idiom of 213c3 and d4 is a little different.

e9 οὐκ ἂν φθάνοιμι: cf. 185e4 n.   **e10 μεταξὺ ἐπιλαβοῦ** lit. 'take hold of me in the middle (*sc.* of my speech)', i.e. 'interrupt me'.   **e11 ἑκὼν γὰρ εἶναι:** cf. 176d2 n.

215a1 ἄλλο ἄλλοθεν: i.e. one ingredient from one period or set of events, and another from another, not in strict order.   **a2 ἀτοπίαν:** cf. 175a10 n.   **a3 ὧδ' ἔχοντι** 'for a man in my condition'.   **εὐπόρως... καταριθμῆσαι** 'recount' (or 'enumerate') 'fluently' (lit. 'with easy provision') 'and in order'.

215a4–222b7: Alcibiades' speech

Socrates may be compared to a satyr in appearance and (superficially) in behaviour, but what is within him is godlike. What he says to me has an extraordinary effect on me, like that of supernatural music on its hearers. As an adolescent, such was my admiration for him that I tried to seduce him, believing that I could have no better erastes, but he withstood the temptation. On campaign at Potidaea, he displayed greater endurance than anyone. He saved my

life in battle; and his courage on the retreat from Delium was exemplary.
There is no one like him, past or present; and his arguments are incomparably
penetrating.

Plato's chief purpose in this speech is to show us that Socrates put
into practice the morality implicit in Diotima's theory. In part of the
speech the framework of an encomium (cf. pp. 11 f., 123) is discernible,
though the handling of illustrative detail is exceptionally dramatic
and lively. The story of the attempted seduction of Socrates (217a3–
219e5) shows his σωφροσύνη (219d5), what follows shows his ἀνδρεία
(219e6–221c1, cf. 219d5 n.), and both the beginning and the end of
the speech can be regarded as praise of his peculiar σοφία.

The εἰκών ('image', 'likeness') with which Alcibiades begins
(215a4–b4, cf. 216c5–7) exemplifies a common form of Greek wit
(hence 215a5 ἐπὶ τὰ γελοιότερα; cf. 214e4f.), attested in comedy (Ar.
Birds 801–8, *Wasps* 1308–13) and used also in *Meno* 80a–c. The speech
as a whole falls into four parts:

(i) 215a4–216c3. It is important that it should be Alcibiades who
pays this tribute to the power of Socrates' moral teaching, for
Alcibiades – undoubtedly, as boy and youth, very close to Socrates –
was regarded by many in Plato's time (cf. Lys. 14.16f., 29f., 35–40)
as a traitor guilty of inflicting great and deliberate harm on Athens,
and Socrates was blamed for his 'teaching' of such a 'pupil'. Xen.
Mem. 1.2.12–48 defends Socrates on the grounds that both Albiciades
and the future tyrant Critias abandoned their association with him
and rejected his exhortation and criticism (cf. 216a2–b6) when they
found the lure of political power irresistible – an interesting admission
that argument can influence action only when addressed to those
who are well-disposed to its presuppositions, and that although
Socrates had the power to enthral and inspire he did not have the
power to keep those who did not wish to stay.

(ii) 216c4–219d2. To understand what the story of the attempted
homosexual seduction meant to Plato's readers, we must first note
that Alcibiades does not embarrass his audience or move them
deeply; he makes them laugh (222c1), for he reveals how, as a handsome and conceited boy, he had tried to seduce a man by using, one
after another, the conventional ploys of a man seducing a boy (cf.
217c7). The story is charged with comic paradox, felicitously
expressed. To appreciate its point, most of us need to translate it into

heterosexual terms and imagine Socrates as a healthy man who converses tranquilly, and then falls soundly asleep, when a beautiful girl has crept naked under his blanket and put her arms round him. Plato undoubtedly wishes to suggest that physical relations are inimical to the pursuit of metaphysical truth with the same partner on other occasions. This may not be true, and even if it is true not everyone will regard it as a good advertisement for metaphysics, but it is dictated by Plato's psychology; he regards the human soul as composed of three contending elements of which two, the 'appetitive' and the 'spirited', must either be controlled by the 'rational' or control it. *Rep.* 588e–589a speaks of the unrighteous man as 'feasting the monster and the lion' and 'starving the human', and in *Phdr.* 254e it is the task of reason, as 'charioteer' of the soul, so to intimidate and humiliate the 'black horse' that it struggles no more against his control.

(iii) 219d3–221c1. Potidaea, a subject-ally of Athens on the north Aegean coast, revolted in the summer of 432 and received help from Corinth; an Athenian expeditionary force won a hard-fought battle between Potidaea and Olynthus late in the summer and began a siege of Potidaea which lasted until the city surrendered at the end of 430 (Thuc. 1.56–65, 2.70). The battle in which Socrates and Alcibiades participated (220d5–e7) is presumably the battle before the siege; the reference to wintry weather (220a6–b7) suggests that they stayed there at any rate for some months, and Thucydides' manner of reference to the siege suggests (2.31.2, 58) that it was conducted by the original force throughout; yet in *Chrm.* 153a–c we encounter Socrates back in Athens very soon after the battle. Unless (improbably) the *Chrm.* passage refers to a different battle – fought and lost in the summer of 429 (Thuc. 2.79) – it is historically false, or Plato has combined in Alcibiades' narrative two military occasions which do not belong together, or winter came very early to the north Aegean coast in 432.

(iv) 221c2–222b7. In the last section Alcibiades reverts to the εἰκών with which he began, and incorporates in his praise of Socrates' uniqueness a characterisation of Socratic λόγοι, which approach great moral issues through everyday analogies and examples; it is a deft touch of realism that Alcibiades is made to introduce this (221d7) with the words 'I forgot to mention, in what I said to start with, . . . '.

215a6 φημὶ γὰρ δή 'for in my opinion. . .', a formula used when an opinion is expressed with great confidence; cf. 212b4f.   **a7 σιληνοῖς:** 'Silenus' is sometimes the name of an individual, father of the satyrs (as in Eur. *Cyclops*; cf. 222d3f. n.), sometimes a category of satyr (cf. the plurals 'Panes' and 'Erotes').

b1 ἑρμογλυφείοις: evidently a general term for the workshops (∼ γλύφειν 'carve') of makers of domestic statuary, since the 'herm' which stood at every front door was their staple trade.   **b2 οἳ διχάδε . . .3 θεῶν** 'which when opened in two are revealed as containing statues of gods inside'. Perhaps this was a temporary fashion in late fifth-century Athens; no examples have survived, nor are there any references to such a type of statue except in late passages dependent on this one.   **b4 Μαρσύᾳ:** a legendary satyr ('silenus' in Hdt. 7.26.3) who competed in music with Apollo and was flayed by the god.   **τό γε εἶδος:** Socrates had a snub nose and protruding eyes (*Tht.* 143e), typical features of satyrs in Greek art; he is again compared (implicitly) with a silenus in Xen. *Smp.* 4.19.   **b5 τούτοις:** satyrs in general, whereas in b8 ἐκείνου we return specifically to Marsyas. **b7 ὑβριστής:** the usual hybris of satyrs is sexual assault, when their natural shamelessness is fortified by wine and overcomes their natural cowardice; Socratic 'hybris' (cf. 175e7 n.) is very different, as Alcibiades' narrative will show.

c2 ἃ γὰρ. . .3 διδάξαντος 'for the music which Olympus played I call Marsyas' music, since Marsyas taught Olympus'. Certain tunes were believed to have been composed by Olympus, who has no historical context; he is associated in *Ion* 533b and *Laws* 677d with mythical figures (including, as here, Marsyas).   **c5 κατέχεσθαι:** Arist. *Politics* 1340a8–12 refers to Olympus' music as giving the hearer the sensation of being possessed by a supernatural force.   **καὶ δηλοῖ. . .6 εἶναι** lit. 'reveals, because it (*sc.* Olympus' music) is divine, those who need the gods and initiation-rites'; cf. *Minos* 318b, where it ἐκφαίνει τοὺς τῶν θεῶν ἐν χρείᾳ ὄντας, and on the point of this cf. e1 n.   **c7 ψιλοῖς:** in *Laws* 669de this word ('bare') is applied to prose as opposed to poetry and to music as opposed to accompanied song.

d2 ῥήτορος: here simply (as very often in classical Attic) 'speaker', without any connotation of habitual or professional speaking (contrast e5). **d5 γυνή**: possibly 'woman' precedes 'man' here because women were regarded as much more impressionable and unstable (*GPM* 99f.). **d6 εἰ μὴ ἔμελλον** 'were I not in danger (*sc.* by so doing)...'. Since he goes on to describe vividly how he is affected by Socrates, either he has in mind (and suppresses) a description which would express his feelings much more extravagantly, or all the emphasis lies on ὀμόσας; but the latter could hardly make the others think him drunker than he is, whereas the former might.

e1 κορυβαντιώντων 'those affected by the music of the corybantes'; the corybantes were a mythical group associated with the goddess Cybele, and the special feature of their cult was the drum- and pipe-music which induced a curative frenzy in those who were 'possessed' in the sense 'deranged' (cf. *Ion* 533e, 536c, and E. R. Dodds, *The Greeks and the irrational* (Berkeley and Los Angeles 1951) 77–80). **e4 Περικλέους**: the superiority of Pericles in oratory was un-challenged; Eupolis fr. 94 is a remarkable tribute to him seventeen years after his death ('the *only* speaker who left the sting behind in the hearer'). **e6 ὡς ἀνδραποδωδῶς διακειμένου**: cf. 210d1–3 ὥσπερ οἰκέτης...δουλεύων.

216a5 ἐμαυτοῦ...6 πράττω: i.e. I neglect my own soul. In *Ap.* 29d Socrates portrays himself as reproaching others for concerning them-selves with (ἐπιμελεῖσθαι) money, reputation and standing instead of wisdom, truth and the moral improvement of their own souls. **a6 βίᾳ...7 φεύγων** 'I force myself to stop my ears and run away from him, as from the Sirens.' Men who heard the Sirens' song stayed with them and died, and Alcibiades would have 'died' politically had he not stopped his ears as Odysseus stopped the ears of his crew with wax (Hom. *Od.* 12.37–54, 154–200).

b2 αἰσχύνεσθαι: almost 'feel inferior to...'. **b5 τιμῆς**: cf. a5 n., and on the motive power of the desire for honour and high standing cf. *GPM* 226–36. **δραπετεύω**: a harsh word; δραπέτης is 'runaway', 'deserter'. **b6 ὡμολογημένα**: cf. a4f. ἀναγκάζει γάρ με ὁμολογεῖν.

c3 οὐκ ἔχω ὅτι χρήσωμαι 'I don't know how to deal with...'; cf. 190c3 n.

d2 ἐρωτικῶς...καλῶν cf. p. 2. **d3 ἐκπέπληκται**: cf. 192b7 n. and

211d5 ἐκπέπληξαι. ἀγνοεῖ...4 οἶδεν: one does not expect a satyr, even when sober, to be learned. *Ap.* 21b–22e is the classic exposition of Socrates' 'ignorance'. ὡς κτλ. lit. 'as is the appearance of him', i.e. 'so far as his appearance goes'. The expression has no exact parallel, and some editors punctuate strongly after οἶδεν, with no further punctuation before the question mark at σιληνῶδες; but this gives a curious blend of a declaration (introduced by ὡς = 'I can assure you that...') with a question. d6 πόσης οἴεσθε: expressions such as 'how do you think?', 'how much do you imagine?', etc., whether parenthetic or (in varying degrees) incorporated into the syntax of the sentence, are somewhat colloquial: 'you just can't imagine how...!' d7 ἴστε: imperative, 'know...' = 'let me tell you, ...'.

e1 οὐδ' ἂν εἷς: cf. 192e6 n. e2 τιμήν: i.e. an attribute (natural or acquired) which makes him envied and highly regarded. e3 οὐδέν 'of no account'. e4 εἰρωνευόμενος...παίζων: εἰρωνεία (unlike 'irony') is 'mock-modesty', 'pretended ignorance'; in *Rep.* 337a Thrasymachus speaks (in no friendly tone) of 'Socrates' accustomed εἰρωνεία'. On παίζων cf. 172a4; σπουδάζειν (cf. e5 and 197e6 n.) is its opposite.

217a1 χρυσᾶ lit. 'golden', not uncommonly used where we would say 'divine'. a2 ἔμβραχυ ὅτι lit. 'in brief, whatever...'. ἔμβραχυ is an emendation of ἐν βραχεῖ, on the strength of *Theages* 127c ὅτου ἂν δέῃ ἔμβραχυ; in *Grg.* 457b ἔμβραχυ περὶ ὅτου ἂν βούληται and *Hippias Minor* 365d ἔμβραχυ ὅτι βούλει there is a variant ἐν βραχεῖ. ἐσπουδακέναι...3 ὥρᾳ 'that he was keen on my beauty'; ὥρα, 'season', 'time', when applied to a person, means the time of life at which a person is most attractive, and is often translatable as 'beauty'. ἕρμαιον: cf. 176c1. a4 ὡς ὑπάρχον μοι lit. 'as it being available for me', i.e. 'in the belief that it was possible for me...'. χαρισαμένῳ: cf. p. 3. a5 ἐφρόνουν: cf. 198d6.

b3 γάρ: almost '– as I was saying –'. b6 ἄν: with an imperfect or aorist indicative, ἄν can give a frequentative sense; *MT* 56, 86.

                                      iterative

c3 οὐδέν...ἦν 'I got nowhere', 'I was no further forward'; naked wrestling obviously gave a bold erastes an opportunity for suggestive

physical contacts which he could pretend were accidental if they
aroused resentment. **c4 ἤνυτον** 'progressed', 'achieved my aim'
(~ ἀνύτειν). **c5 κατὰ τὸ καρτερόν** lit. 'according to strength', i.e.
'by direct assault' (cf. Hdt. 1.212.2 'in a straight fight'). **καὶ οὐκ
ἀνετέον** 'and that I must not give up' (~ ἀνίημι). **c6 ἰστέον...
πρᾶγμα** 'I must know how things stood'. **c7 προκαλοῦμαι:** often
'challenge' (there is a touch of that in c1), sometimes 'put forward
as a proposal', here 'invite'.

d4 διελεγόμην...νυκτῶν 'I kept the conversation going far into the
night'; νύκτες, instead of νύξ, is often used when a time of night is
referred to. **d5 προσηνάγκασα** 'I succeeded in pressing him...'.
d6 τῇ ἐχομένῃ ἐμοῦ 'next to me', i.e. 'next to mine'. **d7 οἰκήματι**
'room'.

e3 τὸ λεγόμενον '– that which is said –', i.e. 'as the saying goes'.
οἶνος...4 ἀληθής: the proverb οἶνος καὶ παῖδες ἀληθεῖς (in typical
proverb-form, ⌣⌣ – ⌣⌣ – ⌣ ⌣ – –, cf. 174b4 n.), cited by Photius,
obviously means that drunken men, through carelessness, and
children, through natural candour, tell the truth. Since παῖδες can
mean 'slaves' as well as 'children' or 'boys', there may have been
another proverbial expression, 'wine without slaves' (i.e. '...when
no slaves are present'), referring to the circumstances in which a man
discloses his intimate thoughts and feelings more completely than at
any other time; or again, an expression 'wine both without slaves and
with them', referring to a drunken man's indifference to whether his
secrets (including dangerous conspiratorial secrets) are overheard or
not. This may even be an improvised modification by Alcibiades of
'wine without slaves', since slaves are in fact present (218b5–7).
e4 ἀφανίσαι: almost 'allow to be forgotten'. **e5 ὑπερήφανον:** the
word can be laudatory (e.g. *Phd.* 96a, *Grg.* 511d, though there is a
faint touch of irony in both); in 219c6 below it is jocularly derogatory.
εἰς ἔπαινον ἐλθόντα 'when one has embarked on praising him'; on
ἐλθόντα...μοι cf. 176d3 n. **e6 ὑπὸ τοῦ ἔχεως:** the definite article is
probably neither generalising nor a reference to a particular species
of snake, but indicates the snake assumed by the popular notion
expounded in the next sentence.

218a1 πᾶν...2 ὀδύνης: screaming, raving and begging for death,

conduct unmanly and contemptible in Greek eyes, since indifference
to the pain of wounds was required of the citizen-soldier.   **a2 ἐγώ...**
b5 λεγομένοις: the sentence of which δεδηγμένος τε (a2)...καὶ ὁρῶν
(a7)... is the skeleton is twice interrupted, by the parenthesis τὴν
καρδίαν (a3)...ὁτιοῦν (a7) and by the parenthesis Σωκράτη (b2)...
λεγομένοις (b5), and after the second parenthesis it is simply abandoned, so that we never come to a finite verb of which ἐγώ can be the
subject. Moreover, the first parenthesis, where we expect a finite verb
(because of the introductory γάρ), has none, so that we have to treat
γάρ as introducing the amplification (πληγείς τε καὶ δηχθείς) of
δεδηγμένος κτλ. (cf. *GP* 67f.).   **a3 τὸ ἀλγεινότατον** 'the most painful
part' rather than 'the most painful bite', as τὴν καρδίαν...δηχθείς
shows.   **καρδίαν...4 ὀνομάσαι** 'the heart or soul or whatever we
ought to call it'; Alcibiades' uncertainty reflects the readiness with
which 'heart' and 'soul' are interchangeable in many Greek expressions.   **a5 ἔχονται** 'get a grip'.   **a6 ἀφυοῦς:** ἀφυής is the opposite of
εὐφυής (209b6), i.e. 'lacking good natural qualities and abilities'.
a7 Φαίδρους: the plural of a proper name often means 'people like...'
or '...and people like him'; there may also be a suggestion here that
Alcibiades' vision is impaired by drink.

b2 καὶ ὅσοι ἄλλοι lit. 'and as many others (*sc.* as there are)', i.e. 'and
all the rest'; cf. 178a and 180c for references to the unnamed participants at the party.   **b4 βακχείας** 'frenzy'; cf. 215e1 n.   **b6 βέβηλός
τε καὶ ἄγροικος** 'profane and vulgar'; the former is a rather technical
word (sometimes literally 'uninitiated', hence not entitled to hear the
secrets of a mystery-cult), the latter a very general derogatory word
(cf. 194c2 n.).

c1 ποικίλλειν lit. 'complicate', 'embellish' (cf. 182b1 ποικίλος),
hence 'beat about the bush'.   **c2 ἐλευθέρως** 'freely', because a free
man (ἐλεύθερος is the opposite of δοῦλος) is able to speak his mind.
c6 τί μάλιστα 'what exactly?'   **c8 μνησθῆναι** 'mention it', 'speak
of it'.   **πρός με:** cf. 177a5 n.   **ἐγώ...9 ἔχω** 'this is how it is with me',
amplified in πάνυ κτλ.   **μὴ οὐ:** cf. 197a2 n.   **c10 οὐσίας...d1 φίλων:**
cf. 183a6f.; Alcibiades is making the kind of promises which one
would expect the erastes to make to his eromenos.

d2 πρεσβύτερον 'of greater importance'; cf. *Rep.* 548c 'honouring physical training πρεσβυτέρως than cultural'. ὡς ὅτι βέλτιστον: with a superlative, to give the sense 'as... as possible', ὡς and ὅτι are common alternatives; the combination ὡς ὅτι is rare, and perhaps analysable as 'in the way in which... would be as... as possible'. On submission to an erastes as a means of self-improvement cf. 183b5–185c2, and in particular 184e1 συμβάλλεσθαι ∼ 218d3 συλλήπτορα. **d3 κυριώτερον:** cf. 180b7 n. **d6 εἰρωνικῶς:** cf. 216e4 n. ἑαυτοῦ lit. 'of himself', i.e. 'characteristically'; cf. Ar. *Wasps* 1002 'I did it unintentionally and not τοὐμοῦ τρόπου'. **d8 οὐ φαῦλος:** almost 'no fool'; e5 οὐκ ὀλίγῳ... διανοῇ explains the point of this.

e2 ὁρῴης ἄν 'you must be seeing, I think, ...'; cf. 175e3 n. **e3 διαφέρον:** cf. 215c7. **e4 κοινώσασθαι** 'strike a bargain'. **e6 ἀντὶ δόξης ...κτᾶσθαι** lit. 'acquire truth of beautiful things in return for opinion', i.e. 'acquire what is truly beautiful in return for what only seems to be so'; on δόξα cf. 202a5 n.

219a1 χρύσεα χαλκείων: in *Il.* 6.232–6 Glaucus exchanges armour with Diomede, giving golden armour in exchange for brazen (for 'Zeus took away his wits'). Socrates means that what Alcibiades wants from him, the acquisition of moral improvement, is of gold, whereas what Alcibiades offers in exchange, the 'possession' of physical beauty, is of bronze; the analogy will not stand up to detailed scrutiny. **a2 οὐδὲν ὤν:** cf. 216e3f. ἤ τοι...3 ὄψις 'the sight of the mind'; cf. 212a1 n. **a4 †λήγειν ἐπιχειρῇ†:** since elsewhere ἐπιχειρεῖν is 'attempt', 'embark on...', 'attack...' or 'put one's hand to...', with an animate subject, the text is highly suspect; Plato may possibly have written ἐπιλείπῃ (without λήγειν), a word of which he is fond in *Rep.*, 'fail in...', 'fall short of...'. τούτων ἔτι πόρρω 'still a long way from that'; contrast πόρρω τῶν νυκτῶν in 217d4. **a5 ταῦτα** 'as I've said'. **a6 οὕτω** 'that being so'.

b3 ἀφεὶς ὥσπερ βέλη 'having, as it were, loosed my arrows'. τετρῶσθαι: this was not very perceptive of Alcibiades, but he thought his beauty irresistible (cf. c5 and 217a5f.), and Socrates had not expressed indignation or revulsion. **b5 ἀμφιέσας:** a double accusative is normal for verbs meaning 'put...round...'. **b6 τρίβωνα:** the τρίβων was a short and unpretentious cloak (Socrates wears one in *Prt.* 335d), and Alcibiades has put his own himation over it as a top

blanket; a himation was normally so used. **b7 τούτῳ τῷ δαιμονίῳ:**
the repeated demonstratives, b5 τούτῳ, b6 τοῦτον, b7 τουτουί and
τούτῳ, are like a jabbing finger; Alcibiades speaks half in exasperated
admiration, half in denunciation (cf. c5 n.).

c1 ὡς ἀληθῶς qualifies δαιμονίῳ; cf. 202d13 n. **c5 τι εἶναι** 'that I
(*sc.* really) was something!'; cf. 219a2, and *Ap.* 41e 'if they think that
they are something, when they are nothing'. **c5 ὦ ἄνδρες δικασταί:**
the normal mode of addressing the jury in court; Alcibiades speaks
facetiously as if he were prosecuting Socrates for ὕβρις; and on
ὑπερηφανία (c6) cf. 217e5 n. **c7 οὐδὲν περιττότερον:** περιττός is
'extra', often with the connotation 'excessively elaborated' (or
learned, inquisitive, expensive, etc.); here the comparative is an
adverb qualifying καταδεδαρθηκώς, 'having slept... in a way that did
not involve anything *more*...'.

d3 τὸ δὴ μετὰ τοῦτο 'then, after that'; adverbs and adverbial phrases
of time and place sometimes incorporate a neuter article (e.g. *Critias*
120a ἐπώμνυσαν δικάσειν τε...τό τ' αὖ μετὰ τοῦτο μηδέν...παρα-
βήσεσθαι), and demonstratives are very commonly reinforced by δή,
e.g. 199c2 μετὰ ταῦτα δή, 201a ἐπὶ δὴ τούτοις. **διάνοιαν:** usually
systematic rational thought (cf. 219a3), but here 'feelings' or 'frame
of mind' is more appropriate. **d7 οὖν:** ὅπως + οὖν, normally written
as one word, ὁπωσοῦν, means 'in any way whatsoever', not 'however...', but the latter is the sense required here. Possibly we should
compare *Prt.* 322c 'So Hermes asked τίνα οὖν τρόπον δοίη...' (i.e.
'...asked "How, then, am I to give...?"'; cf. *GP* 426). **d8 προσαγαγοίμην** 'win him over'.

e1 χρήμασι...2 Αἴας: 'unwoundable by money' = 'incorruptible'
(πανταχῇ 'from any quarter'). Ajax was not invulnerable to weapons
in any magical or supernatural sense, but simply (as portrayed in the
Iliad) very hard to wound because of his fighting skill and vast shield.
ᾧ τε ᾤμην 'and (*sc.* as for) that by which I thought...', i.e. my beauty.
e5 ταῦτά τε...6 ταῦτα: the narrative to which Alcibiades now
proceeds is a further explanation of his 'enslavement' (e3), hence '*for*
all these things had happened to me previously, and later...', i.e. 'for
apart from all that I have described, *later*...'. **e7 συνεσιτοῦμεν:** it
seems from Thuc. 6.98.4, 100.1, 8.92.4 that members of the same φυλή

were put together as a military unit, but evidently they were not compelled to mess together, for Socrates and Alcibiades belonged to different φυλαί, Antiochis and Leontis respectively. **πόνοις** 'hardships', the usual term for the soldier's efforts and privations. **e9 ἀποληφθέντες...στρατείας** 'cut off somewhere, the sort of thing that (*sc.* happens) on campaign'.

220a2 εὐωχίαις: cf. 203b4. **τά τ' ἄλλα...3 ἐκράτει** 'in particular, although he didn't want to drink, he beat everyone at it when he was forced to'. **a5 καὶ αὐτίκα** lit. 'even straightway', i.e. 'any time now'; the prophecy is fulfilled in 223c2–d12. **a7 δεινοί...χειμῶνες:** cf. p. 165. The Thracian area, home of the North Wind, was thought of by the Greeks as uncommonly cold; cf. Ar. *Ach.* 138f. (an envoy delayed there by snow and the freezing of the rivers).

b1 οἵου δεινοτάτου: οἷος δεινότατος 'such as is most formidable' would be logical, but in actual usage such phrases, although formally relative clauses, are commonly put in the same case as the words to which they refer. **b3 ἐνειλιγμένων...4 ἀρνακίδας** 'having wrapped their feet in felt and fleeces'. **οὗτος δ':** δέ is not a connective here, but contrasts οὗτος, as subject of the main clause, with the 'genitive absolute' clause πάντων κτλ.; cf. *GP* 181f., and a fifth-century inscription ('the aliens in Chalcis, as many as do not pay taxes to Athens..., the others δέ are to pay taxes to Chalcis'). **b7 ὑπέβλεπον:** however modest Socrates was in speaking of himself, resentment of his superiority must not be underrated in explaining the hostility which made his eventual condemnation possible.

c1 καὶ ταῦτα μὲν δὴ ταῦτα lit. 'and that is that', but the formula is not dismissive; its point lies in the continuation δ' αὖ, 'and again...'. **c2 οἷον...ἀνήρ** is taken from *Od.* 4.242 (ἀλλ' οἷον κτλ.) and 271 (οἷον καὶ κτλ.). **c3 ἐπὶ στρατιᾶς:** metrically guaranteed in Ar. *Wasps* 354, 557, but that is not a reason for emending 219d9 ἐπὶ στρατείας, given that in Aesch. *Agamemnon* 603 and *Eumenides* 631 ἀπὸ στρατείας is also guaranteed. **συννοήσας...4 σκοπῶν:** τι is object of both participles. The behaviour of Socrates described here (down to d6) seems to manifest not a mystical experience, but concentrated intellectual scrutiny of a problem; cf. 174d4–175c6. **c5 ἀνίει:** cf. 217c5.

c8 Ἰώνων: the Athenians had a large allied contingent at Potidaea (Thuc. 1.61.4), and most of the allies were Ionian.

d1 χαμεύνια 'palliasses'.   **d4 προσευξάμενος τῷ ἡλίῳ:** most Greeks regarded the sun as a god, and found Anaxagoras' theory that it was a blazing lump (*Ap.* 26d) disturbing. It was customary to propitiate a god with a prayer on encountering him, and sunrise is an encounter. **d5 εἰ δέ...μάχαις** 'or again' (lit. 'and if you wish'; cf. 209d4) 'in the battles (*sc.* in which he fought) –', as if going on 'he showed outstanding courage', but at d6 ὅτε the sentence makes a fresh start. **τοῦτο...6 ἀποδοῦναι** 'for it is right to render him this (*sc.* tribute)'. **d7 τἀριστεῖα:** wishing to give a competitive character to as many things as possible, the Athenians awarded a 'prize for valour' after a battle.

e1 ἀνθρώπων: with οὐδείς 'no man'.   **ἀλλά** 'but' (as normally in Greek) is preferred to 'and' because of the contrast with the preceding negative, οὐκ ἐθέλων.   **e2 ὅπλα:** important not only because of their monetary and artistic value, but because to return from battle (even wounded) without one's equipment was to give rise to slanderous rumours that one had discarded it in order to run away faster. **e5 ἀξίωμα** 'standing', through his social and political connections. **e8 Δηλίου:** towards the end of 424 the Athenians were defeated by the Boeotians near Delium in south-eastern Boeotia (Thuc. 4.89–101.2); their retreat became a disorderly flight (*ibid.* 96.6–8).

221a2 ἵππον ἔχων: as one of the large force of cavalry which fought at Delium (Thuc. 4.93.2, 94.1).   **ὅπλα** '(*sc.* hoplite) equipment (*sc.* only)'.   **a3 Λάχης:** a general in 427–425 and 418, killed in that year at the battle of Mantinea. Plato's *Laches* is named after him; he is there presented as a man lacking in subtlety, but ready to listen to Socrates, whose conduct at Delium he greatly admires (*Laches* 181b).

b1 ἔμφρων 'self-possessed'; cf. 194b8.   **b2 τὸ σὸν δὴ τοῦτο** '(*sc.* to quote) that line you wrote'.   **b3 βρενθυόμενος...παραβάλλων** 'swaggering and looking from side to side', an adaptation of Ar. *Clouds* 362. The context here, and especially ἠρέμα παρασκοπῶν, indicate the alertness and curiosity of a man in command of the situation, not nervous glances, let alone rolling the eyes.   **b5 τούτου**

τοῦ ἀνδρός: 'this man' may = 'I', particularly in poetry (e.g. Soph. *Ajax* 78) and sometimes in a boast or threat; Alcibiades is looking at the situation either through Socrates' eyes ('if anyone's going to lay hands on *me*...') or through the eyes of the pursuers (thinking 'let *that* man alone!'). **b7 σχεδὸν γάρ τι** 'for as a rule'. **b8 οὐδὲ ἅπτονται** 'they don't even touch', 'they don't lay a finger on...'. When a battle is won and the defeated are in flight, the pursuers prefer to take no risks and kill only the easiest victims (cf. Thuc. 7.81.5 on the Athenian flight from Syracuse).

c3 τῶν...ἐπιτηδευμάτων: the sense required is 'on the subject of his other activities', and words meaning 'say' or 'think' are occasionally followed by a genitive in such a sense, e.g. Hom. *Od.* 11.174 'tell me πατρός τε καὶ υἱέος..., whether they still receive the honour due to me...'. In the present case the need to incorporate also περὶ ἄλλου probably accounts for the choice of construction. **c7 Βρασίδαν:** a Spartan commander of outstanding skill, energy and courage, killed fighting at Amphipolis in 422 (Thuc. 5.10.8–11). **c8 Περικλῆς:** cf. 215e4 n. **Νέστορα καὶ 'Αντήνορα:** the aged Nestor is described in *Il.* 1.248 as 'clear-voiced ἀγορητής', and he was so remembered in popular tradition (e.g. Ar. *Clouds* 1057); the Trojan Antenor is 'wise' and ἀγορητὴς ἐσθλός (*Il.* 3.148–51).

d4 εἰ μὴ ἄρα εἰ κτλ. 'except perhaps if one were to...'; cf. 205e6 n.

e2 ὀνόματα καὶ ῥήματα: cf. 198b5 n. **e3 περιαμπέχονται** 'wrap round themselves', 'are clothed in...'. **e4 δοράν** 'animal-skin', 'hide'. **ὄνους...βυρσοδέψας** 'he talks about pack-donkeys and... hmm (τινας)...smiths and cobblers and tanners'. The Platonic Socrates often takes humble crafts as an illustration, or as a starting-point, of an argument about intelligence, experience and moral goodness; Callicles protests rudely in *Grg.* 490c–491a, and cf. Xen. *Mem.* 1.2.32–7 (a threatening protest from Critias and Charicles).

222a1 ἰδὼν ἄν: we expect an optative later, but in a3 meet the future εὑρήσει: 'anyone who saw them opened up...will find...'. ἄν with the future in Attic is rare, and usually emended when a manuscript text presents it, but in the present case a change of course in the sentence is acceptable; whether any of his hearers *will* ever penetrate to the heart of Socrates' arguments is something on which Alcibiades vacillates (cf. 216e5–217a2). **a3 τῶν λόγων:** with μόνους; cf. ἀνθρώ-πων in 220e1. **a6 καλῷ κἀγαθῷ:** cf. 204a5 n.

b1 Χαρμίδην...Διοκλέους: Charmides, related to Critias, is intro-duced in the dialogue named after him as a youth of dazzling beauty (154a–155e); Euthydemus was also beautiful, as is clear from Xen. *Mem.* 1.2.29, 4.2.1 (the sophist after whom the dialogue *Euthydemus* is named is another person). **b3 παιδικά...4 ἀντ' ἐραστοῦ:** this puts Alcibiades' own experience (217a–219d) in a nutshell. **ἃ κτλ.** 'and I warn you, Agathon, not to be deceived in that way (ἃ) by him'. **b7 ὥσπερ...γνῶναι:** first in *Il.* 17.32 ῥεχθὲν δέ τε νήπιος ἔγνω, ' (*sc.* even) a foolish man understands (*sc.* something already) performed', then Hes. *WD* 218, with παθών for ῥεχθέν, '...when he has under-gone (*sc.* the consequences)', both making the point 'think *before* you act'.

222c1–223d12: The end of the party

222c1 γέλωτα: cf. p. 164. **c2 παρρησίᾳ** 'frankness', harking back to 217b1f., e1–4. **ἐρωτικῶς ἔχειν:** cf. p. 4. **c4 γάρ** 'for (*sc.* other-wise)'. **κύκλῳ περιβαλλόμενος:** lit. 'putting it on himself' (cf. 216d5) 'all over' (cf. *Phdr.* 251d5, 'stung κύκλῳ'), i.e. 'completely disguising his intentions'. **c6 ὡς ἐν παρέργῳ δή** 'ostensibly as an afterthought' (or '...as a minor consideration'); here, as often, δή implies an accusation of pretence. **c7 ὡς** 'as if...!'

d1 διαβάλλειν: often 'slander', but here 'make...quarrel', 'set at odds'. **οἰόμενος δεῖν:** cf. 173a2 n. **d3 τὸ σατυρικόν...σιληνικόν** 'your "satyr-play", or, rather, "silenos-play"'. The satyr-play, humorous in tone and normally using a chorus dressed as satyrs, rounded off each set of three tragedies at the City Dionysia; Socrates is referring playfully to the comparison on which Alcibiades embarked in 215b6. **d5 μηδέν...γένηται** 'don't let him gain anything by it'. **παρασκευάζου ὅπως** 'take care that...'. **d7 κινδυνεύεις** 'it could well be that you...'; cf. 174b5.

e1 τεκμαίρομαι...ὡς κτλ.: lit. 'I use as evidence...the fact that...'. **e2 διαλάβῃ** 'keep apart'; a conjecture of Rettig, very strongly indi-cated by χωρίς, for διαβάλῃ. **οὐδὲν...ἔσται:** cf. d5 n. **e4 ὑποκάτω ἐμοῦ:** cf. p. 11. Alcibiades had taken a place between Agathon and

Socrates (213a7–b5), so that the order was: Agathon, Alcibiades, Socrates. Socrates now invites Agathon to move 'below' him, to give the order: Alcibiades, Socrates, Agathon. Alcibiades offers to compromise (e8) on the order: Alcibiades, Agathon, Socrates. **e6 οἷα αὖ πάσχω** 'the way I'm treated, again!' **e7 περιεῖναι** 'get the better of...'. **e10 ἀλλ' ἀδύνατον...13 ἐπαινεθῆναι:** Socrates' objection is based on the convention adopted in 177d2–4 and reaffirmed in 214c2–5. **οὐ δήπου κτλ.** 'he'll praise me again – won't he? – instead of being praised, rather, by me'. Cf. Thuc. 2.12.2 'they sent him away πρὶν ἀκοῦσαι', i.e. '...and did not listen to him'. It is possible that μᾶλλον is the relic of a variant, μᾶλλον ἤ, on πρίν.

223a3 οὐκ ἔσθ'...4 μεταναστήσομαι 'I can't possibly...' (cf. 178e5) '...I simply *must*...'. **a6 ταῦτα ἐκεῖνα** 'there we go again!'; cf. 210e5 n. **a7 μεταλαβεῖν** 'get a look-in at...'. **a8 ὡς** is exclamatory, 'how...!'

b2 κωμαστάς: cf. 212c7 n. **b4 εἰς τὸ ἄντικρυς** 'straight on in'. **b6 ἀναγκάζεσθαι:** the understood subject is 'all of them'.

c1 μακρῶν: cf. p. 9. **c3 καθεύδοντας καὶ οἰχομένους:** i.e. some asleep and others gone; for καί cf. *GP* 292 and, e.g., '100 killed and wounded'. **c6 οὖν:** cf. 172a3 n.

d2 ὑπονυστάζειν: 'getting a bit drowsy'. **τὸ μέντοι κεφάλαιον:** cf. 205d1. **d3 προσαναγκάζειν** 'press'. **τοῦ αὐτοῦ...6 εἶναι:** the argument, strikingly unlike what is said by Socrates in *Ion* 531e–534e, is not developed elsewhere in Plato, and reconstruction of the form it might take is a useful exercise for students of ancient philosophy. **d7 ἑπομένους:** cf. 210a4. **d9 κατακοιμίσαντ' ἐκείνους** 'after getting them off to sleep'. **d10 ἕ:** Hermann's addition of this word, referring to Aristodemus as subject of ἕπεσθαι, is indispensable; from καὶ ἐλθόντα onwards the subject is again Socrates. **Λύκειον:** a sanctuary of Apollo Lykeios, with a gymnasium, lying to the east outside the city wall. In *Euthyphro* 2a1f. it is treated as Socrates' favourite haunt; cf. *Lysis* 203a1, b2, *Euthd.* 271a1. By spending the day after the party in his usual way Socrates continues to demonstrate that striking immunity to the effects of alcohol on which Alcibiades remarks in 220a4–6.

INDEX

References in Index 1 are to passages of the Greek text; in the other indexes, to pages.

2. PROPER NAMES

3. GREEK WORDS

4. GENERAL